PRIMARY TEACHING **WITHDRÁWN**

Primary Teaching

Robin J. Alexander
University of Leeds

HOLT, RINEHART AND WINSTON
London · New York · Sydney · Toronto

Holt, Rinehart and Winston Ltd: 1 St Anne's Road,
Eastbourne, East Sussex BN21 3UN

British Library Cataloguing in Publication Data

Alexander, Robin
  Primary teaching.
  1. Elementary school teaching   2. Elementary schools—Great Britain
  I. Title
  372.11'02'0941   LB1776

ISBN 0–03–910519–9

Typeset by Inforum Ltd, Portsmouth
Printed and bound in Great Britain by Mackays of Chatham Ltd.

Last digit is print no: 9 8 7 6 5 4 3 2 1

Acknowledgements

This book's exploitation of the education literature is both substantial and evident. No less obvious, I hope, but nevertheless in need of particular mention, is its indebtedness to the many members of the primary community — teachers, advisers, teacher educators and of course children — with whom I have worked during the past twenty years: this book is nothing if not grounded in that experience.

More specifically, I must thank the following: Alan Blyth, Maggie Ing and Vic Kelly for helpful comments on chapter drafts; Elizabeth Alexander for providing alternative perspectives on familiar issues; and those primary and middle-school teachers from the various Yorkshire LEAs who, as members of the advanced primary diploma course at Leeds University, have shared, tested, supplemented and generally helped develop many of the ideas elaborated in these pages.

R.J.A.

Contents

Introduction

This book is about the task of the teacher in primary schools, its institutional and professional context, and the way it is conceived, practised and justified.

It is as well to stipulate immediately the scope of the term 'primary' as used in the following pages. Primary pupils, under the Education Act 1944, are those under the age of twelve. In local authorities having no middle schools and little nursery provision 'primary' remains a straightforward designation for schools catering for children aged between five and eleven either in single units or divided into infants (5–7) and juniors (7–11). The arrival of middle schools and the extension of nursery education have complicated matters. The former have varying age-ranges (8–12, 9–13, 10–13), are deemed primary (8–12) or secondary (9/10–13), and are preceded by first schools for children aged 5–8, 5–9 or 5–10. Some local authorities term their first schools 'primary' to avoid confusion about where, in a 9–13 middle school, the primary stage stops and the secondary starts. Nursery provision can take the form of separate establishments or of classes attached to primary or first schools, thus extending the scope of 'primary' downwards to age 3–4.

'Primary' is also used to connote less a stage than a style of education, characterised pre-eminently by what is loosely termed a 'child-centred' approach to teaching and organisation. Thus the National Association for Primary Education, committed to extending the influence of post-Plowden progressivism, annexes both middle and nursery schools by taking primary to mean '3–13'. This perhaps overstretches the term: experientially and developmentally, the three- and thirteen-year-old are a long way apart; and the nursery teachers and the subject specialist at the top end of a middle school may have very little in common beyond the fact that they are both teachers. It is as difficult to accommodate such diversity within a single term or a coherent discussion as it would be with, say, university and middle school teachers.

The stipulative definition of 'primary', then, for the purposes of this book, is 'the education of children aged 5–11'. This is not a purist contraction of the term back to its 1944 meaning, but reflects the need for any generalisations about primary teaching to remain valid regardless of the institutional or ideological circumstances of particular schools. If one excludes both the distinctive approaches in current nursery education and the subject specialisation characteristic of the upper two years of middle schools, one is left with practices dominated above all else by the *class-teacher* system — one teacher for the child's total educational experience for a minimum of a year. Moreover, since nursery provision is not universal and middle schools are a minority (and some would say threatened) element in the education system, the 5–7/5–9/7–11/5–11 patterns of organisation, and the class-teacher system with which these are almost invariably associated, constitute the most generally applicable operational definition of 'primary'.

FOCUSING ON THE PRIMARY TEACHER

Books on primary education take many forms but a substantial proportion seek to purvey a particular view of how primary schools should be, and to convert others to that view. Although the present work contains its share of author opinions and values, its main concern is to promote analysis and critique. Thus I am not interested in arguing with Plowden: 'No advances in policy, no acquisitions of new equipment have their desired effect unless they are in harmony with the nature of the child, unless they are fundamentally acceptable to him' (CACE 1967, p. 7); or with Rhodes Boyson 'forget the trendy sixties. The child cannot find it all out by discovery. He needs to be told, he needs to be taught' (Boyson 1982). I am interested, however, in examining the origins and functions of such statements, and in considering their relationship to what we now know, or assert, about the nature of primary teaching 'as it is'. At the heart of this book's analysis is the primary teacher rather than the primary child. The purpose of this perhaps heretical-seeming focus is not to foster an alternative ideology to that of child-centredness. The concern with the teacher arises because it is the teacher more than anyone else who defines the child in child-centred (or in any other approach), who defines children's attributes, states what their needs are, predicts their potential and evaluates their achievement. It could be argued, then, that knowing oneself as a teacher is one of the basic prerequisites for true child-centredness.

PRACTICE AND THOUGHT

Such reflexiveness presupposes all sorts of attitudinal and intellectual attributes in the teacher. It also implies a view of professional conduct in which the quality of the teacher's thought is as significant as the quality of his or her action. This too may be heresy: for the teaching profession has tended to adopt a somewhat dualist view of its activities, in which the notion of practice as little more than a manual activity, deprived of intellectual rigour and rationality, has been prominent, while informed, critical debate and reflection on practice have been seen more as the concern of theorists in 'ivory towers', divorced from the real world, than of practitioners.

Such a mindless conception of practice is of course uniquely unflattering to any professional group concerned, as teachers are, with the development of the minds of others. But it also weakens their professional claim which, like that of other professions, resides as much in a supposed field of expert knowledge drawn upon in a discriminating and considered way to meet individual needs and circumstances as in executive skills.

It is also the case that teachers' ideas and practices come from many sources, some of them highly elusive and almost impossible to identify, let alone to generalise about. Teachers are the product not merely of their training but of their unique intellectual attributes, their personality, attitudes and cumulative experiences. Their own experiences as children (or parents) may profoundly influence their approach to the children they teach. From their early days as pupils they may have acquired models, consciously emulated or unconsciously imitated, for their own teaching. Their political and religious beliefs, their moral values, their aspirations and fears for the future of themselves and others may affect their conception of the primary curriculum, particularly that hidden dimension which acts so potently upon the child's social and moral understanding, more than they care to admit.

None of these influences is denied in what follows. On the contrary, the book's recurrent message of 'teacher: know thyself' is an explicit acknowledgement of their impact. But while a biography of one or two teachers might encompass the unique to the depth required, a book about teaching as such has to deal more with what teachers have in common, with their shared experiences, ideas and situations.

All primary teachers have in common three overlapping areas of experience and consciousness: that of being, as we have noted, a class teacher; that of working in a particular kind of institution, a primary school; and that of having undergone a particular pattern of professional training. Though approaches to class teaching, school organisation and initial training vary, they also have much in common and it is upon this that we shall focus.

Experience acquires meaning: it is reflected upon, interpreted, justified. What binds together these three sets of experiences both for the individual teacher and for the primary profession as a whole is the community of ideas and discourse which the experiences generate and sustain. They acquire shared meanings and justifications. In turn these influence subsequent experience and practice, and the culture of primary education consolidates itself, becomes more distinctive, exerts an increasingly strong influence upon its individual members. Primary teachers from Cumbria and Cornwall can communicate without difficulty on professional matters by virtue not so much of their classroom practices, which may vary, but because of shared assumptions about the job they are both doing which each can take for granted. This suggests two requirements for a book about primary teaching. One is to explore teaching in terms of ideas as well as practices: the thinking, reasoning, assumptions, knowledge and beliefs which underlie teaching acts in primary schools, as well as the outward, observable forms and consequences of those acts. The second is to focus upon the three central shared areas of professional experience to which these ideas and acts relate; the classroom, the school and the training course. This book endeavours to meet both of these requirements.

TEACHERS, SCHOOLS AND TEACHER EDUCATION: THE NEED FOR COMPREHENSIVE ANALYSIS

Including detailed consideration of teacher education in a book about primary teaching is, surprisingly, unusual. There are numerous books about primary education which, whatever their qualities in other respects, barely mention primary teacher training or restrict their commentary on it to a few well-worn prescriptions or brickbats. Conversely, there are many discussions about ideas and practices in teacher education which examine the latter in its own terms, without exploring the appropriateness of the training course to professional needs or, at a deeper level, the consistency of a course's implied model of professional action with what actually happens in the classroom.

If the literature is compartmentalised, so will be the discourse. And so indeed it is. Training and teaching, whatever the efforts of particular individuals and institutions, have become separate worlds. Conceptually, as I have argued, since training is one of the central shared experiences of primary teachers, it must feature in any purportedly comprehensive discussion of primary teaching. But there are also powerful practical needs. The ivory tower/chalk face, theory/practice rhetoric symbolises not merely an institutional gulf but a linguistic and intellectual one. Educationists agree on the need for dialogue, but dialogue presumes a common language of discourse. Dialogue also depends upon mutual acceptance of the need for self-critique. The character of the training process and of teaching must both be regarded as problematic. Critique in turn requires understanding of what is being appraised. Many professions are intimately engaged in the task of selecting and training their new fellow-members to an extent which, for various reasons, the teaching profession is not (or not yet). If there is, as conventional wisdom has it, ignorance among teacher trainers about the real world of teaching in schools, there is equally ignorance in the teaching profession about current intentions and practices in initial training.

The final justification for a comprehensive approach is at once professional and political. This is the era of accountability and central government intervention in matters hitherto left to the discretion of heads, schools, LEAs, training institutions and validating bodies.

The earlier, somewhat vague talk about a 'core curriculum' for schools has been replaced by a narrower, neo-Victorian utilitarianism which uncompromisingly identifies economic and industrial need as the main or even sole determinant of curriculum priorities and puts the arts, humanities and social sciences at risk. Similarly, in teacher education the hitherto generalised recommendations about course content have been replaced by the beginnings of a much more exact prescription, not always, as we shall see, particularly apposite to primary teaching. And, throughout the education system, institutions and providing authorities are increasingly obliged to account to central government and the public for their curriculum policies: not necessarily a bad thing, but sufficiently contrary to the established British tradition of curriculum laissez-faire to make teachers facing such demands acutely vulnerable, because where serious curriculum discourse at institutional level has not been demanded by external agents it may not have been promoted internally.

All these considerations dictate professional debate about, in the present case, primary teaching, primary schools, primary teacher education and the relationships between them. For in the absence of debate of sufficient sharpness and persuasiveness at the professional level, the initiative passes to those whose preference may be for simplistic prescription backed by political power, rather than open discourse.

CHILD, CURRICULUM, TEACHER

Few juxtapositions illustrate better the way the educational climate has changed than the opening sentences of the 1967 Plowden Report and the 1981 government paper entitled *The School Curriculum*:

> At the heart of the educational process lies the child (CACE 1967)

> The school curriculum is at the heart of education (DES 1981a)

The second reads like a conscious and defiant parody of the first, and indeed its intentions tend to be perceived by serving primary teachers as iconoclastic: while the Plowden statement produces a warm glow, the recent DES statement engenders in many a cold shiver.

What is notable about much discourse in the primary world is its tendency to polarisation. This is one of the recurrent concerns in the present book and the first three chapters refer frequently to the language and assumptions of such discourse. The aim here is to avoid tired polarities like child/curriculum or child/subject and to operate on the basis of a simple, commonsense, and relatively neutral model of the educational process. The title of Part 1, 'Teacher, Child and Curriculum', encapsulates this model. The educational process as currently conducted in schools centres on a relationship between the *teacher* and the *child*. This relationship is constituted of transactions, events and experiences — planned and unplanned, deliberate and incidental — which are justified by reference to a value system, a notion of what it is to be educated. These transactions, together with their justifications and outcomes in terms of the child's learning, constitute the *curriculum*. Teacher, child and curriculum are interdependent and inseparable. A discussion of the educational process which excludes any one of them loses its validity. Yet it is one of this book's contentions that primary discourse and practice have tended to treat the three dimensions as mutually exclusive, and that this tendency has been reinforced, both structurally and conceptually, in teacher training.

The book attempts to enact this basic model, to reconcile and keep in equilibrium its 'child', 'curriculum' and 'teacher' dimensions. Throughout, the teacher dimension is pervasive since the overall direction is towards analysis of the process of being and becoming a primary teacher. But the child and curriculum dimensions are also prominent: they are isolated in separate chapters (2, 3, 4 and 5) yet also brought together by the nature of the analysis.

The overall structure of the book reflects the three shared contexts of primary teaching referred to earlier, though not exclusively. Part 1 is particularly concerned with the job of being a class teacher, with practice and with the ideas and ideology with which practice is associated. Part 2 examines the ways in which primary teachers have been trained and considers relationships between such patterns of training and some of the strengths and weaknesses of classroom practice and discourse which emerge in Part 1. Part 3 considers the culture and organisation of the primary school, its impact on the teacher and the child's curriculum, and the question of how far current approaches to school management and decision-making enable the primary school to meet the challenges of social and educational change.

The book can be read at two levels. It was conceived, as the foregoing makes clear, as a unified critique which assumes significant connections between the various elements examined in Parts 1, 2 and 3 — child, curriculum, teacher, classroom, school and training institution. But with a diverse readership in mind the book is so constructed that each of its three parts is reasonably self-sufficient.

PART ONE

TEACHER, CHILD AND CURRICULUM

1

The Class Teacher and Primary Ideology

WHAT IS PRIMARY EDUCATION?

Working with primary teachers and children one gains a powerful sense of professional consensus over the kinds of educational practices connoted by the word 'primary'; a consensus, moreover, tinged sometimes with an element of moral superiority when reference is made to other parts of the education system, particularly secondary schools. Probing a little to discover what it is that members of the primary profession, and the schools in which they work, have in common, one encounters amidst the expected diversity of ideas and organisation the solid bedrock of a set of beliefs and claims concerning the nature of childhood, the learning process and the curriculum, which are subscribed to regardless of particular school circumstances.

During the late 1960s and early 1970s, in the years between the optimism of Plowden and the gloom generated by a combination of financial crisis (following the 1973 oil price rises) and anti-progressive educational critique (associated with the Black Papers, the William Tyndale affair and the 1976 Ruskin College speech of the then Prime Minister, James Callaghan) the American penchant for uncritical acclaim of English traditions reached new heights. Planeloads of professors and teachers, the latter in pursuit — in between the Tower of London and Anne Hathaway's cottage — of easy credits for master's degrees and doctorates, descended on primary schools in certain parts of England, chiefly Oxfordshire, Leicestershire, the former West Riding of Yorkshire and London. (One Oxfordshire primary head finally called a halt when he arrived at his school one morning to find a coachload of US teachers waiting, direct from Heathrow and uninvited.) 'Open education' became a growth industry, and American writers like Featherstone, Silberman and Rogers provided an adulatory commentary on primary education which conveyed the distinct message that what they described and applauded was universal practice.

One American writer who attempted a more dispassionate and analytical appraisal was Barth (1975), who offered a set of 'assumptions about children, learning and knowledge' which 'underlie the practices and utterances of open educators'. Despite the dramatic shifts in the educational climate since then, and the decreasing prominence of words like 'open' and 'progressive' in the educational vocabulary, one still finds remarkably unanimous commitment among serving teachers to many of these assumptions, particularly the following:

> Children are innately curious and display exploratory behaviour quite independent of adult intervention.
>
> Active exploration in a rich environment, offering a wide array of manipulative materials, facilitates children's learning.
>
> Play is not distinguished from work as the predominant mode of learning in early childhood.
>
> Children will be likely to learn if they are given considerable advice in the selection of the materials they wish to work with and in the selection of the questions they wish to pursue with respect to those materials.
>
> Children pass through similar stages of intellectual development, each in his own way, and at his own rate and in his own time.
>
> Intellectual growth and development take place through a series of concrete experiences followed by abstractions.
>
> Knowledge is a function of one's personal integration of experience and therefore does not fall into neatly separate categories or disciplines.
>
> There is no minimum body of knowledge which it is essential for everyone to know.

A more extended and complex taxonomy of open education was offered by Walberg and Thomas (1971): to the above list, which emphasises curiosity, active learning, sequential development and subjective knowledge, they add characteristics of teachers. For example:

> The teacher respects each child's personal style of thinking and acting.
>
> The teacher sees herself as one of many sources of knowledge and information in the classroom.
>
> (Walberg and Thomas 1971)

Why does one find such unanimity among primary teachers in respect of sentiments like these? This is a question we shall explore in this and the following chapters, but first, clearly, one must seek to discover the extent to which the sentiments are consistent with the practice.

The myth of progressivism?

Discovering what was actually going on during this period — as Simon (1981) points out — is not easy. Nevertheless, his historical review is thorough, fully documented and persuasive. Simon reminds us that Plowden itself found only 10 per cent of primary schools to be 'good or even outstanding' and that two thirds were 'adequate', 'mediocre' or 'bad'. However, since Plowden was treated as an inspirational document, and one which ostensibly legitimised the progressive aspirations of thousands of teachers, one might expect a survey ten years later to show a substantial change in these proportions. The HMI primary survey (DES 1978a) failed to provide that evidence. It was one of several rather sobering empirical studies which we shall refer to in this book which contribute to a now fairly comprehensive picture of primary practice as occasionally exciting, usually competent in the so-called 'basics' at least, but not infrequently mediocre or inadequate. Of course all such adjectives require qualification: by what criteria is teaching judged exciting, competent, mediocre or inadequate? Such qualification is postponed until we discuss in more detail the studies concerned, but the point to make here is that the combined message of Ashton et al. (1975), Sharp and Green (1975), Bennett (1976), King (1978), Bassey (1978), DES (1978c and 1982a), Galton and Simon (1980), Simon and Wilcocks (1981) is that primary rhetoric and primary reality can be a long way apart. The accusations of the Black Paper authors (Cox and Dyson 1971) of the 1970s and of Rhodes Boyson, still, in the 1980s, over the supposed neglect of reading and mathematics, were a long way wide of the mark: the basics have received consistently high priority — it is the rest of the curriculum, as we shall see, that should give most cause for concern.

Primary 'facts'

So are we any nearer to identifying the quintessential character of primary education, that which produces the palpable atmosphere of solidarity, of enlightenment in the face of philistinism, when two or three or a hundred are gathered together in the name of 'primary'?

I suggest that our response to the rhetoric–reality gap should not be to dismiss the rhetoric but to acknowledge its pervasiveness and seek to understand why it persists. Rhetoric, then, is one undeniable fact of primary education. Beyond that we encounter so little uniformity of practice that we might feel inclined to ask whether the word 'primary' is anything more than a label denoting a stage of compulsory schooling (and even there, since the advent of middle schools, we have problems of definition). What propositions about primary children, teachers and schools will hold in all, or at least most situations? There would seem to be two, concerning the principal actors in primary schools, children and teachers, together with two immediate consequences for primary teaching.

Two propositions and two imperatives

Developmental range and diversity

The pupils in primary education are children aged between 5 and 11: if psychologists are right, most of these children have achieved 80 per cent of their intellectual growth, 50 per cent of their adult vocabulary and 50 per cent of their educational attainment by the age of eight or nine (Kellmer-Pringle 1980), though how one quantifies these things is another matter. In other words, though precise ages and stages must always be open to doubt the primary phase is marked by a substantial, variegated and very significant period of human development. This, moreover, takes place in a varied, pluralist environmental and cultural context, with children coming from backgrounds which have a wide variety of values, habits and aspirations.

The class teacher system

The institutional contexts of primary education are also varied: large and small schools; first, infant, junior and JMI; horizontal and vertical grouping; open-plan and box classrooms. So too, especially since the abolition in most authorities of the 11-plus, are the educational values cr philosophies that the schools espouse and the curricular and teaching practices that these engender. Beyond this variation, however, the one fixed point in primary practice is the class teacher system: one teacher for all or most of the child's schooling for a period of one year and often for longer. This, more than anything else, is what distinguishes primary from secondary teaching.

Together these two basic propositions about primary education create two imperatives for the teachers concerned.

The 'whole child'

The first imperative is for each teacher to develop a comprehensive, rounded view of each child. I use the phrase 'the whole child' as aspiration rather than achievement: it is surely arrogant, as well as philosophically questionable, to claim that one can ever 'know' another person in his or her entirety. But class teaching, to be successful, at least requires the teacher to aim in this direction, trying to understand the many facets of the child's development, his or her interests, aspirations, abilities and potential — verbal, expressive, physical and so on.

The 'whole curriculum'

The second imperative for the class teacher is the obligation to conceive, plan and implement (apart, perhaps, from some occasional remedial reading or music) the whole curriculum to be experienced by each child during that period of a year or more. I shall argue later that this whole curriculum responsibility is too frequently, in both schools and training institutions, underestimated.

Primary class teachers thus stand in a relationship to both child and curriculum which is fundamentally different from that of their secondary colleagues. Their professional knowledge and skills have to be holistic: the relationship, interpenetration and cumulative meaning for the child of the various curriculum elements necessarily concern them to an extent that they cannot concern a secondary teacher.

PRIMARY IDEOLOGY AND THE REQUIREMENTS OF CLASS TEACHING

Present-day primary schools are the direct descendants of the nineteenth-century and early twentieth-century elementary-school tradition which provided a basic mass education, with the three Rs at its core, for working-class children. It is important to retain this historical perspective when considering primary education in the 1980s. The primary tradition is very recent indeed: as Blackie (1967) points out, the Hadow (Board of Education 1931) re-organisation of elementary into primary and secondary was fully completed in 1965, a mere two years before the publication of Plowden, and there are still many former elementary-school teachers now serving in primary schools: some still occasionally lapse into the terminology of 'standards' ('Standard 7' was the top class of the elementary school). What Blyth (1965) calls the 'developmental' tradition (i.e. what is conventionally known as child-centredness) is a recent overlay on a pattern of education which in two vital respects — the persistence of class teaching and the view of literacy and numeracy as the 'basic' or core elements of the curriculum — represents an unbroken tradition stretching back to 1870 and earlier.

Thus, when it is argued that class teaching obtains in primary schools 'because it is best for the young child' this is manifestly inaccurate as a causal statement: the generalist class teacher is there by historical accident and such justifications as can be offered for class teaching in terms of the child's educational needs have been added subsequently. They may be valid, but equally they may be rationalisations rather than rationales.

The developmental, or child-centred, tradition has had an uneven impact, for it is but one of three to some extent competing traditions in primary education: the developmental (particularly strong in infant and first schools), the elementary (particularly in junior schools and departments which were often physically separate from infants — witness the labels still carried above older school doorways), and the secondary (subject) tradition with the arrival in middle schools of ex-secondary subject specialists. The latter produces a tension — often reflected dramatically in the transition from class to subject teaching in the third or fourth year — which many middle schools fail to resolve: it may well be exacerbated by HMI's recommendation (DES 1983c) that middle-school subject teaching should be strengthened and extended.

We can now begin to understand why there is the apparent paradox, as revealed by studies like the HMI primary surveys (DES 1978a, 1982a), of routine teaching dominated by the basics coupled with a progressive rhetoric which argues strenuously that primary education is so much more than this. They represent two distinct traditions: one there for historical reasons, pragmatic, unprincipled except by reference to the narrowest Victorian criteria of utility (which in the 1980s are beginning to re-assert themselves); the other set up specifically in opposition to that tradition, reflecting the influence of educational idealists like Froebel and Montessori and manifesting itself especially in early childhood education (Selleck 1972). The true paradox, however, is not the co-existence of these traditions, since, after all, the presence of both reactionary and radical, or traditional and progressive elements (and all shades in between) is to be expected in a venture as value-laden as education. It is that the progressive rhetoric is apparently espoused across most of the range of actual primary practice (except perhaps for the extreme of the traditional end of the continuum) despite a wide variety of practices, some of which, as we shall see, are totally inconsistent with the rhetoric.

In seeking to understand why this should be so, we shall need to introduce the concept of ideology. 'Ideology', Nisbet (1967) suggests, is 'a pattern of ideas, both factual and evaluative, which purport to explain and legitimize the social structure and culture of a particular social group or society, and which serves to justify social actions which are in accordance with that pattern of ideas'. I apply the term ideology to what, quasi-neutrally, the primary profession usually calls its 'philosophy', that is to say the network of beliefs, values and assumptions about children, learning, teaching, knowledge and the curriculum which I exemplified earlier by quoting from Barth's analysis of progressive writing in the 1960s and 1970s. Such beliefs and values can be interpreted as arising in substantial measure from the particular historical, institutional and professional situation of primary teachers as much as from objective analysis of the child and the educational process. The class-teacher system came first; it required no justification in a system of mass education at public expense other than economic and administrative: it was the cheapest and most straightforward means of educating children to the minimal levels required. But the twentieth century has witnessed the increased professionalisation of teachers: the professional claim had to be backed by a convincing corpus of expert knowledge which could stand comparison with the self-evident subject-knowledge base of specialist teachers in secondary, further and higher education. There was a need to develop a conceptual framework for the practice of class teaching which — whatever its educational benefits for the child — would support and sustain class teachers, provide them with a professional identity, and 'prove' that the approach with which they were saddled by virtue of historical accident was the best one from the child's point of view. Child-centredness, whatever its educational merits when examined dispassionately, provided the best available ideology to meet the primary class teacher's situation.

We shall develop and apply this idea further in the next two chapters. First, however, the substance of the ideology needs to be spelled out and commented on in greater detail. Since it is of course presented publicly not as ideology but as a set of principles grounded in objective knowledge of children, pedagogy and curriculum, it is essential to treat it in these terms and to test its rationality, coherence and consistency, together with the extent to which it is matched by practice. We start with a generalised look at the language of child-centredness and then, in Chapters 2 and 3, look in greater detail at its substance and relationship to empirically explored practice.

THE LANGUAGE OF CHILD-CENTREDNESS

Nobody familiar with the culture of primary schools can doubt the pervasiveness of two elements. First, there is the language of child-centredness, the verbal expression of an ideology which remains in the 1980s as powerful and sometimes vehement as it was in the 1960s. This language has considerable potency for inducing a warm, consensual solidarity. From the mouth of a non-teacher, viewed initially and inevitably with suspicion, the rhetorical question 'But we teach children, not subjects, don't we?' is a ticket to professional approval and acceptance; it disarms suspicion, sets heads nodding and confirms ally status. Second, many primary schools, especially infant and first schools, have a physical appearance and an interpersonal climate which seem to confirm the seriousness of the intentions:

> The children behave responsibly and cooperate with their teacher and with other children . . . A quiet working atmosphere is established . . . Teachers attach great importance to children learning to live together amicably and gaining a sense of social responsibility.
> (DES 1978a, p. 108)

> The (first) schools . . . have established the same good relationships — both within the school community and outside it with parents and others — found in primary schools looked at in the national survey . . . overall the quality of the materials and the standard of display, the care and arrangement of the equipment and apparatus, and the general orderliness in the school contributed to the good aesthetic quality of the surroundings . . .
> (DES 1982a, pp. 55 and 38)

British primary schools, then, can be welcoming, attractive, friendly and purposeful environments, a refuge from the sometimes socially insecure and environmentally dismal world outside.

In developing a critique of some aspects of primary ideology, I wish in no way to deny the value of the kind of school climate with which at best it is associated. Rather, my argument is that the primary school's strengths in respect of climate and interpersonal relations are sometimes offset by weaknesses in respect of curriculum and pedagogy — not always obvious to the uncritical outsider (or insider) since such weaknesses may not significantly diminish the defining characteristics of 'busyness' and 'enjoyment' (King 1978), the sense of purposeful and valuable activity — curriculum and pedagogy being aspects of the teacher's task where emotional commitment to an ideal is no substitute for intellectual engagement. As ideology, child-centredness may be effective; as educational rationale it is sometimes deficient. In the first instance this deficiency arises from the abuse of language to secure the unthinking emotional response.

The problem is partly the self-evident nonsense, well explored by Entwistle (1970), of that statement 'we teach children not subjects'. (Of course you teach children, but so do your secondary colleagues; they teach subjects to their pupils: are you saying you don't teach yours anything?) This is a simple matter of case abuse — 'subjects' being accusative but 'children' sliding covertly between accusative and dative to suit the argument.

Some of the difficulties arise because such statements reflect an addiction to aphorisms and maxims, particularly of a pseudo-Confucian variety, which require the pointed juxtaposition or opposition of two key concepts. Thus the meaning of a sentiment becomes less important than its euphony and its aura of timeless, even rustic, wisdom. So when someone asserts that 'children learn to write by writing', the statement, ás is the essence of aphorism, has the effect of terminating further discussion: it says in a few pithy words all that needs to be said. This is a pity, because if one dwells upon such an adage for a second or two, or substitutes (as is often done) alternative verbs — 'paint', 'sing', 'count', 'sit', 'stand' — it becomes not so much profound as profoundly banal.

More serious is the seemingly deliberate use of fallacy, false dichotomy, category mixing and other devices for creating the illusion in an uncritical audience of a secure argument.

Take these three examples from one representative text for teachers:

Experience, not curriculum.

Child, not curriculum.

Rather than curriculum, let us concern ourselves with the individual's sense of time, his rhythm and moods.

(Marsh 1973, pp. 76, 11 and 132)

Here the concern for 'child' and 'experience', which no reasonable person will reject, are deliberately presented as incompatible with a concern for 'curriculum'. But what children experience in school as a result of the deliberate policies and actions of their teachers *is* their curriculum, so that a commitment to 'experience', the child's 'sense of time', 'activity' and so on is a curricular commitment. But in the language of child-centredness, a concern for the child's curriculum is presented, simply and irredeemably, as incompatible with a concern for the child. A similar process operates with another standard polarity: 'learning, not teaching'. King (1978) points out that the Plowden Report's index has 34 entries on 'learning' and none on 'teaching'. Yet teaching is, of course, nothing if not the process of bringing about learning: what else is a paid primary teacher doing if not teaching? Underlying this false dichotomy is a conceptual misrepresentation of 'teaching' as mere 'telling' or 'instructing' — one employed by progressives' critics as much as progressives themselves (exemplified in the Rhodes Boyson quotation given earlier: the child 'needs to be told, he needs to be taught'). In primary ideology 'teaching' is rejected as a concept because of its Dickensian empty-vessel connotations ('Now, what I want is, Facts. Teach these boys and girls nothing but Facts. Facts alone are wanted in life . . . '). By so rejecting the word 'teaching', teachers fall into a trap of their own making and provide weapons for their critics — they can be accused of knowingly denying their contractual obligations: instead they should seek to render the meanings of 'teaching' more comprehensive and flexible, indicating a range of teacher acts leading to children's learning.

Category mixing, revealing the same basic misconceptions about one or both of the activities being contrasted, is most forcefully demonstrated in utterances which concern knowledge. Thus Kirby (1981) argues that schools must not deal with knowledge as they 'are places of encouragement, rather than indoctrination', and Pluckrose (1979) juxtaposes 'subjects' with 'learning by rote'. In both cases there is a confusion of *curriculum content* (what) — whether 'knowledge' or 'subjects' — with *pedagogy* (how). Indoctrination and learning by rote are methods, independent of content.

The most famous example of this yoking of content and method to produce guilt by association is the statement in the Hadow Report (Board of Education 1931) 'The curriculum is to be thought of in terms of activity and experience rather than of knowledge to be acquired and facts to be stored'. Actually, this contains a second untenable yoking together — of 'knowledge' and 'facts' — and this leads me to what I see as a serious and dangerous weakness in much child-centred discourse, the use of misrepresentation and caricature. In this case 'facts' and 'knowledge' are a false equation since facts are but one sort of knowledge. It is significant that such devices are used most prominently in relation to the question of knowledge in primary education, for it invites the teacher to respond 'If knowledge is mere inert facts I want none of it': we shall see later how the 'knowledge as facts' rhetoric relates directly to the endemic curriculum insecurity of the primary class teacher, to which current patterns of teacher training contribute substantially.

A typical view of what knowledge-free child-centredness is to replace is found in Kirby (1981, p. 11):

> mass teaching, chanting of tables, mechanical reading round the class . . . rigid timetables and the silencing of bells . . . the same textbook for every child.

The problem of knowledge, which faces everyone involved in the educational process, is squarely resolved in primary ideology by equating it with 'inert facts' 'imposed' on the child, through the 'rigidity' and 'fragmentation' of 'subjects': a conception of knowledge identical, as we have seen, to that portrayed in the opening paragraphs of Dickens' *Hard Times* and so tellingly contrasted with Sissy Jupe's 'personal knowledge' of the horses her father trains but which she is unable to 'define'. Excluded from such a portrayal are basic distinctions between propositional and procedural knowledge and between 'knowing' and 'understanding', consideration of the distinctive concepts and modes of inquiry of culturally evolved disciplines, and sensitivity to the basically problematic nature of the whole knowledge question. So caricatured, and in such an overtly populist manner, the problem of knowledge can be dismissed. It is a direct appeal to anti-intellectualism and 'gut' reaction. Such use of caricature is not new. Selleck remarks:

> When Montessori said 'in such a school the children, like butterflies mounted on pins, are fastened each to his place, the desk, spreading the useless wings of barren and useless knowledge which they have acquired', she was not interested in describing the past; she wanted her reader to react to it unfavourably . . . When description was attempted it was more often with a few and bold strokes so that the resulting pattern was simple and dramatic and therefore memorable, but ultimately a caricature. It seized upon obvious features of the nineteenth-century elementary school, looked at them out of context and left them so ingrained on the mind that all else was inconspicuous . . .
>
> (Selleck 1972, p. 72)

Kirby's 1981 vision of a non-progressive classroom (above) is exactly matched by that of the principal of Maria Grey Training College in 1918:

> rigid timetables, clanging bells, silent cloakrooms, cramping desks and absurd rules . . .
> (Selleck 1972, p. 53)

Primary discourse abounds in such throwbacks. The vocabulary, the sentiments, the saints and villains are the same now as a century ago. Given the extent of social and educational change since then, it is hard to see how such language can retain any credibility as a vehicle for serious discussion about primary education.

This language yields further devices for generating the necessary emotional response. For example it can be rich in organic metaphor, giving the process of child-centred education the immediacy of life fully savoured:

> The rhythm of work . . . an ebb and flow between the material and the processes of sketching, observing, looking for references . . . This gives a sensual base to the educational process, where concentration on increasing awareness and sensitivity is a priority . . . No need for the externally-imposed authority of the teacher.
> (Marsh 1973, p. 14)

In case it is argued that this sort of language appears in published texts but not in staffrooms, compare the following from a recent curriculum memorandum in an infant school:

> It is important that the natural flow of activity, imagination, language and thought be uninterrupted by artificial breaks such as subject-matter.

The language lulls and cradles, suggesting an affinity with a romantic conception of the natural order, a regression to childhood innocence and security, a pot-pourri of firelight and warmth against the cold night. 'At the heart of the educational process lies the child': Plowden's use of the words 'heart' (rather than the more neutral 'centre'), and 'lies', with the image of the child recumbent, dormant and maternally cradled, seems hardly accidental. The first of the two extracts above is followed by a chapter in which the phrase 'ebb and flow' appears five times in not many more pages. Note, in deliberate contrast, the roughness of the punch line 'No need for the externally-imposed authority of the teacher': all major words there carry an unequivocal and consistently brutal message, and the vocabulary used to characterise non-child-centredness is invariably of this order — harsh, suggestive of restriction, repression, violence even: 'nourish', 'sensitive' versus 'crude', 'inert', 'restriction', 'impose' (Marsh 1973). Note, too, how in the second extract 'subject-matter' is relegated to the status of something extraneous to the educational process, an 'artificial break'.

Another author actually personifies those responsible for shattering the dream:

> Froebel referred to the teacher as a gardener and the children as plants. Many people have broken into this garden . . . parents, administrators, providers of resources and tax-payers . . .
> (Kirby 1981, p. 132)

Here, apart from the highly questionable inference that the teacher is accountable to nobody, which at this stage is not my main concern, the significant element in the portrayal is that the child-centred cocoon enfolds *the teacher* as well as the child. The teacher partakes of that childhood innocence identified by King (1978) as one of the central elements in primary ideology: together child and teacher provide mutual warmth and protection against a hostile world of taxpayers, administrators, and, yes, the child's own parents.

We can also note how the 'cocoon' image extends beyond the classroom into other spheres of primary influence like the LEA advisory service and initial training. In the latter case the element of teacher possessiveness about 'their' children can be matched by that of primary tutors towards their students. Rejected by both can be not merely other adult influences but forms of professional discourse more rational than that exemplified above. 'Infants are different', it is asserted, and, of rationality, 'primary teachers don't talk in such abstract terms'. Childhood educators, we might suggest (adapting the most celebrated maxim of one of their chief sources of inspiration, Rousseau), have their own ways of thinking, seeing, feeling . . . and talking. They even have their own way of publishing: many books for primary teachers have the thick paper, large print, lower-case letters, short words, abundant pictures and cosy titles (frequently beginning 'Let's . . . ') used for the children's own books. Surely this confusion of roles between the immature pupil and the adult, paid professional is excessive to the point of self-indulgence. Teachers may want the warmth and security of a child-centred cocoon for their pupils, but if their activities are to have any relevance to the world beyond school in which the child is growing up they must recognise that their own place is outside the cocoon, facing and engaging with social realities, working out the best form of curricular response to them.

CONCLUSION

In this chapter we have considered some of the difficulties of defining 'primary' in terms which would gain universal agreement while retaining some indicative or diagnostic value. The basic features of primary are, first and pre-eminently, the prevalence of the class-teacher system with its holistic implications for the teacher's task, and, second, a pervasive ideology which is generally espoused regardless of the diversity of organisational and pedagogical practices. We used the term 'ideology' advisedly and began to develop the argument, which will be used at various points in this book, about the way in which recent primary ideology relates to the pre-existing elementary tradition, from which primary schools have grown, of class teaching and a curriculum dominated by a utilitarian concept of 'basics'. By this analysis the educational argument or 'philosophy' in primary ideology can be seen, in part at least, as post-hoc rationalisation rather than as rationale from first principles. We then considered the language through which primary ideology is expressed, and highlighted its heavy use of aphorism, false dichotomy, caricature, and other devices which serve to diminish and debase basic educational concepts like 'curriculum', 'knowledge' and 'teaching' to the extent that a failure to engage in serious discussion of them can be 'justified', paradoxically, as 'child-centred'. We also exemplified the metaphorical density and emotionalism of this language, and its appeal to populism and ignorance, and showed how, whatever their original function in the context of mass elementary education, the fact that neither language nor message has altered for a century suggests that they no longer constitute a valid vehicle for serious discourse about modern primary education. They have become ritualised and sloganised beyond redemption.

2

Knowing and Understanding Children

Commitment to, and a deep understanding of, children as unique individuals are the main bases of the primary teacher's professional claim. The commitment is inherent in the notion of 'being a primary teacher'; the understanding is seen as deriving from the constant proximity of teacher and child, generated by the class-teacher system.

In the discussion which follows it is important to bear in mind one simple proposition (or truism) concerning human relationships: that merely being with someone constantly over a long period of time does not necessarily generate a deep understanding of that person.

This chapter will consider evidence about the actual, as opposed to the claimed, character of the class teacher's 'understanding of children' and will show how the teacher's knowledge of the individual child may be mediated through an overarching view of children and childhood in general and subject to a variety of contextual and other influences and filters. However, it must be emphasised that study in this area is recent, tentative and difficult: if actually coming to understand someone is a complex process then for a researcher to characterise that understanding empirically is doubly so. At best such studies as are available in this area are suggestive. They provide a basis for productive speculation rather than 'evidence' or 'proof'.

DEVELOPMENTALISM AND READINESS: THE DOMINANCE OF PSYCHOLOGICAL MODELS

One such suggestive inquiry is that of King (1978), whose sociological study of teachers and children in three infant schools involved close, recorded, non-participant observation and interviews over a period of a year. King's teachers operated within a strongly articulated child-centred ideology which had four elements:

1. *Sequential developmentalism* — the idea that the child passes through a 'naturally-ordered sequence of physiological, psychological and social development' where while the rate of development will vary from child to child the sequence and stages will be the same. Linked with developmentalism was the notion of 'readiness', particularly in relation to reading — the idea that children's capacity to cope with specific sorts of learning is determined by the developmental stage they have reached.
2. *Individualism* — the principle that children are unique and must be catered for on the basis of analysis of individual 'needs'.
3. *Play as learning* — see Plowden (CACE 1967, p. 193): 'Play is the principal means of learning in early childhood'.
4. *Childhood innocence* — the notion that while children are capable of unacceptable behaviour they are guiltless of malicious intention: the fault lies elsewhere and they therefore need to be protected from the 'harmful and unpleasant aspects of the outside world'. King suggested that this element in the ideology is pervasive among infants' teachers, far less so among teachers of juniors.

King argues that teachers' 'typifications' of each child (the 'understanding' that we need to explore) were built up over the first half-term or so, and were always consonant with this framework, and thus in important respects both restricted and restricting. Assessment of children tended to avoid intellectual attributes connoted by words like 'bright' and to incorporate instead constructs connoting attributes of personality and behaviour — 'mature/immature', 'silly/sensible', 'quiet/noisy'. The Rousseau-esque 'innocence' element enabled the child, and to some extent the teacher, to be absolved from responsibility for lack of progress or poor behaviour. These tended to be explained in terms of a 'family-home background' theory which placed the blame for failure squarely on the home, tacitly or explicitly characterised in terms of the 'cultural deficit' model identified in Sharp and Green's earlier (1975) study of a progressive primary school and explored in the now substantial sociological literature on the cultural contexts of educability and language.

Silver and Silver, towards the end of their detailed history of a south London primary school from 1824 to 1974, pinpoint the significance of 'individualism' thus:

> The most profound distinction between the contemporary primary school and the monitorial school of 1824 . . . is that the discussion is about 'each child', not the infant poor.
> (Silver and Silver 1974, p. 177)

This is useful as confirmation of the 'individualism' element in King's hypothesised primary ideology, but it also reminds us that when the precursors of today's primary schools existed 'by definition, for the infant poor', the gross material privations and prospects of most of the children attending them gave obvious point to 'family-home'/'cultural deficit' explanations.

The 'sequential developmentalism' element is also powerful, and I shall show in Part 2 how it is strongly reinforced in teacher education courses — as has been, until recently, the 'cultural deficit' explanation of pupil failure. Clearly, an understanding of how children develop is an essential element in professional knowledge. Explored in depth, the work of Piaget, Bruner and others has pedagogical potency, and this is reflected, particularly in Piaget's case, in his influence on primary mathematics and science, especially through published project materials. Piagetian stage and stage-independent theories provide the main rationale for Nuffield mathematics, for example, the teachers' handbook of which is dedicated 'with gratitude (and permission) to Jean Piaget' (Nuffield Mathematics Project 1975) and the Schools Council project Science 5–13 explicitly sequences its learning objectives according to Piagetian stages (Ennever and Harlen 1975). More than those of any other theorist, the ideas of Piaget have become internalised in the profession and made part of teachers' everyday discourse. However, this prompts two major reservations, one about the validity of the theory as such, and the other about the way it is used to inform primary teaching.

A full critique of Piagetian theory is clearly beyond the scope of this book, and is in any case available elsewhere (e.g. Brown and Desforges 1979, Donaldson 1978, Modgil and Modgil 1982). However, some of the more familiar reservations can be recorded here. One relates to the role of language in the research procedures. Its function as the vehicle for the supposed demonstration of children's cognitive levels and capacities was a crucial one, and some critics see the use of language in typical Piagetian tests more as a barrier than an aid to researcher understanding, for children were, in effect, required to operate in accordance with the researcher's language rather than their own. Donaldson, for instance, showed how the researcher's language could be alien and ambiguous, challenging children to guess the researcher's particular meaning of key words like 'more' on which hypotheses about conservation depended. Another objection relates to the social circumstances of the experiments. The children responded to cues and leading questions; they were placed under pressure to opt for one from a limited number of possible answers; they were sometimes implicitly invited to consider the manifestly ridiculous as a viable alternative. The overriding objection, then, is that the child's language and thought could not be so much explicated as filtered, redirected or hindered by the research methodology. Moreover the Piagetian 'replications' (raw material for the 1960s and 1970s higher-degree industry) might not so much test as merely illustrate the theory (Shayer 1979): by repeating an experimental procedure in every detail, any inbuilt weaknesses would be carried forward and thus a confirmation of the procedure's 'findings' was a foregone conclusion. Casting a procedure in a radically different way could produce dramatically different findings, as Donaldson's work on 'decentring' showed. She found that outside the tight confines of the Piagetian research procedure very young children might give ample evidence of deductive reasoning abilities, and argued that assertions about children's 'limited capacity for reasoning and abstract thought', which are now part of the everyday conceptual framework for primary teaching, were not only inaccurate but damaging.

The more serious issue, then, is how theory of this nature is applied. Brown and Desforges (1979) showed how professional discourse is dominated by confident assertions about 'stages' and 'readiness' legitimised by reference to Piaget's work. The inevitable consequence is a tendency: (a) to underrate children's capacities in a number of directions, particularly logical reasoning and abstract thought; (b) to impose on children's cognitive development a framework of firm horizontal hurdles which, although it purportedly allows for individual differences, may be presented in so dogmatic, crude and generalised a manner that dispassionate attention to the uniqueness and complexity of the individual mind ceases to be possible.

The connection between an over-rigid concept of developmentalism and the consistent evidence of under-expectation in primary classrooms (Burstall 1970, Goodacre 1968, Brandis and Bernstein 1974, Nash 1976, Sharp and Green 1975, DES 1978a and 1982a) seems irresistible. Remarks like the following (from the NUT response to the 1978 HMI primary survey) are familiar symptoms:

> The Union would not agree with [HMI's] analysis of what is suitable in the teaching of history to young children; the passage of time is a very difficult concept for children of this age to grasp . . .
>
> (NUT 1979, p. 25)

Note here the way that decisions about children's learning are to be taken not on the basis of their motivation or interest, or by reference to that close analysis of 'individual' needs which is central to primary ideology, but on the basis of fixed assumptions about children's capabilities at given ages. In this respect of course the 'sequential developmentalism' and 'individualism' elements in King's analysis of primary ideology contradict each other, and one assumes — since evidently developmentalism can be shown to be applied in practice — that 'individualism' is mere rhetoric.

Similarly, in the same document:

> Advanced reading skills such as skimming need a level of sophistication beyond the reach of most primary children. To suggest that they should be taught at this age betrays a lack of knowledge of children's conceptual development on the part of HMI.
>
> (NUT 1979, p. 19)

Note here how the language of sequential developmentalism rules out all alternative analyses: 'level', 'beyond the reach', 'age', 'conceptual development'. Note too the implied firmness of the 'levels' and especially the way the status of final truth or indisputable fact is accorded to that 'knowledge of child development' invoked to refute HMI's suggestion that higher-order reading skills are sometimes neglected in older primary children once initial reading skills have been mastered. (It is worth mentioning that alternative and contrary 'knowledge' in relation to higher order reading skills is available elsewhere: Southgate, Arnold and Johnson, 1981.)

For 'understanding children', then, one might read 'understanding children's development', and, for the latter, 'being able to define children in terms of predetermined developmental stages.' It is then not so much an *understanding of children* as a *definition of childhood*, and what we need to be wary of in practice is the risk of the developmental emphasis ruling out alternative forms of 'understanding' and alternative ways of perceiving and interpreting children's behaviour.

An investigation of children's problem-solving by an experienced teacher provides a good example of the way in which excessive commitment to developmentalism can exclude alternative hypotheses, diagnoses and explanations. The teacher asked a group of top infants to devise means for weighing an elephant. A boy produced a picture of a mechanical device. A girl concentrated on the problems of enticing the beast onto a weighing machine, on its likely reluctance, and on the dangers to the people involved. The teacher judged the boy's answer as 'sophisticated for his age' and the girl's as 'twee'. His analysis was formed exclusively by assumptions about the extent of logical thinking achievable by children of given ages. It failed to allow for alternative modes of thinking — in this example the girl's perception of the 'problem' as a behavioural and an affective one seems as valid as the boy's view of it as mechanical. If any explanatory theory can be applied to the two children's responses, given their total difference conceptually, it is that of the relationship between sex and cognitive style. This possibility did not occur to the teacher, even at the commonsense level of being alert to the implications of the fact that he, a man, preferred the boy's answer.

From subjects to developmentalism: a new compartmentalisation?

So far we have considered what one might term the 'horizontal' dimension of developmentalism: the way the conceptual frameworks for some teachers' everyday professional expectations and diagnoses seem to be dominated by ages and stages. But there is also a 'vertical' dimension, which takes the form of a classification of children's development into several distinctive aspects. The study of primary teachers' aims by Ashton, Kneen, Davies and Holley (1975) classified children's development under six headings:

(a) intellectual;
(b) physical;
(c) aesthetic;
(d) spiritual/religious;
(e) emotional/personal;
(f) social/moral.

By way of defence against the objections of writers like Hirst and Peters (1970) the authors cite this classification's pedigree in 'standard works on child development' which use these or similar headings, and they stress that the classification is to be used loosely. The appeal to 'authorities' is no real defence, of course, and in any case the claimed looseness and flexibility are not reflected in the subsequent report or its follow-up (Ashton, Kneen and Davies 1975). In the latter the authors develop a strategy for translating such developmental aims into action by superimposing on them that other 'standard' classification of human attributes, into 'knowledge', 'skills' and 'qualities'.

The first point to make about the developmental classification is that it is open to dispute on conceptual and psychological grounds. No evidence is advanced that human development actually proceeds along such channels. Rather that is simply a theoretical model of human development, and while in the first three the separation of 'intellectual' from 'physical' and 'aesthetic' betrays a familiar dualism, the rationale for 'spiritual/religious', 'emotional/personal' and 'social/moral' is hard to discover.

Are these categories of human development that have been observed, or do they denote culturally evolved patterns of desired behaviour? Is this how humans actually develop or how we would like them to develop?

However, were this indeed simply a flexible working framework such objections and questions would be of little account in practical terms, but because it is applied in conjunction with the knowledge/skills/qualities classification to curriculum discourse and practice, it constitutes, in essence, a curricular statement of some importance. Not only, as Hirst and Peters point out, are cognition and feeling kept firmly apart, but the entire matrix is riddled with anomalies. Thus, under the heading 'aims related to aesthetic development' (art, music and so on) the 'knowledge' column is left empty and the aesthetic component of the child's development (and hence, in terms of primary ideology, of his or her curriculum) is conceived, apparently, in terms of 'skills' and 'qualities' alone. The extreme restrictedness of this view of aesthetic education needs emphasising: it is defined as involving no knowledge and little intellectual activity. Similarly 'spiritual development' is defined in terms of 'knowledge' of the Bible, Christian beliefs and world religions, the 'qualities' of conforming with Christian precepts, and no 'skills': a curious view of spirituality, to say the least. And among the 15 'social and moral development' aims there is just one concerned with knowledge, that of knowing 'those moral values, relating to people and property, which are shared by the majority of members of society', and the 'skills' and 'qualities' overwhelmingly emphasise knowing and conforming to social norms like honesty, industriousness, persistence, conscientiousness, obedience and so on. Taken together the 'spiritual', 'social' and 'moral' aims seem the antithesis of those concerns for empathy and autonomy central to child-centred ideology. Overall, one is left with the impression that the (presumably representative) sample of primary teachers whose efforts produced this study conceived of human development, human achievement and the curriculum in somewhat restricted terms. 'Knowledge' in particular plays a minor role (15 aims as compared with 29 'skills' and 28 'qualities') and is clearly perceived in low-level propositional terms — general knowledge, grammar, vocabulary, rules and norms, etc.: a view of some significance in the context of the 'child, not knowledge' part of child-centred ideology.

The plea of 'looseness' carries little weight, for this classification or modified versions of it have widespread currency at LEA and school levels, most notably in assessment and record-keeping systems and in school curriculum schemes and guidelines (see p. 193). Such documentary frameworks for practice or for the assessment of children's progress have proliferated in recent years. I have yet to read one which treats its own classification as problematic in the way that subject categories are invariably treated.

One is left wondering whether the 'fragmentation', 'rigidity' and 'compartmentalisation' attributed to the subject-based curriculum have really been eliminated or whether they have simply reappeared in another guise, ideologically more congenial, but conceptually equally questionable — from the imposition of subjects to the imposition of developmentalism, from the 'artificial barriers' of subject boundaries to those of developmental levels and strands — for there is nothing natural about a developmental theory. How flexible and open is it possible for professional thought and discourse about children and the curriculum to be, given the tightness and conceptual weakness of the developmental matrix within which it can become imprisoned? Which is the more serious in its consequences for children's education, a view of 'art' as a distinctive area of the curriculum involving induction into capacities to use and respond to the elements of colour, tone, form, texture, line and so on (i.e. a subject) or a view of 'aesthetic development' as comprising no more than some basic manipulative skills and a sense of pleasure? In terms of under-expectation and under-achievement, it could be argued, the child stands to lose more from the imposition of a narrowly conceived developmentalism than from a subject-based curriculum. The boundaries between subjects are vertical: unlike developmental boundaries they incorporate no assumptions about what a child can or cannot learn, achieve, or do at a given age or stage.

I commented earlier that the statement 'child not curriculum' not only is an unhelpful polarisation but also enshrines a contradiction, since defining what the child should experience and learn in school is a curricular activity and indeed there can be no meaningful concept of education without curriculum. What has to be explored by teachers and others pursuing such an exclusively child-centred (or curriculum-centred) view of education is the issue of which in the end is more in the child's educational interests, a structure for conceptualising ways of knowing and understanding or a structure for defining childhood. (Needless to say, as one who dislikes dichotomies, I would argue that neither on its own is an adequate basis for curriculum planning.) But in any event, close analysis of frameworks such as the one discussed above reveals that the use of the word 'development' is at best misleading and at worst evidence of self-deception on a large scale. For the lists of intellectual, aesthetic, physical and other aims are grounded not in developmental analysis but in what is essentially a species of epistemology. Thus, for example, the restricted view of 'aesthetic development' is entirely inconsistent with evidence actually available on children's aesthetic development from workers like Eisner (1976), Lowenfeld and Brittain (1982), Griffiths (1945) and others and with theoretical and empirical study of creative processes. Instead it seems to reflect, in its arbitrary catalogue of 'skills' and 'qualities' the limited conceptualisations of those who have engaged neither with aesthetic development nor with aesthetic experience and activity to any significant depth but have only their own limited experiences first as pupils and then as teachers of a traditionally low-status and ill-taught curriculum area on which to draw. The word 'development' is then invoked to give the resulting muddled and impoverished conceptualisation legitimacy in terms of child-centred ideology: 'art' is subject-centred but 'aesthetic development' is child-centred.

Development and knowledge: are they really incompatible?

The 'developmental needs' approach represents the most substantial articulation of a counter-argument to that of writers like Hamlyn who start from the basis of the given-ness of culturally evolved areas of knowledge: 'The best person to say how the teaching of mathematics should proceed is the mathematician' (Hamlyn 1970).

Actually, mathematics is a poor example in the primary context because it is one of the few areas of the curriculum where logical (as opposed to psychological) imperatives are allowed to carry substantial weight, and if one were to substitute 'art'/'artist' or 'history'/'historian' for 'mathematics'/'mathematician' the professional contentiousness of such a statement would be more readily appreciated.

Embedded in the developmental view of the child's curriculum is the assumption that logic and psychologic, or epistemology and child development, are irreconcilable. Undoubtedly there is a tension between, on the one hand, a concern to preserve the concepts and structures of culturally evolved, 'adult' versions of different ways of making sense and responding to experience (see Hirst's 'forms of knowledge' — Hirst 1965 and 1974), and, on the other hand, a concern to provide young children with learning experiences consistent with the way they think, make sense of and respond to experience. As Blyth argues (UCET 1982): 'An emphasis on growth and development in children is not easily reconciled with an emphasis on ways of knowing'. But the emphases ought not to be treated as mutually exclusive, for the epistemology/ development tension is at the heart of curriculum. To explore it in relation to each area of learning is not merely productive but essential, for learning has to be both developmentally apposite and culturally meaningful. One of the most unsatisfactory elements in child-centred discourse is its tendency to rule epistemological considerations out of order and thereby simply to dodge this central tension.

If we reflect for a moment on our own experience of outstanding teachers, we may well need to acknowledge that their success was due not only to interpersonal and pedagogical skills but to an ability to structure curriculum experiences which reflected both an engagement with this tension and a resolution of it. Sybil Marshall's celebrated account (1963) of her work as a teaching head in a Cambridgeshire village school, something of a cult book in the child-centred canon, is not in fact an endorsement of Rousseau's maxim that 'Childhood has its own way of thinking, seeing, feeling' (Rousseau 1911, p. 54) or of his consequent insistence that education should not be in any sense a preparation for adult life. Marshall's writing is dominated instead by a concern to achieve a meaningful relationship between 'child art' and 'art', a continuity between early aesthetic experience and a later capacity to understand and respond to 'the arts'.

> To believe in their own potentiality for creativity was for the children the first half of their journey towards being educated beings. The other half could be completed only when they could see their own lives surrounded, sustained and indeed explained by the general experience of humanity . . . To be able to approach the classic works of art without fear, and with pleasure, interest, understanding and love is to be able to tap the inexhaustible well of past human experience.
>
> (Marshall 1963, p. 171)

Nor is this sense of continuity without empirical foundation. For example, while Kellogg's analysis of thousands of young children's drawings showed a consistent developmental sequence building upon basic scribbles and a vocabulary of elemental shapes like circles, squares, crosses, suns and radials as a child moved towards early pictorial representation, it also showed the child reaching for supposedly 'adult' artistic elements like composition, perspective, contrast, tone, texture and so on, without teacher guidance or 'imposition' (Kellogg 1969). As with rhythm, timbre, dynamics, pitch and melody in music, such elements appear to be fundamental to creative activity and response at any developmental level and in any cultural context.

Such continuity, in fact, is hardly surprising, given the nature of human development and the cultural evolution of knowledge; what is remarkable is the unquestioning allegiance in the primary world to the view that there is no connection between the adult's and the child's cognition and world view, that the adult, somehow, is severed from his or her childhood, that human history is transition from the primitive (yesterday) to the advanced (today). This view, moreover, is inconsistent with the very theory drawn on to legitimate the child-centred rationale: the concrete-to-abstract sequences of Piaget and Bruner are recurrent, not once and for all, and maybe it would be salutary for primary teachers in training to study how adults, as well as children, think, learn and tackle problems, and to examine, compare and put in perspective ideas and artefacts — artistic, political, religious and philosophical — from different cultures and different periods in history. The standard child-development course is an extraordinarily limited framework for the understanding of human development, human attributes and human potential which the teacher needs.

While not claiming to tackle this challenge in the breadth implied above, several recent curriculum projects make a significant contribution in as far as they show how, in different areas of learning, cultural, epistemological and psychological considerations can be reconciled to produce curriculum experiences which are meaningful and valid by both 'adult' and 'child-centred' criteria. The Science 5–13 materials combine Piagetian developmental analysis and a 'discovery' approach to learning with objectives and experiences which are consistent with the scientist's perception of his activity: 'observing, exploring and ordering observations'; 'posing questions and devising experiments or investigations to answer them'; 'appreciating patterns and relationships'; 'interpreting findings critically', and so on (Ennever and Harlen 1975).

Similarly, the Bruner-inspired project 'Man A Course of Study' (MACOS) employs anthropological and ethological perspectives to engage children's capacity to attempt to define what is essentially human about human beings in terms of attributes such as language, tool-making, social organisation, the prolongation of childhood and humanity's urge to explain its world. In terms of that narrow developmentalism discussed earlier this area of inquiry would seem to be, by virtue of its potential abstractness, beyond the conceptual 'level' of even older primary and middle-school children; yet MACOS uses visual resources, a rigorous approach to the structure and progression of concepts and an inquiry-based methodology in a way which seeks to represent in practice Bruner's maxim that 'any subject can be taught effectively in some intellectually honest form to any child at any stage of development' (Bruner 1963, p. 33).

The work of Blyth and his colleagues achieves a comparable reconciliation or synthesis for history, geography and social science (Blyth, et al 1976) — that indeterminate and confused area of the curriculum where if the above subject labels are not used, a variety of umbrella terms are available, none of which may necessarily mean in practice what it implies conceptually: integrated studies, social studies, environmental studies, humanities, topic work, projects, etc.

The authors make a useful distinction between 'subjects' and 'disciplines': the former are areas into which a school curriculum is divided for timetabling or staffing purposes, while the latter are modes of study, inquiry and explanation which are distinctive (and indeed 'disciplined') as to their underpinning structures, concepts and modes of operation. If subjects are — as in primary parlance — 'arbitrary' (and by this view they may well be) then disciplines are not. But, in any case, neither subjects nor disciplines are treated as ends in themselves by this project but are available as resources for the study of 'man in place, time and society'. Thus this area of the curriculum can as readily be planned on the basis of 'themes' resembling (superficially at least) the familiar primary 'topic' as 'subjects'. On the other hand, and consistent with the arguments about science and art above, the discipline base of the project's themes provides what so many primary topics (for example as castigated by HMI in the two primary surveys) lack: a seriousness in pursuit of truth (as opposed to unexamined information) about the child's world. Ultimately, however embryonic the style of engagement with, say, the historian's tools of inquiry and interpretation of evidence, it is this underlying integrity of purpose which enables this kind of environmental studies topic to transcend mere 'busyness' and become educative.

Each of these projects preserves, appropriately 'translated' to meet children's perceived cognitive capacities and interests, the key features of the ways of knowing concerned; and each defines these key features in 'process' rather than 'content' terms, with an emphasis on modes and tools of inquiry, types and uses of evidence, methods of verification, skills of observing, recording, seeking and applying information, rather than the accumulation of 'information' gained by means unexplored and unchallenged. This is a view of knowledge a long way removed from the content-heavy, process-free, 'empty vessel' characterisation which in child-centred ideology is used as a basis for dismissing 'subjects' and 'knowledge'; on the other hand it is a view of knowledge with which advanced workers in the disciplines concerned — science, history, geography, sociology, anthropology — can identify, while the exclusively content characterisation would gain little approval. Yet, ironically, the child-centred objection to subjects and knowledge arises precisely because these are seen as 'adult' concepts and characterisations 'imposed' on the child. Clearly the epistemological dimension of primary ideology requires further exploration, and this we shall attempt in Chapter 3.

It is significant that none of the approaches outlined above has proved easy to implement. Teachers' difficulties with Science 5–13 necessitated a follow-up project to help them achieve 'match' between learning experiences and children's abilities (Harlen et al 1977), while the MACOS approach is expected to be used only after an intensive in-service course. Similarly the Place, Time and Society project (Blyth et al 1976) started as an approach, a means of generating professional discussion and curriculum planning, but the team were forced to produce conventional teaching materials to meet professional demands for answers rather than questions. Reconciling 'growth and development' with 'ways of knowing' is as much an intellectual as a practical problem: it appears to challenge teachers' professional knowledge and intellectual tenacity to an extent that the easy rhetoric of 'needs and interests' and those busy-seeming but educationally dubious topics on 'transport' or 'witches' do not. Clearly, then, we shall need to consider the extent to which initial training provides the knowledge and intellectual capacities for this kind of professional challenge.

THE CHILD AND SOCIETY: ANOTHER UNNECESSARY DICHOTOMY?

The answer to the basic educational question 'What should the child learn?' is, as we have seen, neither exclusively psychological nor exclusively epistemological: it requires us to consider and juxtapose both dimensions. However, the question is perhaps pre-eminently a cultural one in as far as psychological and epistemological constructs are culturally evolved and embedded, and curriculum decisions are about choices, values and alternative scales of priorities. Here the weighting of much primary discourse is particularly unsatisfactory, for while there is some (if negative) consideration of knowledge, cultural and value issues tend to go by default. Thus, the 'developmental needs' approach to curriculum planning exemplified in the Schools Council Aims study and its follow-up (Ashton, Kneen, Davies and Holley 1975, Ashton, Kneen and Davies 1975) produces a list of 72 aims (in order of priority) for primary education which represents a straightforward and instrumental scale of cultural values, the necessary contentiousness of which is apparently not perceived. The device the researchers used to highlight the cultural dimension if anything exacerbated the problem: all the aims were categorised as either 'societal' or 'individual':

> The purpose of primary education is to begin to equip the child with skills and attitudes which will enable him to take his place effectively and competently in society, fitting him to make a choice of an occupational role and to live harmoniously in his community.
>
> (societal)
>
> The purpose of primary education is to foster the development of the child's individuality and independence enabling him to discover his own talents and interests, find a full enjoyment of life in his own way and acquire his own attitudes towards society.
>
> (individual)
>
> (Ashton, Kneen, Davies and Holley 1975, p. 38)

Between the original study and its follow-up the surveyed teachers shifted 'in the direction of emphasizing the societal purpose' (Ashton 1981, p. 27).

This polarisation of the child and society is endemic to primary discourse. It manifests itself in the everyday utterances of teachers — 'Society demands . . . ', 'Society expects . . . ' — and in the characteristic literature of child-centredness:

> We cannot harmonise the needs of society in a curriculum. Any consideration of aims should be based on what we know about individuals and their basic desire to seek a meaning and to make their world . . . With such a starting point one need not worry about what children 'ought to know in mathematics' . . .
>
> (Marsh 1973, p. 83)

The previous chapter gives other examples: the world 'out there' expressing its alien demands is contrasted with the child's inner world and the 'garden' or cocoon of child-centred schooling.

Clearly the polarisation is untenable: the child is a member of society; so is the teacher. Society and the individual define each other.

Such statements seem to reflect an underestimation of the cultural context and cultural significance of the teacher's actions in the classroom. Nor is there much offered in the major policy documents to which teachers naturally turn for guidance. Plowden contented itself (CACE 1967, Chapter 15) with being 'both hopeful and fearful' about the future shape of society and offered the fall-back responses of 'flexibility' and 'adaptability' which at best are extremely difficult objectives to achieve in any operable sense and, at worst (since the words are frequently invoked but rarely explicated), are a device for dodging the hard social analysis and competing value positions which are involved. Similarly, the 1978 HMI primary survey, while commendably redirecting attention to primary curriculum issues, fails to address itself to the question of the cultural justifications for the curriculum specifications it offers: 'Taking primary schools as a whole, the curriculum is probably wide enough to serve current educational needs.' (DES 1978a, para. 8.67). What these 'current educational needs' are the survey does not say; the omission is presumably justified by the bland assumption of cultural consensus and uniformity.

The Schools Council primary aims study is the starting point for White's attack on the child–society polarity. He argues that the kind of thinking I have exemplified above reflects a long tradition of professional insularity:

> of all members of the teaching profession, (the primary teacher) has traditionally been the least politically aware. Her typical milieu has been the world of art and crafts, of movement and drama, of learning to read and count. It has typically been a cosy, inward-looking world, quite cut off from the complexities of politics.
>
> (White 1982, p. 203)

He then argues for a new role. The primary teacher:

> will need to be a person of wide horizons . . . will need to be more knowledgeable, more reflective about society and its values than her present-day counterpart.

And he suggests some of the implications in terms of professional knowledge and teacher training:

> A deeper understanding of political realities necessitates some knowledge of economics, sociology, applied science, social and political history . . . A deeper reflectiveness about aims and their realization depends among other things on something of a philosophical understanding . . .

Cultural analysis for curriculum purposes is extremely difficult, and fraught with the risk of accusations of value bias. On the other hand, ignoring value issues will not banish them: every curriculum decision is imbued with them and the teacher who argues 'We mustn't impose our values on the children' displays not so much neutrality, as professional self-deception.

What might help here is a wider range of models of curriculum needs than is yet available. One approach is to start with a list of the most pressing 'social issues' demanding an educational and curricular response; current contenders might include multi-culturalism, sexism, the decline of urban industrial environments, technological change and its impact on environment, lifestyles, employment patterns and prospects, value pluralism and moral dissensus, challenges to and instability in the existing social order, and at the global level the gap between rich and poor nations and the acceleration of an arms race involving weapons of mass destruction. Even supposing one could achieve some consensus on the items in such a list, the moral issues raised by each are formidable.

Or one can start with an attempt to derive educational aims from a coherent cultural model rather than from a possibly arbitrary or contentious collection of 'issues'. One such is offered by Stonier (1982) whose analysis of 'post-industrial' society produces the following priorities:

(a) education for employment (flexibility and entrepreneurial skills);
(b) education for life (understanding the world; understanding oneself);
(c) education for the world (technological literacy; humanistic literacy; a global political and economic perspective; individual survival skills);
(d) education for self-development (artistic, physical and social skills; communication skills; organisation skills);
(e) education for pleasure (education for leisure; gaining employment through learning)

(Stonier 1982)

Stonier's analysis is explicitly 'societal' rather than 'individual' in Ashton's terms, in that he argues that the challenge to education is 'to understand what is now happening to our society, and to respond to it imaginatively and . . . effectively' (Stonier 1982, p. 299). Yet each of the aims reflects a concern for the situation of the individual in society as well as for society as a whole: using societal analysis as the starting point he effectively avoids the individual/society polarisation which inevitably ensues from the exclusively child-centred position.

A similar approach underlines some recent attempts to devise a 'core curriculum'. One of the most extensive such ventures was undertaken by Skilbeck and others at the Australian Curriculum Development Centre (CDC 1980), which produced a broad specification for curriculum content on the basis of several stages of analysis: (a) a list of 'universal aims of education', operable in any context; (b) a list of 'aims for Australian schools' reflecting the implications of the espoused Australian commitment to 'parliamentary democracy, the rule of law, full and active participation in civic and social life, and fundamental democratic values'; (c) specifications of aims produced by different authorities; (d) the characteristics of pupils; (e) the capacities and resources of schools; (f) school experience and examples of successful practice; (g) theory, research and practice relating to learning processes.

The CDC model is thus far more than a reconciliation of 'individual' and 'societal' and certainly is well ahead of comparable British official attempts to define overall aims and core content which (e.g. DES 1981a) tend to be so vague and unexceptionable as to have little practical value. What is particularly significant is that it incorporates a comprehensive model of curriculum, acknowledging context, processes and purposes as well as content, and in particular it rejects the (official British) perception of a 'core' as a set of subject labels and offers instead two sorts of interrelated 'core learnings' as a basis for selection. First, *processes*:

(a) learning and thinking techniques;
(b) ways of organising knowledge;
(c) dispositions and values;
(d) skills and abilities;
(e) forms of expression;
(f) practical performances;
(g) interpersonal and group relationships.

Second, *areas of knowledge and experience*:

(a) arts and crafts;
(b) reasoning and values;
(c) social, cultural and civic studies;
(d) science and technology;
(e) communication;
(f) environmental studies;
(g) mathematics;
(h) work, leisure and lifestyle;
(i) health education.

Again, the individual and society are here indivisible and the model has a coherence which the imposition of the 'developmental' matrix (see pp. 22–27) on the random list of 72 aims in the Schools Council project fails to achieve.

A further possibility is the kind of framework for generalised cultural analysis offered by Lawton (1983). A culture is perceived as having eight 'structures' or 'sub-systems': social; economic; communication; rationality; technology; morality; belief; aesthetic. All of these are 'cultural invariants' or basic aspects of any society. They provide the framework within which analysis of the unique characteristics of particular cultures can be explored and against which a coherent view of social change (such as is essential to the teacher, education being nothing if not future-oriented) can be developed.

Four main objections are conventionally offered in the primary world to such approaches. The first is that since the primary child, even at age 11, is several years away from leaving school, cultural imperatives have insufficient immediacy to require attention. The second is that the value issues raised are too formidable: for those who can begin to work out a private response to such daunting social issues as those I identified earlier, let alone a curricular response for primary children, their contentiousness seems to dictate a quick retreat into action-excusing words like 'adaptability' and 'flexibility'. Third, many argue in accordance with the 'cocoon' principle that young children's security should not be disturbed by confronting them with issues that the mature adult has difficulty in coping with. Fourth, the 'developmental' argument is introduced in support of the contention that the relative conceptual abstraction of such issues and the kinds of moral dilemmas they pose make attention to them at any stage prior to the formal operational inappropriate. Since this transition is conveniently held to coincide with the child's transfer to secondary school this excuses further discussion. Though we have dealt with the final objection earlier in this chapter, some sort of case can be made in respect of the other three. But it should be stressed that giving curriculum discourse a cultural dimension demands nothing so simplistic as putting race, microtechnology, unemployment and the Bomb on the child's timetable, but rather ensuring that as a minimum such issues, or rather the knowledge and modes of analysis which define and clarify them, need to be firmly on the agenda of teachers and teacher educators, simply because curriculum is a cultural artefact: culturally embedded values and assumptions are what it is justified by, and a concept of curriculum purportedly independent of these is an impossibility.

The matter is more complicated than this, however, for the pervasiveness and power of television and the circumstances of many families and domestic environ-ments have caused such issues and realities to penetrate children's consciousness and feed their fears to an extent that perhaps dictates that primary schools can no longer maintain their traditional conspiracy of silence. For example, children are increasingly aware, as are adults, of the possibility of imminent nuclear annihilation. Somehow they have to cope with that, and with the knowledge that politicians, the Church and large sectors of the population can apparently acquiesce in genocide as political policy while remaining, seemingly, personable, kindly and caring. 'Childhood innocence' has to take quite a battering: such knowledge tests to its limits the faith children need to be able to place in adults as rational, moral and protective. So, whether they like it or not, teachers will indeed have to work out specific educational responses to such issues, because as specific issues these now confront children.

Something of this is expressed in the Schools Council paper *Primary Practice* — surprisingly, given the tendency of such documents towards consensual blandness of the sort illustrated earlier, though in this case perhaps we were witnessing a defiant parting shot from a body already under sentence of ministerial execution. The authors argue that primary teachers should focus on 'what seem likely to be the most pressing issues of the twenty-first century', among which they list computer literacy, rights and duties in a democratic society, consumer education, multi-culturalism and multi-ethnicity, and — controversially — Third World studies, conservation, energy and pollution, and peace studies (Schools Council 1983, pp. 29–30). Perhaps this list does no more than catch the early to mid-1980s mood of national pessimism and interna-tional nervousness. On the other hand, it might just represent a trend of profounder long-term significance: the beginnings of a greater preparedness, endorsed by the primary profession's leaders, to look outwards from the classroom as well as inwards at the child.

It must be emphasised, however, that what is needed here is balance. There is also an extreme 'society-centred' view, as restricted in its way as the cocoon version of child-centredness. This — exemplified in central government pronouncements and policies since 1979 — equates society with the economy and uses technological development as the sole yardstick for social progress. Its consequence for the child's education is an updated version of the nineteenth-century utilitarian curriculum. The view of 'culture' informing educators' decisions needs to be comprehensive, pluralist and open: the view of 'society' guiding recent educational policy is one-dimensional, ideologically partisan and closed.

PEDAGOGY: THE CLASS TEACHER AND THE REALISATION OF THE CHILD'S 'POTENTIAL'

I have suggested that the class-teacher system in primary schools, being a legacy of nineteenth-century mass elementary education, predates the child-centred ideology by which it is justified:

The class teacher . . . has the knowledge and professional judgment necessary to decide on the appropriate curriculum content, organization and methods best suited to individual children

(NUT 1979, p. 35)

Certainly the argument seems superficially convincing: the primary class teacher sees the child all the time, across the total spectrum of learning. Secondary teachers see their pupils for a small proportion of that time, and in a limited curriculum context. Therefore primary teachers 'know' their pupils better and their professional diagnoses are more reliable.

I have also suggested, however, that unassailability as a diagnostician is not an inevitable consequence of this temporally more extensive acquaintance: which do competent doctors need more of in order to make their diagnoses — time with the patient or professional knowledge and skill? And do secondary mathematics teachers make a better or worse job of diagnosing their pupils' mathematical ability and needs than primary class teachers operating in the same curriculum area?

The critical questions I propose to consider now in connection with 'knowing and understanding children' are:

1. What evidence do we have about the nature of that knowledge of children on the basis of which the class teacher makes his or her everyday professional judgements?
2. What evidence do we have about the effectiveness of the various pedagogical approaches associated with primary class teaching and justified in terms of the above knowledge?
3. What other theoretical or empirical observations might be made about the class teacher's claim to know and to be able to develop the child's 'potential'?

Everyday knowledge of children

The empirical exploration of how the teacher builds up a picture of the children he or she teaches, and of the sources of such information as he or she uses, is a very new field in educational inquiry. The methodological difficulties are well defined by McNamara and Desforges (1978) and Desforges and McNamara (1979). Even the extensive work on teacher expectation and pupil performance, to which we referred earlier, pays relatively little attention to the mechanisms by which these expectations are formed.

At the simplest level, three particular kinds of 'knowledge' can be pinpointed:

(a) formal information, gathered as a result of testing and the making and transmission of pupil records;
(b) what Becher, Eraut and Knight (1981) call 'grapevine' information, prominent in the staffroom, focusing especially on children who are thought to display extremes of behaviour, personality or ability, and providing the teacher with advance information on the 'reputation' of a child (and its family);
(c) informal information gathered or constructed by teachers themselves on the basis of everyday interaction and evaluation in the classroom.

These areas offer only starting points. Each raises difficult questions. Assessment via *formal* testing or other publicly verified procedures can only deal with very limited and specific areas of school work and is much less important than the continuous *informal* (even unconscious) evaluation of the pupil by the teacher. Moreover, formal assessment of cognitive ability is not always readily separable from informal appraisal of, or reaction to, aspects of behaviour — attention span, persistence, responsiveness, and so on — so that assessment cannot be treated apart from the broader questions of classroom interaction and teacher perception. Similarly, 'grapevine' information is in obvious ways highly selective and susceptible to prejudice.

So, if we focus on the more significant question of how teachers build up a detailed picture of the individual pupils they teach, it is necessary to look not just at specific forms of information-gathering but also at the complex processes of classroom interaction and the theories, values and ideologies of the individual teacher. The first point is, of course, that teachers do not establish separate and private relationships with each pupil but face a whole class and each individual relationship is mediated through the whole class (Lortie 1975). And this is an important factor determining teachers' perceptions. Subject to a massive bombardment of information the teacher has to select, and tends to focus on the extremes of ability and behaviour (Morrison and McIntyre 1973). Hargreaves (1967) found that teachers learned the names of 'good' and 'bad' pupils much more quickly than those who were average. Thus, profiles of pupils are not built up by teachers on some kind of 'rational' or even intentional basis, but out of social engagements.

Second, theoretical models of interaction or decision-making draw attention to important questions — person perception, stereotyping, sensitivity to pupils' needs, processing of information and so on — but tend to over-emphasise the rational, conscious and purposeful aspects of the teacher's behaviour. As Jackson (1968, p. 151) puts it: 'The immediacy of classroom life, the fleeting and sometimes cryptic signs on which the teacher relies for determining his pedagogical moves and for evaluating the effectiveness of his actions call into question the appropriateness of using conventional models of rationality to depict the teacher's classroom behaviour.'

Jackson, Lortie and others go so far as to argue that there is very little in the way of 'educational knowledge' shared by teachers. The aims of teaching are vague, and success can rarely be quantified. Thus Lortie (1975, p. 136): 'The teacher's craft . . . is marked by the absence of concrete models for emulation, unclear lines of influence, multiple and controversial criteria, ambiguity about assessment and timing, and instability in the product.' Jackson goes even further. He found that teachers relied upon subjective feelings to monitor their own teaching. Unlike astrophysicists or garage mechanics, teachers seem to lack a technical and specialised professional language, relying upon a very simple and markedly particularised discourse: 'Rarely, if ever, did they turn to evidence beyond their own personal experience to justify their professional preferences' (Jackson 1968, p. 181). McNamara and Desforges (1978) and Desforges and McNamara (1979) suggest that this kind of argument against teachers possessing a coherent and viable 'craft knowledge' is predicated on inadequate research — too little investment of time and an inability to elicit the knowledge that is embedded in the concreteness and particularity of teacher language. But they too clearly see the inadequacy of looking for some simple and coherent set of explicit attitudes.

Against this background of methodological complexity perhaps the most convincing material stems from close observations of classroom processes coupled with exploratory teacher–observer discussion after the events to establish their meanings and explanations and the sorts of knowledge on which the teacher has drawn. Here, as indicated earlier, King's study of infant classrooms offers substantial insight:

> Typification, assessment, teaching, learning, controlling, were all aspects of the same flow of action and interaction in the classroom and they were all consonant with the teacher's recipe ideologies, particularly those of development and individuality.
>
> (King 1978, p. 58)

The sources for typifications, mediated by the child-centred framework, included 'public' and 'private' knowledge relating to children's compliance with the teacher's behavioural code or 'hidden curriculum', their relationships with other children, their learning progress, their family/home background and so on. Social class assumptions and constructs played some part — a point more strongly argued in Sharp and Green's study (1975) where the characterisation of working-class and middle-class family circumstances and aspirations was markedly stereotypical, and at secondary level by Keddie (1971), who suggested that teachers' knowledge of pupil ability had mainly to do with social-class-oriented judgements of their moral, social and intellectual behaviour. Moreover, in some expectancy research (e.g. Nash 1973) the key social class attribution could even be incorrect: children's actual home circumstances could be very different from teachers' perceptions of them.

Attempting to represent such complexity diagrammatically is a dangerous exercise, but if we treat the attempt with due caution it may help to draw together some of the main strands of our discussion so far (see Figure 2.1). In particular, we can show that: (a) a teacher's knowledge of a given child is subject to 'filtration' and 'signal interference'; (b) teachers as educators act on children in accordance with a view of them which they are largely instrumental in constructing; (c) this view, even granted sometimes the availability of considerable formal information, cannot really be claimed to be either objective or absolute.

The recent empirical material on teacher expectations and typifications does not of itself repudiate the claimed efficacy of the class-teacher approach as a means of promoting learning, but it certainly calls into question the validity of the confident claim that the class teacher knows the child best. Moreover, it casts doubt upon the wisdom, and fairness, of putting the child under the charge of one teacher's 'knowledge' of him or her for a period of a year or more, especially where the framework is simplistic, and there is little construct modification, a high incidence of labelling and/or a failure at the level of interpersonal relationships. The class teacher's 'knowledge of children' can be distinctly double-edged.

Against such reservations have to be set the traditional arguments about continuity, stability, the value to the young child of the carefully nurtured micro-culture of the single unchanging classroom, and of curriculum coherence (if it really exists: see Chapter 3).

The effectiveness of class teaching

Empirical evidence on the effectiveness of the pedagogy associated with the primary class teacher role is recent and slender (though expanding). Everyday discourse tends

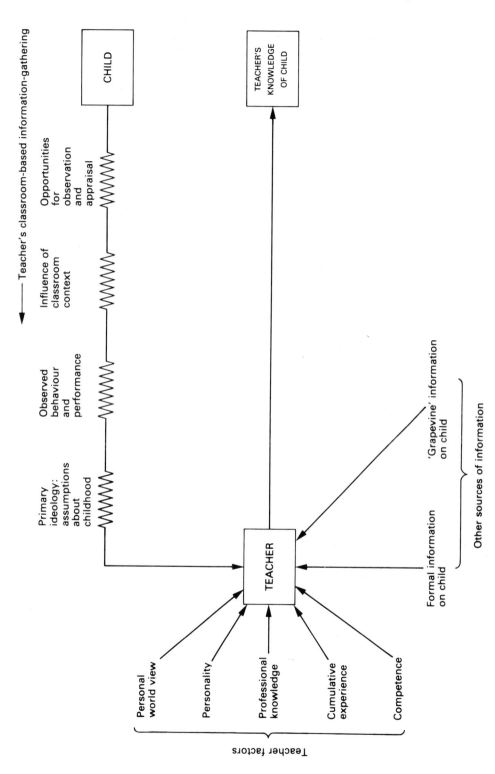

Figure 2.1 *'Knowing the whole child': processes and influences*

to be framed by highly generalised terms like 'formal' and 'informal' which are not only too vague to be useful, but also have strong evaluative overtones (formal = old-fashioned, rigid, authoritarian, didactic; informal = progressive, flexible, responsive, heuristic). The much-publicised Lancaster study of Bennett (1976) attempted through the use of questionnaires and cluster analysis to refine the terms and purported to show via a pre-test/post-test programme the effectiveness of 'formal', 'informal' and 'mixed' styles of teaching. However, the combination of media oversell and subsequent methodological and statistical critique (Gray and Satterly 1981) makes this study an unreliable one in the present context.

The 1978 HMI Primary Survey (DES 1978a) adopted a similarly dichotomising view of primary pedagogy — 'didactic' versus 'exploratory' and, of course, 'mixed methods' — and through the use of the concept of 'match' purported to show both the incidence and effectiveness of the three styles. Of the teachers, 75 per cent used 'mainly didactic' teaching methods, 5 per cent 'mainly exploratory' and 20 per cent 'mixed'. Crude though it was, this analysis of incidence pointed up one very significant issue, later confirmed in the ORACLE study (see below), namely the extent to which primary professional practice and primary ideology contradicted each other: progressivism emerged as a distinctly minority pursuit. Moreover, the survey appeared to show that children of 'didactic' teachers scored higher on tests than those of 'exploratory' teachers, but that 'mixed' methods were the most effective in terms of both test scores and match ratings.

The ORACLE research (Galton, Simon and Croll 1980, Galton and Simon 1980, Simon and Willcocks 1981) is the most extensive to date and incorporates a rather more sophisticated typology of teaching styles than either Bennett or HMI. Like HMI, but unlike Bennett, the ORACLE team used classroom observation, but their study was unique in adopting a highly pre-structured and systematised schedule for classroom interaction analysis. Together the studies confirm that the predominating ideological commitment since before Plowden to group work, individualisation, informality and exploration is not strongly reflected in practice. On 'treating each pupil as an individual' for example — a key component in the ideology as King (1978) showed — the ORACLE team found that while pupils' work was largely individualised (as opposed to corporate) and the bulk of the teacher's time was spent on private individual exchanges with specific individual children in turn, the exigencies of class size meant that each child received individual attention from the teacher for a very small proportion of lesson time (Galton, Simon and Croll 1980). Moreover, teachers who used individual interaction tended to operate most frequently at the instructional, 'monitoring' and routinely supervisory levels, rather than in providing probing or open-ended higher-order cognitive interactions of the sort Galton and Simon showed to be so significant for effective learning.

A similar picture emerges for group work. Like individualisation it features prominently in progressive rhetoric, and the physical arrangement of children into groups (rather than rows or pairs) provides one of the most obvious visual contrasts between many primary and secondary classrooms. Yet, within such groups, learning was mostly individual rather than as genuinely collaborative as the notion of 'group learning' implies, and teachers who worked mostly at the small group level tended to use largely didactic teaching methods. 'Grouping' thus emerges as an organisational device rather than a means of promoting more effective learning, or perhaps exists for no reason other than that fashion and ideology dictate it.

Just as the approbatory image of 'individual' and 'group' work is strongly questioned by the ORACLE evidence, so, conversely, the use of classteaching is in some respects rehabilitated. (To avoid confusion I use two words 'class teaching/class teacher' to denote the universal organisational arrangement in primary schools that this book focuses on, of having one teacher for the whole year and the whole curriculum, and one word 'classteaching' to denote the particular pedagogical practice of the teacher treating the class as a single unit and engaging their attention from the front of the room.) In the child-centred ideology classteaching is seen as the antithesis of individualisation, as treating children as identical, as failing to allow for individual differences in ability and motivation; it is strongly tinged with connotations of fact transmission, rote-learning and even indoctrination (Selleck 1972).

Galton and Simon's work shows how the teachers they termed 'class enquirers' (i.e. classteachers) made frequent use of open as well as closed questions and emphasised problem-solving and the exploration of ideas. This approach was more likely to produce those 'higher order cognitive interactions' between teacher and child than the versions of either 'individual' or 'group' teaching that they observed. Classteaching is of course the style most familiar in secondary schools, and it has to be pointed out that in the generally larger classes in primary schools the number of children actually engaged in productive teacher–pupil interactions in the context of classteaching can be very small.

Clearly, whatever methodological reservations they provoke, such findings call into question the rhetoric of 'individual', 'group' and 'class' teaching upon which the justification for the class teacher role partly depends. When one combines such analysis with the strong ideological framing and sometimes inflexible, typificatory or stereotypical character of the professional 'knowledge of children' which emerges from the other classroom studies discussed earlier, the educational arguments in favour of generalist class teaching begin to look increasingly thin, and less and less in the child's educational interests.

It is also interesting to note the way the message of such research can be missed or distorted at the professional level when it implies critique of mainstream ideology and practice. Thus Kirby remarks:

> The keywords to successful learning, according to the ORACLE project, are active attention and involvement on the part of the children.
>
> (Kirby 1981, p. 31)

This re-interpretation of ORACLE in vaguely Hadow/Plowden terms effectively shifts the responsibility from the teacher to the child. The real keyword of ORACLE is 'interaction', the onus for promoting which was placed squarely on the teacher. In its implications for careful analysis, planning, structure, progression and the systematisation of the teaching-learning process, 'interaction' in the ORACLE sense has little in common with that self-justifying 'busyness' (King 1978), so often connoted when Hadow and Plowden are invoked in support of 'activity and experience'.

The class teacher and the development of the child's 'potential': further observations

For HMI (DES 1978a and 1982a), the concept of 'match' between a child's perceived ability and the learning experiences provided for him by the teacher was a major concern. HMI offered evidence of variation in teachers' matching ability relating to teaching style (didactic/exploratory/mixed) and to curriculum area. I shall argue more fully in Chapter 3 that the findings on the curriculum aspect of match have profound implications for teacher education, as indeed HMI have now realised, in their recommendations about curriculum consultancy and staff responsibilities (DES 1978a, 1982a, 1983a and 1983b). But of course 'match' demands, broadly, two sorts of professional knowledge — of the child and of the range of appropriate curriculum experiences.

Blyth (UCET 1982) uses the terms 'professional knowledge' and 'curricular knowledge' to distinguish understanding of children from understanding of curriculum. The distinction is necessary, but the labels are unsatisfactory since they might encourage the view that curriculum knowledge and expertise are distinct from, or somehow less centrally 'professional' than, knowledge of children and educational processes. I would prefer 'professional knowledge' to be an umbrella term, meaning exactly what it implies — the full range of knowledge a professional needs in order to undertake his job (see Hirst 1979) — and to use further, more precise, terms to define the components of such professional knowledge.

Primary ideology rests heavily on the view that 'knowledge' of children is infinitely more important than curriculum knowledge, but if the validity of the former can be shown, as we have seen, to be so open to doubt, and if the latter is either deemed unimportant or is not available, then the basis of primary teachers' professional-knowledge claim begins to look alarmingly suspect: at least their secondary colleagues can fall back on their 'subject knowledge'.

Actually, the primary curriculum knowledge issue is far more complex than the phrase 'subject knowledge' implies, as I shall show in Chapter 3. Meanwhile, concentrating on the familiar notion of 'potential', two fundamental points need to be made.

First, if the assessment of *performance* is difficult (despite the formidable batteries of tests now available), how much more problematic is the assessment of *potential*. If we know our objectives or criteria, and have a reasonably good assessment method or instrument we can say, with some confidence in the reliability of our judgements, whether or not, or to what extent, a child has achieved the objectives or met the criteria. But the jump from what a child actually has done to what he or she might or might not be able to do is much more hazardous. HMI's 'match' findings show potential being consistently underrated. Tempest (1974), Ogilvie (1973) and others report that teachers had difficulty in identifying very able children. The various 'giftedness' checklists now available from LEAs and research projects are not so much objective indicators as sensitisers to the possibility that the teacher's initial informal assessments might be inadequate; but having been alerted to the possibility of talent the teacher still has few clearcut means for establishing in what direction that talent lies. Problematically, potential is unknowable, in an absolute sense, though we can and do claim to know what a child *might* be able to achieve in specific areas or in very general terms on the basis of IQ scores, reading ages and the like. But what of the child's potential in curriculum areas where we have provided limited or no learning opportunities, or have not assessed his or her performance with any precision? And what if our teaching has been in some respects ill-conceived or ill-matched in relation to the child's abilities (whatever they may be — the Catch 22 of assessing potential)? The problem with 'potential' is that it implies first a fixed, predetermined level of ability and, second, that the actual areas of knowledge or skill are also in some sense mapped out in advance. Yet what does seem to be fairly certain is that what children achieve is in part at least a product of the opportunities with which they are provided and the expectations others have of them: the better the teaching and the higher the expectations the more children may achieve and the greater 'potential' they thereby demonstrate, thus rendering more and more obsolete the use of concepts like 'potential' or even 'ability' which are absolutely fundamental to current educational thought and practice.

Of course, we should distinguish between immediate and long-term potential. The day-to-day decision about what the child should do next rests on a short-term appraisal of immediate needs based on very recent performance: the idea of learning as a progressive process which can be planned for demands this sort of appraisal. However, it is not (or should not be) in any sense a permanent appraisal, but needs to be open to continuing modification in the light of our monitoring the child's performance through a sequence of learning experiences. This transitory, constantly revised appraisal process is rather different from such assessment of longer-term potential as we have to make from time to time, for example when advising parents or making formal records, and which becomes increasingly crucial to children's life-chances the further up the education system they move. However, the two sorts of appraisal are linked, in that when we make a longer-term assessment of potential, while we might look more globally at a child's work rather than at an immediately recent and limited part of it, we are still, in essence, hazarding a prediction of future performance on the basis of past achievement. The quality of the longer-term prediction will depend on the quality of those short-term, day-to-day appraisals which guided our decisions leading up to the point of longer-term prediction.

So that while it is important, as HMI imply through their focus on 'match', to establish as reliably as possible what a child might be capable of in order to make appropriate curriculum decisions and recommendations, an over-confident assessment — especially if it is a considerable under-expectation or over-expectation — may be damaging. Since such over-confidence is usually a product of ignorance or insensitivity the damage may be compounded. The troubling thing here is that the more we come to know about children, about teaching and learning, and about the immense diversity and openness of knowledge, the more we have to accept that our best judgement of what a child can do, good though it is, is an approximation — not an absolute judgement but the most reliable and impartial which circumstances and our experience, knowledge and skills allow.

The strength of the class-teacher system is that it puts the teacher in as strong a position as possible to make this judgement (by comparison with a secondary colleague who may see a pupil for three sessions of 40 minutes each week). But ultimately we are dealing with uncertainties: even as both a teacher and a parent I would hesitate to say that I *know* what my own children's educational potentials and needs are, but some of their teachers, whose acquaintance with the children is far slighter than mine, will claim that knowledge with an assurance which privately I find disturbing, though publicly I recognise that professional credibility depends on their demonstrating such assurance. It is this element of uncertainty at the root of some of the most important of our professional judgements which makes teaching in its way so much more complex and demanding an activity than many other professions: at least, that is, for the teacher who is sufficiently experienced, self-aware and modest to perceive and accept the uncertainty.

The second point to make about 'potential' is that it tends to incorporate implicit attributions of causality. We have seen how recent sociological studies confirm in different ways primary teachers' use of what King (1978) terms a 'family-home background' theory to explain discrepancies between their views of how children should be and the way they actually are, and that teachers themselves are rarely seen as contributing to such discrepancies. The reasons for seeking explanations outside the classroom for lack of success in it have to do, one assumes, with the complex, demanding and potentially self-undermining character of teaching. Professional self-esteem is necessary for confident classroom decision-making and for many teachers the incidence of pupil failure or at least under-achievement is so high that to turn more than a modest proportion of it back on oneself would be excessively damaging and inhibiting.

This explanatory framework, as we shall see, is initially provided in teacher training: psychology and sociology of education courses (or their integrated/thematic counter-parts) tend to investigate in depth the characteristics of learners and their family background. Pedagogy is frequently explored in a reificatory way, in terms of the processes rather than their agent (e.g. questioning, assessing, organising rather than the questioner, assessor or organiser). Little theoretical or otherwise detailed analytical attention is devoted to the teacher other than to the external professional persona and observable actions: motivations, constructs, cognitive processes and personality — the way each teacher thinks, feels and views his or her task — remain unexplored.

Thus 'potential' emerges, by default rather than intention no doubt, as a function of the child's attributes of (a) innate intelligence, (b) developmentally determined cognitive levels, and (c) culturally influenced attitudes and motivations, but not as a function of teacher action or teacher–child interaction. Yet if, for a change, one applies a different theoretical perspective, that of, say, psychoanalytic rather than developmental theory, an alternative hypothesis about 'potential' becomes available.

Drawing on Jungian models, Storr (1960) argues that the individual's self-realisation is achieved only through mature personal relationships and that the development of the individual and the development of relationships with others are inseparably linked. Moreover, outstanding genius apart, the individual's potentialities do not simply emerge, but require to be evoked by compatible circumstances, and particularly through relationships with someone who has something of the 'same gift or interest which is seeking expression'.

Storr uses this as an argument first for education by teachers rather than parents, and second for education by many teachers rather than one or a few: 'The varieties in temperament and the differences in hereditary endowment are extensive, and the more people with whom the child and adolescent can come into contact the more quickly he can find himself.' The mechanisms are projection, identification, model-ling, development of the potentiality leading eventually to dis-identification or 'growing out' of the other person whose possession of an admired characteristic has evoked the same in the child. Autobiographical writing is full of examples of indi-viduals coming into contact with an adult, frequently, but not necessarily, a teacher, whose possession of a particular ability was strongly admired and led to the develop-ment of the same ability in the child. One of the staunchest of child-centred advocates, Pluckrose, recalls developing 'a love of poetry because I respected at an impression-able age a teacher who cared for words' (Pluckrose 1975, p. 4).

This alternative approach to the issue of 'potential' raises important questions vis-à-vis the confident claims made for class teaching in this regard. To what extent can a teacher recognise aspects of a child's personality and potential that he does not possess himself? Can he evoke them if latent? Can he develop them? Can he achieve these things if his own level of education is modest or, in major areas, deficient (as is, inevitably, the case for all of us)? Can he achieve these things while espousing an ideology which holds that curriculum knowledge — in the sense of deeper personal understanding of, say, mathematics, science, the arts, and so on — is at primary stage unimportant by comparison with 'knowledge' of the child as mediated through a somewhat restricted concept of developmentalism? Does this not effectively invali-date his claim that he 'knows' the child? Does it not demonstrate that knowledge of the child requires some depth of curriculum knowledge? Does it not mean that by neglecting his own knowledge, the teacher may deny himself one of the means whereby he may identify or cause to be evoked the child's potential? In sum, by this analysis, is not the ideological rejection of curriculum and knowledge a demonstration not of child-centredness but of its antithesis?

Thus, on psychological grounds the claims for class teaching can be either substan-tiated or undermined, depending on which psychological theories and models one applies. The notion of 'ideology' which I discussed, in Chapter 1, as a value system related to justifying and preserving position and identity, would partly explain why developmental psychology has been so readily accepted as the main component in primary professional knowledge and why, in a profession not generally impressed by theory and research, Piaget receives such unqualified acclaim. Interactive personality theory calls into question the class teacher's claim: cognitive developmental theory reinforces it. Class teaching came first, a legacy of the elementary tradition in subsequent search of an 'expert knowledge' rationale: developmentalism provides that rationale.

There is one catch and one further cause for concern in this complex and admittedly speculative area. The catch is that the HMI primary survey's use of the concept of 'match' between children's potential and the curriculum experiences provided pre-sumes that HMI's capacity for recognising and assessing potential was greater than that of the class teachers they observed. The presumption is inherent in the survey, and indeed in the concept of an inspectorate which makes public its findings and expects them to be acted upon. One might term this, in view of the spate of such survey material in recent years, presumptiousness rather than presumption. This reservation, on the other hand, while it calls into question the validity of HMI's match ratings does not invalidate the concept of 'match' itself which is immensely suggestive, even if empirically elusive.

The cause for concern arises from the probability that children have potentialities both in areas of school curriculum provision, and in areas where there are no such experiences and opportunities. If potential is indeed evoked and realised as discussed above not only is there likely to be under-achievement and under-expectation in areas where at least it can be identified, but one can also reasonably assume the existence in our child (and adult) population of unrealised potential in other areas on a vast scale, and a waste of human resources for which the word 'tragic' is for once not an overstatement.

CONCLUSION

In this chapter I have taken the cornerstone of primary ideology — the class teacher's claim to a deep personal understanding of the children he or she teaches, on the basis of which he or she can accurately define and administer to their curriculum needs — and have suggested that it is open to question on both conceptual and empirical grounds.

I considered first the dominance of 'developmentalism' in the professional perspective, the potential inflexibility of pre-determined developmental 'levels', and the extent to which such an explanatory theory necessarily rules out alternatives. I suggested that it might constitute not so much an *understanding* as a *definition* of children and childhood, and went on to explore the extent to which the developmental matrix can 'impose' a structure every bit as 'rigid' and compartmentalised as that of the subjects which it replaces.

Moreover, far from offering an alternative to a knowledge-based view of primary education, the developmentalist approach may sometimes derive less from genuine developmental analysis than a view of curriculum knowledge and skills redefined as developmental needs: a view which in even basic epistemological terms is sometimes anomalous and inadequate.

Staying with the question of knowledge I challenged the assumption that logic and psychologic, or child development and epistemology, are incompatible, as, of course, in primary ideology they are held to be, and gave examples to show that their reconciliation or synthesis comes about in the first instance through the adoption of a more comprehensive and process-oriented conception of knowledge than that normally at the heart of the anti-subject, anti-knowledge view.

I then tackled a further dichotomy which I regarded as unnecessary and unhelpful: that of the child and the teacher on the one hand and society 'out there' on the other. Not only is such a dichotomy conceptually untenable in the obvious sense that child and teacher are as much part of 'society' as parents and politicians, but its imposition leads to a neglect of the analysis of the relationship between curriculum and culture which should be fundamental to teaching.

Next I looked more closely at the mechanisms by which everyday 'understanding of children' is achieved in the classroom and argued that while the recent research on teacher expectations and typifications is methodologically problematic it might at least suggest that understanding children is not an automatic function of the class-teacher system as such, but of the pre-existing perceptual and conceptual constructs and frameworks of the teacher. In some cases, therefore, the class-teacher system might prove a positive disadvantage to the child.

Nor does the evidence on the pedagogy of class teaching bear out the standard claims in respect of that 'individual attention' associated with child-centred ideology.

Finally, I considered the vexed matter of 'potential': the accurate assessment of which is another pivotal element in primary ideology. Not only is such assessment likely to be restricted by teacher typifications and professional constructs, but it seems to relate closely to the quality of teacher–child interaction and the teacher's capacity to 'evoke' latent potential. Using an alternative perspective I suggested that evoking the full range of a child's potential may be beyond the scope of one person, particularly a person of limited experience and education, and that interaction with a variety of adults, gifted in different ways, could be more successful. This raises a number of serious and fundamental questions about the actual, as opposed to the claimed, efficacy of the class-teacher system, and reinforces the suggestion that class teaching might actually be contrary to the child's interests, particularly, perhaps, after the early primary years once the argument for the security provided by the one teacher and a permanent 'home' in the school becomes less powerful.

Throughout this discussion I have attempted to keep two objectives in view. First, the need to adopt a much broader framework for considering the teacher's 'understanding of children' than the narrow developmental one usually applied, and to show how one's capacity to understand children in the context of making educational decisions on their behalf has essential epistemological, cultural and pedagogical dimensions. In particular it requires that we look as much at ourselves as at the children we teach, for 'understanding' is essentially an attribute of the person who claims it, not of the objects of that understanding (children) or the situation in which they are located (school). My second objective has been to get beyond ideology, if not to the 'truth' about 'understanding children', at least to a point where unshackled and informed speculation about the best way to educate them becomes possible. Such speculation is the essence of curriculum discourse, not separate from it, and in turning now to 'curriculum' I am conscious that this might imply a contradiction in that if the present chapter has been 'curricular' by my comprehensive definition, the following chapter might seem to represent a regression to the more limited conception. No contradiction is entailed, however, for the starting point for discussion throughout this book is always existing concepts and practices, so that just as in the present chapter I started with the 'developmental' concept of child-centredness and argued that it was excessively narrow, so in the next chapter I start with the conventional concept of curriculum as a range of explicitly labelled formal activities. My overall message remains intact: that curriculum discourse ought to incorporate and synthesise perspectives on children, knowledge, culture and pedagogy. These perspectives will be elaborated and supplemented in later chapters.

3

The Class Teacher and the Curriculum

Whatever the extent of the ideological commitment to 'child not curriculum', the existential reality of curriculum cannot be denied. Primary children are in school for 25–27½ hours per week, excluding lunch breaks (Bassey 1978). The bulk of that time is spent on activities which can only be defined as 'curricular' in that they are the means whereby the educational goals of the school and its teachers are achieved.

Whether a school's goals actually are achieved, whether children learn what they are intended to learn, and whether they acquire and develop knowledge, skills and dispositions other than those intended — these questions cannot be pursued fully at this point. Nevertheless, it is important to be alert to the issues they raise: the distinction and relationships between the formal and 'hidden' curriculum of a school; the relationship between planned and incidental learning; and the distinction within incidental learning between outcomes considered desirable or undesirable by the teacher.

In particular, we should remember that what teachers intend or assume that children learn can be very different from what they actually learn. At the most mundane level, any parent knows that 'What did you do in school today?' can produce answers bearing little resemblance to the grand statements of open evenings, prospectuses and reports: formal tasks may be dismissed with a shrug while social events — the making and breaking of friendships, interactions with an encouraging or an unsupportive teacher, memorable verbal utterances like peer jingles, teacher jokes or sarcasm, playground taunts or expressions of friendship — all these can seem to loom in formal curricular terms disproportionately large. Philip Jackson sums up the force of the social dimension in schooling in the three words, 'crowds', 'praise' and 'power':

> Learning to live in a classroom involves, among other things, learning to live in a crowd . . . Most of the things that are done in school are done with others, or at least in the presence of others, and this fact has profound implications for determining the quality of a student's life . . . Schools are basically evaluative settings . . . It is not only what you do there but what others think of what you do that is important . . . Adaptation to school life requires the student to become used to living under the constant condition of having his words and deeds evaluated by others . . . School is also a place in which the division between the weak and the powerful is clearly drawn . . . Teachers are . . . more powerful than students, in the sense of having greater responsibility for giving shape to classroom events.

> (Jackson 1968, p. 10)

Although my concern in this chapter is with the formal rather than the 'hidden' curriculum — with the conscious actions and professional constructs of teachers rather than the additional social messages these actions may convey to children or the responses such perceived messages may provoke — the fact that curriculum in action is located in a highly complex and only partly explicated social setting makes the task of defining the 'reality' of the 'formal' primary curriculum an extremely difficult one.

Yet some sort of empirical data on this 'reality' is a prerequisite for any discussion, let alone any critique, of primary curriculum practice. In pursuit of this let us consider, first, four sources: the HMI primary survey (DES 1978a), the HMI first school survey (DES 1982a), the ORACLE research (Galton, Simon and Croll 1980, Galton and Simon 1980, Simon and Willcocks 1981) and the Nottinghamshire primary teacher survey (Bassey 1978). All four studies offer a list of curriculum components. Most give the frequency or proportion of time spent on each component so that it is possible to build up a picture both of the scope and shape of the 'whole curriculum' and of teachers' priorities within it. Bassey's study relies on questionnaire and interview data from teachers, the two HMI surveys rely on direct observation (plus questionnaire data in the case of the 1978 study), and the ORACLE project used extensive observation of teacher actions coded in terms of a pre-specified set of categories. However, even in such a rigorous study, a basic methodological problem remains: how do we define what a child is 'doing' at a given point in time? When he is writing, with a mathematics workcard in front of him, is he developing mathematical concepts and skills, is he actually learning mathematics, or might his thinking and learning be in other directions? Or when he is copying sections of a school library book on reptiles, how do we define this activity in curriculum terms? Is he acquiring factual knowledge? Or developing extended reading and study skills? Or discovering the short cuts to producing the largest amount of writing for the least amount of intellectual effort consistent with what he thinks his teacher means by 'a good piece of topic work'?

The problem here is threefold. First, the straightforward one of formal definition (Is it 'science' or 'topic work'?) which can best be resolved by discovering the teacher's intentions and curriculum nomenclature. Second, the difference between, and divergence of, teacher intentions and pupil learning outcomes. Third, and most intractable, the problem of the relationship between the child's outwardly observable behaviour and his mental activity. Most primary classroom 'observation studies' available to date are tacitly behaviourist and all must incorporate the possibility of mismatch between the child's actual cognition or learning and the observer's inferences. Furthermore, as phenomenologists point out, the quasi-objective observation study both imposes on behaviour the observer's interpretations and theoretical frameworks, and fails to explicate the meanings which the observed behaviours have for the 'actors' involved (i.e. the teachers and children). At a minimum, then, there are in a class of, say, thirty children, thirty-two possible interpretations of curriculum events or 'definitions of the situation' — those of each of the thirty children, the teacher and the observer. The rigorous training given to observers in the ORACLE research project to ensure observer and instrument 'reliability' (Galton, Simon and Croll 1980, pp. 4–28) produced consistency in the ability of different people to code behaviours at regular intervals in accordance with pre-specified behaviour categories. It presupposed the validity of these categories and of the overall procedure. It did not make them necessarily more 'reliable' in a broader sense as means of uncovering what was really going on in the classrooms. 'Reliability' as defined in such research studies can be tautologous and self-validating.

These problems have to be acknowledged, not least because they suggest that teachers' objections to the curriculum framework of documents like the 1978 primary survey — on the grounds of misrepresentation of their professional intentions in terms of inappropriate labels and structures — need to be taken seriously as legitimate methodological objections, however defensive they might at first appear.

THE FORMAL PRIMARY CURRICULUM: SCOPE, PRIORITIES AND CONSISTENCY

Scope

What is the range of curriculum activities undertaken in primary classrooms? Bassey's teachers were asked to list the 'activities and subjects of a normal week for their classes' (Bassey 1978, p. 21).

This produced from *junior* teachers two clear categories:

1. 'general items of activity' (5½ out of 27½ hours per week):
   (a) assembly;
   (b) administration;
   (c) physical education.
2. 'curriculum subjects' (22 out of 27½ hours per week):
   (a) mathematics;
   (b) language — reading, writing, talking;
   (c) thematic studies;
   (d) art and craft;
   (e) music;
   (f) physical education;
   (g) integrated studies.

However, on closer inspection it is clear that the labels in the contentious areas beyond language, mathematics, art and craft, music and physical and religious education denote exactly the same activities as history, geography and science. Thus, 'learning about people' includes learning about 'the locality' and 'more distant places' (geography) and 'people in other times' (history): together they encompass 'social studies' on the 1978 survey list. 'Learning about the physical world' includes 'plans, maps, globes and models' (the tools for geographical study), while 'learning about materials, plants and animals' is self-evidently a species of primary science ('heat and energy', 'the use and operation of machines', 'water', 'animals' and 'plants'). As I showed in Chapter 2, many ostensibly 'developmental' curricular statements are no more grounded in developmental analysis than is Hamlyn's assertion (1970) that the best person to define the mathematics curriculum is the mathematician: 'aesthetic development' as characterised in the Schools Council aims study (Ashton, Kneen, Davies and Holley 1975) reflects an adult epistemology of aesthetic education, but one which demonstrates a serious lack of real engagement with either aesthetic questions or children's development.

The ORACLE project (Galton, Simon and Croll 1980) offers a classification comparable to that of HMI:

1. Mathematics: number work; practical mathematics; abstract mathematics.
2. Language: reading; writing; spoken English; written English.
3. Art and craft.
4. General studies: religious education; history, geography and social studies; science.

In the main text Galton, Simon and Croll refer simply to 'general studies' and explain that the area is 'complex'. In subsequent footnotes they offer the above breakdown into three subject areas, together with a clear differentiation of each into 'topic and project work' and 'single subject work'. The latter are qualitatively different curriculum categories: they denote methods of organising learning rather than ways of knowing and understanding. Looking back at the Bassey lists, which used teachers' own preferred categories, one can now detect an anomaly of some significance. The lists mix subject and organisational/pedagogical categories: the latter are used only in the vexed area of history, geography, science and social studies, the areas where HMI in both the primary and first school surveys were particularly critical of superficiality, lack of progression, under-expectation and lack of 'match', and where, as I shall show, professional training offers minimal preparation.

What other observations might be offered about the scope of the primary curriculum, at this very general level, as revealed in these four studies?

First, there are clear areas of consistency and consensus: mathematics and language feature as distinctive curriculum areas on every list. They seem non-problematic in terms of nomenclature and priority.

Second, there are areas that are more or less consistent, but sometimes have integrated/incidental status: art and craft, physical education and music.

Third, one major area is notable for its inconsistency of nomenclature and the confusion surrounding its character: integrated studies/thematic studies/general studies/history/geography/science/learning about people/learning about the physical world/learning about materials, plants and animals. As I have suggested, this is not simply a problem of terminology, but a fundamental confusion about the very nature and purposes of a major area of the child's curriculum.

Fourth, one area, personal, social and moral development is particularly elusive. It is, variously, explicit, implicit or totally omitted. Yet the Assessment of Performance Unit team investigating the possibility of producing a national test programme in this area asserted:

> Pupils' personal and social development is given the highest priority by teachers, both in school organization *and in curriculum design* . . . At the primary phase, the personal and social development of the pupil has a central place in the education provided . . .
>
> (APU 1981, p. 1, my italics)

The same emphasis to this area is given in all recent official documents on the curriculum. Yet because of its inherently controversial nature the APU decided not to proceed with national monitoring but to offer instead a 'map of the territory' for the use of teachers and others as in Figure 3.1 (APU 1981, p. 7).

The area is acknowledged to be central yet value-saturated. The solution to this dilemma is usually to dodge it: it is rare to find a school or LEA statement as full even as the APU's 24-page pamphlet. Yet, of course, children develop personally, socially and morally whether or not schools conceive of such development in terms of specific, timetabled curriculum activities: their learning in this area is promoted through their everyday interactions, the examples presented by teachers and fellow-pupils and by the 'hidden curriculum' of a school's norms, and values relating to personal and interpersonal behaviour and relationships. The greater risk, it can be argued, is not of overt indoctrination but of a school's being either so squeamish about the issue, or so ignorant of the actual mechanisms of social and moral learning, that it fails to examine its actual impact on the child in this area, and the social/moral curriculum becomes 'hidden' rather than formalised, yet none the less influential. If the question 'How *ought* the child's personal/social/moral education to proceed?' seems too fraught, then the alternative 'What *is* the impact of this school's culture and practices on the child's personal, social and moral development?' is perhaps both more acceptable and more essential.

Curriculum priorities and consistency

The most obvious indicator of curriculum priority is the amount of time spent by the child in each area. However, while in secondary schools such calculations are straightforward, and a timetable analysis will suffice (see Wilcox and Eustace 1981), in primary schools time allocations are more difficult to ascertain. There are four reasons for this. First, the class-teacher system enables teachers to be highly flexible from one day or week to the next whereas a published secondary timetable is necessarily rigid and predictable: thus the typical week, let alone the typical day, may be hard to define. Second, variation in curriculum emphasis: one child might be having extra remedial reading while others at the same time are undertaking a topic. Third, the organisational practice of having different activities going on simultaneously makes

Aspects of development	Dimensions			
	Knowledge	Understanding	Practical application	Attitudes
a) GENERAL DEVELOPMENT				
Persons and personal relationships				
Morality				
Social awareness				
b) RELIGION AND PHILOSOPHIES OF LIFE				
c) SPECIFIC DEVELOPMENT				
Occupational				
Political				
Legal				
Environmental				
Health				
Community				

Figure 3.1

the recording of time allocations very difficult. Fourth, there is the ideological disin-clination of many primary teachers to define their teaching in terms of others' curriculum labels.

These difficulties seem to be reflected most prominently in the analysis by Bassey (1978) of infant pupils' activities. Precise figures are given for the 'general activities' of 'class talk', 'play time', 'administration' and so on, but not for the conventional curriculum areas of mathematics, language and the rest. In contrast the figures from his junior teachers were unambiguous:

Curriculum area	Average number of hours per week for pupil	Percentage
Language	7	30.4
Mathematics	5	21.7
Thematic studies	4	17.4
Physical education	3	13.0
Art and craft	2	8.7
Music	1	4.3

(Bassey 1978, p. 28)

In other words, in crude numerical terms, the 'basics' of language and mathematics take up something over half the child's time, and everyday observations readily confirm in particular the practice of giving children one hour of mathematics every day of the week, usually in the morning (when the child, supposedly, is 'fresh': when he is tired he can undertake art, music, science and the other 'non-basic' activities).

A similar temporal emphasis on the 'basics' is shown in the ORACLE study. Different figures emerged from the pupil and teacher records: Galton, Simon and Croll (1980) point out that they can only be expected to coincide when classteaching (i.e. the pedagogical technique, not the primary organisational device of class teaching) is the nòrm. This discrepancy is particularly marked in creative writing and what they term 'general studies' (religious education, history, geography, social studies, science) because much of the work is topic/project based. Their figures for the 'real' or actual curriculum were as follows:

	ORACLE percentage
Language	35.7
Mathematics	30.0
Art and craft	10.2
General studies/thematic studies	24.3

It would be misleading to juxtapose the ORACLE and Bassey figures as they stand, because the former relate only to observed activities in the classroom, so that once PE and music are included the percentages of each of the four areas above are reduced. However, though a fine calculation on the basis of the authors' data is impossible, if one adds to the ORACLE figures the Bassey allocations for PE and music and recalculates the ORACLE percentages, the figures become remarkably similar.

Thus, as Galton, Simon and Croll remark after comparing figures from ORACLE, Bassey and the Bullock Report (DES 1975), 'teachers seem to be both consistent and accurate in their estimates of time spent on the broader curricular areas' (Galton, Simon and Croll 1980, p. 186).

However, this picture of consensus and consistency is rudely disturbed by the figures which emerged from the HMI primary survey. As Richards (1982) points out, in rough or 'coarse-grained' terms the national curriculum picture, and the educational priorities it represents, is clear, but at the more significant level of analysis of the curriculum as experienced by individual children, there is wide variation. HMI identified 36 items (DES 1978a, pp. 77–79) found to occur individually in at least 80 per cent of the survey classes:

Language: listening and talking

(a) children were taught to
    (i) follow instructions
    (ii) follow the plot of a story
    (iii) comprehend the main ideas in information given to them
(b) children talked informally to one another during the course of the working day
(c) discussion took place between children and teachers when new vocabulary was introduced.

Language: reading and writing

(a) in 7 and 9 year old classes children practised reading from a main reading scheme and from supplementary readers

(b) in 9 and 11 year old classes children read fiction and non-fiction which was not related to other work they were doing in the classroom
(c) in 11 year old classes children made use of information books related to work in other areas of the curriculum
(d) at each age children were encouraged to select books of their own choice
(e) children were given handwriting practice
(f) children undertook descriptive and narrative writing
(g) in 9 and 11 year old classes children did written work on prescribed topics related to other parts of the curriculum

Mathematics
Work was done to enable children to learn:

(a) to use language appropriate to the properties of number, size, shape and position
(b) to recognise relationships in geometrical shapes, numbers, ordered arrangements and everyday things
(c) to appreciate place value and recognise simpler number patterns
(d) to carry out suitable calculations involving +, −, × and ÷ with whole numbers
(e) to understand money and the value of simple purchases
(f) to use numbers in counting, describing and estimating
(g) in 7 year old classes children undertook practical activities involving addition, subtraction, multiplication and division

In 11 year old classes children were taught to:

(h) estimate and use measurements of length, weight, area, volume
(i) work with the four rules of number including two places of decimals
(j) calculate using decimals
(k) use fractions, including the idea of equivalence, and apply them to everyday things
(l) use various forms of visual presentation including three dimensional and diagrammatic forms.

Aesthetic and physical education
The programme of work included:

(a) singing
(b) listening to music
(c) two or three dimensional work showing evidence of observation of pattern *or* colour *or* texture *or* form
(d) in 7 year old classes, practice of skills in gymnastics *or* games *or* swimming
(e) in 9 and 11 year old classes, gymnastic skills
(f) in 9 and 11 year old classes, practice of skills in playing games
(g) in 11 year old classes, swimming lessons

Social abilities and moral learning
Work was arranged to promote the following:

(a) reliability and responsible attitudes
(b) consideration for other people; e.g. good manners, concern, friendship
(c) respect for surroundings and the care of materials and objects in the classroom and school
(d) participation as a member of a group or team, learning to follow rules and obey instructions
(e) involvement in the development of religious ideas and moral values during the school assembly
(f) in 9 and 11 year old classes, awareness of historical change and causal factors in relation to the way people lived or behaved in the past
(g) in 9 and 11 year old classes, work relating to at least one of the following aspects of geography; population, agriculture, industry, transport, or resources within or outside the locality
(DES 1978a, pp., 77–79. Reproduced with the permission of the Controller of HMSO.)

HMI then showed that the 'coverage of items varied from class to class and showed no overall consistency' (p. 74). Some items, such as reading practice and mathematical computation, took place in all classes observed. On the other hand, science did not appear at all on the list reproduced above because it was not undertaken in even the minimum 80 per cent of classes. Similarly, 'some work of a geographical nature' was undertaken in only 60 per cent of the 7 year old classes (though in 90 per cent of the 9 to 11 year old classes) and 'some attention to the study of the past' in 60 per cent of the 7 year old classes, 90 per cent of the 9 year old classes and almost all 11 year old classes.

When grouped into the four main curriculum categories of 'mathematics', 'language', 'aesthetic and physical education' and 'social abilities' (a curiously misleading label for this unregarded rump of the primary curriculum), the percentages reveal a disturbing lack of consistency nationally.

Percentage of classes undertaking all widely taught items in each subject

	7 year olds	*9 year olds*	*11 year olds*
Mathematics	65	76	58
Language	54	43	53
Aesthetic and physical education	73	63	58
Social abilities	65	46	61

(DES 1978a, p. 85)

Percentage of classes undertaking all widely taught items for combinations of two or more subjects

	7 year olds	*9 year olds*	*11 year olds*
Items for language and mathematics combined	42	37	39
Items for language, mathematics, aesthetic and physical education combined	35	28	28
Items for language, mathematics and social abilites combined	33	24	32
All items combined	29	19	24

(DES 1978a, p. 86)

The HMI figures suggest that 'consistency' is a concept in need of careful qualification where the character of primary children's curriculum experience is concerned. On the positive side, following the claims and rumours generated in the post-Plowden years, HMI were able to state in the survey press release (with some relief, no doubt), that:

> High priority is given to teaching children in primary schools to read, write and to calculate, and there is no evidence to support the suggestion that teachers neglect the basic skills.
>
> (DES 1978c, p. 1)

Beyond the 'basics', however, the picture is much more variable: no observational or experimental science in 80 per cent of the classes observed; superficiality and lack of direct observation in art; craft making a smaller contribution to the work than is desirable; a lack of response to the challenge of a multi-cultural/multi-faith society in religious education; fragmentation, superficiality, repetition and lack of progression in history and geography.

The subsequent first school survey (DES 1982a) provided a similar analysis: initial teaching of reading soundly undertaken, but with a subsequent neglect of extended reading skills; written activities competent, but of limited range (insufficient descriptive and expressive writing); spoken language attended to, but listening skills neglected; mathematical computation given priority, but little application to contexts where the skills might be applied; a lack of development in religious education; very little attention to 'the wider circumstances in which they (the children) live', to their situation in time and place; a lack of progression in understanding and skill development in science, though a more positive picture than in the 1978 survey; a neglect of three-dimensional and observational work in art and a failure to realise the 'educational value of art and craft work'; music given little or no role in 20 per cent of the schools and conceived in a limited way elsewhere (in contrast to the 1978 survey which showed specialist teachers promoting it more competently in 7 to 11-year-old classes); lack of progression and challenge in physical development.

It must be remembered that HMI's own investigative framework can hardly be accused of being over-ambitious or unrealistic. As we have seen, the observation schedules reflected what HMI saw rather than what they hoped to see. In a sense then, despite the evident failure of some classes and schools to approach even such institutionally derived norms, HMI's own framework is a limited one educationally: there is little attention in it to the issues concerning personal and social development that I discussed above, little detailed consideration of drama, dance, health education or other curriculum areas which feature in substantial numbers of primary schools, and, in particular, no suggestion whatsoever that existing conceptions of the curriculum for pre-adolescent children and existing curriculum priorities might need to be questioned. In this respect the HMI surveys, particularly the 1978 survey (which is more systematically presented and conceptually less open-ended than its successor) carry the same dangers as a vehicle for professional and curricular development as the Schools Council 'aims' survey of Ashton, Kneen, Davies and Holley (1975). Being grounded in the practices and opinions of serving teachers they have an attractive 'realism' and legitimacy, and feature prominently in initial and in-service discussions of the purposes and character of primary education. But, as we saw in Chapter 2, embedded in the aims study are some highly questionable assumptions about children's development and learning, the nature of knowledge and the relationship of the child and the educational process to their cultural and societal contexts. Similarly, whatever the extent of criticism of current practices in the HMI surveys, the existing overall curricular frameworks and priorities remain unexamined. Using such documents in the context of a holistic curriculum appraisal can simply confirm just those values, assumptions, prejudices and misconceptions which most clearly need to be challenged. As Dearden comments, referring to the Ashton study:

> Is it thought that sufficiently complicated statistical manipulation of expressed opinions confers legitimacy, or normative force, on the digested results? . . . Surveys of teachers' opinions on aims may have their uses, but they cannot settle what those aims ought . . . to be

> (Dearden 1976, pp. 28 and 29)

In the remainder of this chapter I want to pursue the question of consistency beyond the manifest, formal or observed primary curriculum to the ideas and justifications in which it is located.

THE UNIFIED CURRICULUM

The idea that the curriculum has a unity and almost serendipitous flexibility is basic to British primary education, and is presented as a natural concomitant of the child-centred position:

> In early learning, knowledge is not differentiated into different compartments, but oppor-. tunities are used for teaching particular skills in whatever context they arise
> (NUT 1979, p. 16)

The language of curriculum discourse — 'fragmentation', 'little boxes', 'rigid compartments', 'children not subjects', 'the child's view of the world', etc. — was considered in Chapter 1. What has to be noted, apart from its sometimes vehement character, is its fairly consistent use not so much of positive statements about the child's curriculum as negative assertions about knowledge. The word 'knowledge' itself, and certainly 'subjects', can be taboo in professional circles: introduced in embarrassed terms they are hedged round with apologies and qualifications such as 'I don't mean of course that subjects should be taught separately, I'm just using the word for the sake of convenience'. While the key rationale for curriculum unity may be the 'child's way of looking at the world', the key characteristic of the unified curriculum is less an exposition of that world view than a rejection of subjects. Thus, to extend the argument, the secondary curriculum is characterised as lacking unity or overall meaning, because it is structured on a subject basis and taught by specialists. Curriculum unity, then, is seen as unachievable except through (a) an absence of definable subjects and (b) the class-teacher system: a 'whole curriculum' for a 'whole child'.

At the very least the notions that subject non-differentiation is synonymous with curriculum coherence and that subject structures are incompatible with child-centredness are questionable: and presumably some secondary teachers (who may be as concerned with curriculum coherence as their primary colleagues) would indeed wish to challenge this, though the HMI secondary survey (DES 1979a) provides strong evidence of curriculum fragmentation. However they, and we, might wish to ask whether children's capacity to relate meaningfully their various learning experiences might not be equally, or more, a function of pedagogy — the way those learning experiences are structured and sequenced. What such questions serve to highlight is the way the assertions about the unified curriculum slide unselfconsciously between two distinct *levels* of curriculum: the teacher's claims and modes of organisation on the one hand, and the sense the child makes of these on the other. What the teacher intends or claims and what the child learns can be very different. A teacher's version of the curriculum may have unity, but for the child it may appear as a random and confusing array of disparate activities. The 'meaning' of an experience resides in the capacities of the individual undergoing the experience, not in the claims of the external agents of that experience.

Thus far the argument is conceptual. However, apart from making this basic criticism about the equation of subjects and curricular disunity or incoherence, I wish to concentrate more on practice, and to ask: disregarding for a moment the claims and counterclaims about unity and fragmentation in the primary curriculum, what empirical evidence do we have on such matters?

The observed curriculum and its outcomes

The first half of the present chapter considered evidence about the observable character of the primary curriculum in terms of time allocations, pedagogy and children's learning. The recurrent elements can be summarised thus:

1. There appears to be a divide between the so-called 'basics' of language/reading/ mathematics and the rest of the curriculum as to both the adequacy of provision and the 'match' between children's activities and the learning experience provided.
2. There are wide inconsistencies or discrepancies between individual classes and schools in provision within the 'non-basic' areas of learning, with large numbers of children apparently missing out on major areas.
3. There appears to be evidence of a general impoverishment in the curriculum experiences provided for primary children in areas other than the basics, reflected in low teacher expectations, a narrow range of experiences in each area, circularity and lack of progression within and between school years, and superficiality in some of what was provided.

Three points can now be made in respect of this evidence.

First, the concept of a unified curriculum would seem to be incompatible with curriculum practices which so sharply differentiate, both quantitatively and qualitatively, one area of learning (the basics) from the rest of the child's curriculum.

Second, if we pursue the argument about the need to consider the matter from the standpoint of the child's curriculum experiences rather than the teacher's curriculum claims, a 'unified' curriculum is best conceived as one which is experientially consistent regardless of its structure. Recent evidence suggests that in many schools the external curriculum structure may have a superficial overall coherence (provided, for example, by a lack of subject labels and emphasis on topic/project work), but that what the child experiences may be remarkably inconsistent in quality and character (DES 1978a, 1982a).

The third point is that if curriculum inconsistency is a consequence of the inevitable unevenness in the class teacher's professional knowledge and expertise, this is tantamount to saying that, far from promoting curriculum unity and consistency as is claimed, the class-teacher system may actually militate against these goals. If that is so, the profession might need to weigh more dispassionately than hitherto the relative advantages and disadvantages of generalist class teaching and specialist subject teaching, especially perhaps in the junior age-range where the breadth of the curriculum poses the greatest professional challenge.

The relative status of curriculum experiences

The concept of 'basics' reflects curriculum priorities, a view that certain curriculum experiences have more value than others. Educational priorities are to be expected in every society. But since our particular society is far from static or monolithic as to values, social structure and economic circumstances, one might equally expect curriculum priorities to be neither permanent nor wholly clear-cut.

Instead we have a curriculum firmly divided, for over a century of tumultuous change, into two parts: the high priority areas of 'basic skills' which are defined as reading, writing and mathematics, and the lower priority areas of creative and expressive arts, social and environmental studies, scientific understanding, moral and religious education, physical education and so on. The operational divide is reinforced in primary discourse; the validity of the hierarchy, and the primacy of the activities which are defined as so much more 'basic' than others to the education of children between the ages of five and eleven, are rarely questioned. The research studies themselves tacitly reinforce the value system. Bennett (1976) effectively defined educational 'progress' as test score gains on Moray House and NFER reading and mathematics tests. Galton, Simon and Croll (1980) carefully recorded curriculum activity for language and mathematics under different subheadings (number work, practical mathematics, abstract mathematics, reading, writing, spoken English, creative writing) but 'the rest', some 35 per cent of the pupil's time, were conceived as 'art and craft' plus 'general studies' (see, however, p. 53). The 'products' of primary education were measured in terms of test score gains in reading, spelling, punctuation, use of capital letters and verbal usage; mathematical concepts and problem solving; and some basic 'study skills'. HMI (DES 1978a), despite commenting fairly comprehensively, as we have seen, on activity across the curriculum, chose to undertake systematic appraisal of pupil progress through tests in reading and mathematics only. And their own examination of curriculum consistency shows that, in effect, in the overwhelming majority of schools 'consistency' is a problem not for the basics, where time allocations are fixed and non-negotiable, but for 'the rest'.

The unsatisfactory message of such studies — whatever the authors' intentions — seems clear: if one wishes to evaluate the quality of the education provided for children between the ages of five and eleven one should do so in terms of test score gains in reading, written English and mathematics.

I said that the basics were non-negotiable: in practice this is true of reading, writing and mathematics, but spoken language may still have to be argued for. Despite, when looked at dispassionately, the primacy and universality of spoken language as a fundamental cultural tool of socialised man and its consequent claim to be the only true 'basic', it is still commonly the case that spoken language has more in common with 'the rest' in terms of its inconsistency in time allocation and treatment than with the other 'basics'. This anomaly is an important clue to our understanding of why primary schools have such an apparently fixed and in some senses limited conception of educational priorities. The view owes little to child-centredness, but much to nineteenth-century mass compulsory elementary education — the institutional and legal (if not always ideological) foundation of modern primary education. That system of education aimed for basic levels of literacy and numeracy. The ability to use spoken language — to communicate, argue, reason, generate ideas, express and change opinions and deepen understanding — was not only superfluous to the economic, occupational and political requirements of those who devised the system, but also potentially subversive of them.

The line from the 1870s to the 1980s is unbroken and consistent: the anomaly of spoken language makes any attempts to justify the current notion of basics in terms of more recent child-centred or individualistic ideology seem unconvincing. A genuinely child-centred view of basics would tend to include a more comprehensive list of fundamental skills and attributes — interpersonal skills, empathy, social confidence, moral awareness for example; and what Wicksteed (1982) calls, in a useful attempt to break away from the Victorian legacy, the skills of 'surviving' (technologically and socially), of 'relating' to others and acquiring a practical realisation of human inter-dependence, and of 'celebrating' or responding through, for example, religion or art to the sense of awe inspired by human existence.

Competing justifications for curriculum activities

Just as there is a sharp divide, at the practical levels of time allocation and the quality of teaching and learning, between the basics and the rest, so too does this conflict between societal/utilitarian and child-centred/individualistic justifications tend to undermine the claims for curricular coherence and unity. For it is not so much that the child's curriculum as a whole may be justified in 'societal' or 'individualist' terms (see Ashton, Kneen, Davies and Holley 1975), or that various parts of a curriculum may have different but ultimately complementary justifications, but rather that one conception of curriculum may conflict with or undermine another in a practical context where the value differences are reflected, temporally and pedagogically, in such disparate terms. 'Societal' and 'individualist' are, as I have suggested, unnecessarily viewed as mutually exclusive, but if this conceptual polarity is what informs much curriculum discourse and decision-making (as it is) then it inevitably produces polarity in curriculum practice.

Eisner and Vallance (1974) offer a more diverse framework for characterising the various orientations on curriculum:

1. *Curriculum as the development of cognitive processes*: an orientation which focuses on the 'how' rather than the 'what' of education, on the processes and dynamics of learning, rather than its outcomes.
2. *Curriculum as technology*: a means-ends view of curriculum, which highlights not processes of learning or knowing, but the technology by which knowledge is communicated and learning is facilitated.
3. *Curriculum as self-actualisation or consummatory experience*: a strongly value-saturated orientation on curriculum, concerned with personal purpose, autonomy and growth, and with the present enriching potential of learning experiences rather than future, learning outcomes.
4. *Curriculum for social reconstruction/relevance*: in which goals are societal rather than individualist, and social change and the individual's response to a role in it are key issues. Here the ideological and political dimensions are strong, and typically diverge into 'adaptive' and 'reformist' strands: education to produce individuals who will fit into the current societal structure and dominant value systems on the

one hand, education to produce individuals capable of questioning and reforming these structures and values on the other.

5. *Curriculum as academic rationalisation*: education as cultural transmission via the established disciplines, seen as exemplifying intellectual activity at its best.

From our discussion of the primary curriculum it will be seen that the major tension is between (4) and (3) above: social reconstruction/relevance versus self-actualisation. However, the nineteenth-century 'basics' legacy ('relevance') is 'adaptive' rather than 'reformist' and for this reason conflicts strongly with self-actualisation goals as reflected in child-centred justifications. Recently the 'cognitive process' emphasis (1 above) has emerged as an additional strand, exemplified in some of the curriculum projects I have already mentioned — Science 5–13, Place, Time and Society, Communication Skills, MACOS. It also provides a new rationale for the primary mathematics curriculum. However, it does so within an unquestioned value framework dominated, as I have suggested, by social adaptation: in the end the primary curriculum remains a deeply conservative and conformist response to the situation of the individual in the context of pluralism and social change. 'Process' and 'self-actualisation' goals are undoubtedly present but the shape of a curriculum dominated by a particular notion of 'basics' ensures that they have minimal practical force other than to confuse the claim of curriculum coherence and unity.

Competing epistemologies in the primary curriculum

Eisner and Vallance's final 'orientation' is unfamiliar in primary education but pervades university education and to some extent aspects of the secondary curriculum. It is the legacy of that élite, humanist tradition represented in public and grammar schools in the nineteenth century and historically therefore it and mass elementary education, with an adaptive three Rs curriculum, are diametrically opposed. However, it has re-emerged as a distinctive strand in modern educational thought in the work of Hirst (1965 and 1974) and has been applied to the primary curriculum by Dearden (1968): these would tend to argue that a 'forms of knowledge' approach is intellectually liberating, and therefore far more consistent with self-actualisation goals than primary ideology allows (which, as we have seen, reacts sharply against knowledge as such). Indeed, historically, intellectual autonomy and flexibility through subject disciplines were regarded as essential outcomes of a system of education reserved for future leaders and entrepreneurs.

In rejecting 'knowledge', therefore, primary ideology reacts with some historical conciousness against the fact-inculcation of three Rs elementary education, but fails to discriminate between the latter's version of knowledge and that of academic subjects, whose origins and purposes in élite minority education were very different. Instead a simplistic and undifferentiated model is adduced as a basis for rejecting knowledge in any form (save in the protected 'basics'): knowledge = subjects = facts = indoctrination. And since the 'traditional' curriculum was seen as dealing mainly or exclusively with knowledge as so defined, the model serves as a justification for rejecting the notion of curriculum itself. The logical nonsense of this position has already been referred to, but it will now be seen that at the heart of primary curriculum discourse and practice are epistemological contradictions and confusions. Epistemological analysis must be a central component in any attempt to make sense of current ideas and practices in primary education; moreover it is clear that such analysis needs to retain a cultural and historical consciousness — the historical development of primary schools and the resulting professional situation of primary teachers are major determinants of current primary ideology and practice.

Does the primary curriculum reflect a coherent view of knowledge?

While the thrust of the present chapter appears to be towards a negative answer to this question, we must note an important recent attempt to redefine child-centredness in terms of a positive (rather than iconoclastic or dismissive) view of knowledge. Blenkin and Kelly (1981) show how the current psychological emphasis in child-centred ideology, which we discussed in Chapter 2, overlays an earlier philosophical tradition exemplified in the writings of Rousseau and Dewey and which offers an evolutionary or empiricist definition of knowledge as deriving from experience and being therefore provisional and modifiable, in contrast to the rationalist's belief in *a priori* knowledge existing independently of the knower (this historical line is also traced by Entwistle 1970 and Selleck 1972, though to a more critical conclusion). The empiricist educator will tend to argue that because truth is not absolute, 'to impose the values of this present generation on the next is a form of indoctrination' and that the essence of a curriculum must be its acknowledgement and demonstration of the evolutionary character of knowledge and the plurality of values. The empiricist, therefore, would be opposed not so much to subjects as such, since they can be and are defined according to a variety of epistemological traditions (including the empiricist), as to the rationalist's claim that subjects incorporate absolute values and are therefore to be conceived of hierarchically, some more 'worthwhile' intrinsically than others, their relative status unchanging, and their boundaries fixed and impermeable.

A similar distinction is made by Eggleston (1977) though from a sociological rather than a philosophical standpoint. He identifies two basic curriculum perspectives, 'received' and 'reflexive'. In the 'received' perspective curriculum knowledge is 'given' and non-negotiable, and is structured into fixed and permanent subjects and disciplines. In the 'reflexive' perspective curriculum is seen as reflecting the changing cultural situation of those who create and experience it, and is therefore changeable, negotiable and non-absolute.

Blenkin and Kelly develop this analysis into a defence of child-centred ideology in empiricist terms, invoking the work of Piaget (who saw himself as an epistemologist) to show how the particular philosophical position can be reconciled with what child developmental research would suggest primary teachers should be doing anyway. The case is persuasively presented, tracing a distinctive 'primary' tradition from Rousseau,

Pestalozzi, Herbert, Froebel, Montessori and Dewey, through Piaget and Bruner, to the 'process' oriented projects in science, mathematics, language and environmental studies to which I have already referred.

However, there seem to me a number of practical difficulties in the way of this analysis.

First, such an epistemology may be very different from the actual views or intentions of teachers, and indeed Blenkin and Kelly tend to cite as evidence not the observed everyday practice of primary teachers and children such as we have attempted to uncover in these chapters, but an idealised, prescriptive version represented in published curriculum projects. Their final chapter, 'Recent developments in the primary curriculum', is about the curriculum intentions of project directors and authors rather than the curriculum activities of teachers and children.

Second, the view of primary ideology as representing a positive 'epistemology' conflicts with evidence available in primary writing and everyday professional discourse, such as I have drawn upon so far, that the predominant perspective on knowledge is not so much 'empiricist' or 'reflexive' as merely negative.

Third, the proof of a coherent epistemology would presumably be a coherent and unified curriculum; something the primary curriculum increasingly seems not to be. In this respect too, different epistemologies apply to different curriculum activities. Thus, while it is true that a reflexive, subjectivist or relativist view of knowledge is sometimes invoked to justify non-directive teaching in social/environmental studies, or to excuse the teacher from assessing children's creative writing or art (on the grounds that 'I mustn't impose my values on their creative efforts'), I would suggest that an *a priori*, if not rationalist, position, is much more dominant. It informs approaches to the 'basics' of language and mathematics, where whatever pedagogical mode is used (e.g. a discovery-based approach) the goal is the acquisition of *a priori* knowledge. Moreover, the closer one looks at work actually undertaken in ostensibly empiricist areas like social/environmental studies and science, it is clear that the goal here too is usually the acquisition of information. The 'empiricist' element is in the pedagogy: instead of being told directly by the teacher the child has to look it up and copy it down. The authoritative source of *a priori* knowledge is thus the printed word rather than the teacher, but its character is the same. What is considerably rarer is to find classrooms where a genuinely empiricist approach is used, with all knowledge statements, from whatever source, treated as provisional, as requiring to be tested against observable evidence, where children are encouraged to seek differing, even competing accounts of 'Life in Victorian Times'. Blenkin and Kelly are right to point out that such an approach underpins some recent published curriculum projects, but as yet there is little evidence that it is applied in many classrooms.

Finally, one looks for evidence of the kind of responsiveness to cultural plurality and change which would be the chief hallmark of the empiricist curriculum. Such evidence is hard to find. On the contrary one of the more remarkable features of the primary curriculum, as we have seen, is its resistance to change and its continuing embodiment of an absolutist hierarchy of values.

Thus, it might seem that the truer reality of the primary curriculum is an epistemological muddle, whose justificatory face is empiricist but whose practice is dominated by, if anything, a covert *a priori* epistemology.

The 'fragmentation of subjects'?

Despite the professional antipathy to 'subjects', and despite the taboo nature of the term, there are good grounds for asserting that subjects are a central element in primary curricula of all ideological complexions, and most notably so in the 'basics'. Thus, mathematics is taught mainly as a separate area of learning, its distinctive conceptual structures, principles, terminology and logical sequences untainted by enforced conjunction with other curriculum areas — a fact deplored in the HMI first school survey (DES 1982a). It is presented as a public, received, *a priori* form of knowledge, and the matter of its consistency or otherwise with 'how the young child views the world' is never invoked. Few subjects are less like the way children subjectively make sense of experience, or are more 'artificial' than mathematics: the 'truths' appealed to are beyond the child, absolute and unchanging, and mathematics exemplifies par excellence Blenkin and Kelly's rationalist epistemology. At the same time developmentalism is satisfied because Piagetian theory provides a basis for reconciling the logical and psychological dimensions: the effort which has gone into achieving that reconciliation has not yet been applied to other areas, except perhaps to primary science, which since the 1978 HMI survey and the mid 1970s 'Great Debate' about education has emerged as a 'neo-basic' curriculum area.

Similarly, though not a 'form of knowledge' in Hirst's sense (1965), the teaching of reading has strong subject characteristics: a distinct methodology, a unique conceptual structure and terminology. The technology of digraphs, diphthongs, look and say, phonics, readability formulae, cloze procedure, miscue analysis and so on give it a received, bounded, objective character comparable to that of mathematics. Again, in Blenkin and Kelly's terms it is absolutist and *a priori*.

The same is beginning to be true of spoken language, where the work of Tough (1976, 1977, 1979) provides a set of precise categories — 'self-maintaining', 'directing', 'reporting', 'logical reasoning', 'predicting', 'projecting' and 'imagining' — to enable the child's language to be appraised and diagnosed, and shaped or 'fostered'. The approach is akin to the schedules for analysing classroom interaction used by Galton and Simon which we considered in Chapter 2, and its essence is that language, meaning, intention and communication can all be objectified, regardless of persons and contexts.

It is important to note that the cases of mathematics and spoken language are in epistemological terms vastly different. Mathematics has always been a distinctive form of knowledge, with its internal structures, procedures and concepts well-established and widely agreed upon. But the codification of language and meaning is a wholly different, infinitely more complex and questionable activity, one which needs to be grounded at least as firmly in philosophical and sociological analysis as in the psychological theory which informs Tough's work.

What the established and emerging codified, objectified quasi *a priori* primary curriculum areas have in common, therefore, is not a pre-existing 'subject' character but status as 'basics'. The pattern is clear and consistent: in acquiring 'basic' status, areas of learning divest themselves of integrationist attributes and empiricist claims and become, to all intents and purposes, separate subjects. Thus, currently, primary science is at an interim point in this process, changing from an ill-defined aspect of environmental studies into a distinctive field of activity for which the unambiguous subject label 'science' can increasingly be used in professional discourse and school timetabling without fear of that ideological backlash or professional embarrassment to which I referred earlier.

There seem to be two related factors at work here. One is that the wider societal pressures and perceptions become internalised and operationalised in the school curriculum, and override child-centred or integrationist arguments. The other is that as a consequence of these pressures the curriculum areas concerned become the object of research, development and professional attention. The more deeply an area of learning is investigated, the more it becomes systematised, since such investigation is impossible without analytical categories and frameworks; the less, therefore, it becomes possible to sustain the child-centred argument that the area must be defined in terms of how the child perceives the world.

At the same time, as Goodson (1982) shows, the emergent subject is encouraged in its purpose by lobbyists whose status as 'experts' is bound up with the subject's successful objectification and acceptance.

The process is self-reinforcing, as the case of mathematics, the longest established primary subject, shows. The more extensive and elaborate the codification, the stronger the apparent case for the subject's being given more and more curriculum time, since the subject lobbyist can 'demonstrate' a need by simply pointing to a lengthy list of concepts, principles and procedures and asserting that these cannot be taught in less than 'n' hours. Thus, according to the Cockcroft Committee on the teaching of mathematics (DES 1982b) one-fifth of the child's curriculum should be devoted to mathematics.

Codification and systematisation, apart from reinforcing the subject status of the areas concerned, also greatly widen the gulf between the 'basics' and the rest of the curriculum. Another area where this process is much in evidence is in school and LEA record cards, which have become consistently more elaborate as a response to the increasing accountability pressures from central and thence local government since the late 1970s.

The Inner London Education Authority's primary record (6–11) is typical. It has ten curriculum headings as follows (ILEA 1979):

(a) oral language;
(b) reading development;
(c) written language;
(d) numbers;
(e) measures;
(f) geometry;
(g) sets;
(h) creative abilities;
(i) handwriting;
(j) topics/projects.

The amount of detail requested under each varies considerably. Under 'oral language', comments only are invited: this contrasts with the Avon LEA record card which asks its teachers to record children's progress in oral language in terms of a four-point scale and the Tough categories previously listed. 'Reading development' in contrast, has 15 detailed sub-categories requiring ticked responses. Four sorts of 'written language' have to be commented on ('personal', 'factual', 'imaginative', 'using information' — compare this with Avon's 'expressive', 'transactional' and 'poetic'). Mathematics (sets, numbers, measures and geometry) has thirteen categories — a relatively modest number: Rochdale LEA (1978) has 214 spread over the four junior school years (7–11) and most involve a four-point scale. Four sorts of 'creative ability' are offered — two dimensional, three dimensional, dance/drama and music, two areas of physical skills, and 'topics/projects' lists no skills or concepts but just contains the bald invitation: 'Note any topics/projects worked on during the year and any note-worthy attitude shown by the child' (ILEA 1979).

Most record schemes are consistent with this general pattern — a great deal of detail is invited for language and mathematics, in response to lists of prespecified skills and concepts; broad headings, with the probability of the teachers writing anything they wish, are used for the rest of the curriculum: note that the 'topic/projects' box in the ILEA booklet quoted above does not invite the teacher to specify what, if anything, the child had actually *learned*. Such lack of prespecification could no doubt be rationalised in terms of the intrinsic 'openness', 'flexibility' or 'subjectivity' of the curriculum areas concerned. This would dictate an approach to evaluation which is 'responsive' rather than 'pre-ordinate' (Stake 1975) — that is to say one which 'anticipates idiosyncracy, unpredictability and the uniqueness of individuals' experiences in educational settings' rather than 'establishing the extent to which a course's prespecified objectives have been achieved' (Adelman and Alexander 1982). How-ever, given the available evidence about the disparate quality of teaching and learning in basic and non-basic areas, it is hard to avoid the conclusion that the absence of prespecification in the latter stems less from analysis of what might constitute pupil competences than from the lack of such analysis. It is not difficult to draw up a list of study and inquiry skills for topic work or social/environmental studies which are apposite in any learning situation and which would greatly aid the class teacher in both curriculum planning and evaluation. (See for example two recent environmental/ social studies projects: Blyth et al 1976, Harris 1972).

One of the consequences of this discrepancy is that the inviolability of the tightly codified basic subjects is increased, while, by contrast, the case for those areas about which little can be said except for a few platitudinous utterances about 'self-expres-sion' or 'finding out for oneself' becomes ever flimsier. Thus, without some degree of codification of the skills, concepts or attitudes concerned, curriculum areas like social education, art or drama have apparently no stronger case for, say, an average commit-ment of three hours per week than for twenty minutes, and the latter, being so small, can easily disappear in the week when something untoward happens (which, as every primary teacher knows, seems to be every week).

'Integration' and the anti-'subject' view

That divide between 'basics' and 'the rest', then, is accentuated structurally by a tendency for the former to have subject characteristics and for the latter to be more likely to be integrated, except in areas like music and physical education, where the necessity for a location other than the children's home base or classroom, and sometimes the use of specialist teaching, will provide at least the timetabled distinctiveness of a 'subject' if not the structural elaboration of subjects like mathematics and reading.

In distinguishing between 'non-differentiation' and 'integration' Pring (1976) reminds us that integration properly means the bringing together of areas of inquiry or learning hitherto apart and having distinct pre-existing identities. Integration is a device for illuminating more comprehensively the issues or themes being studied, but requires the distinctiveness of the perspectives of the various modes of inquiry, or subjects, to be retained to some extent so that the multi-dimensional character of the issue can be perceived and demonstrated. While some published projects and schemes in use in primary schools (for example those referred to earlier) apply such a concept of integration, it is more common for 'integration' to mean in practice a non-differentiated exploration of a theme or 'topic' using inquiry procedures generalised and common sense rather than distinctly 'historical' or 'geographical' or 'scientific'. The justification is that

> The environment is manifestly an integrated one and as such it should be treated . . .

and

> Adults divide knowledge into subject compartments for the sake of convenience . . .
>   (Quoted by Oliver 1975)

This, then, is the common-sense exposition of that empiricist epistemology seen by Blenkin and Kelly (1981) as fundamental to primary curriculum thought: its poles are 'the way children naturally look at the world' and 'the way the world naturally is' — 'seamless', undifferentiated, common-sense, everyday and above all 'natural' rather than 'artificial'.

This field has been well worked by philosophers of education (e.g. Dearden 1968 and 1976, Pring 1976, Hirst 1974) and there is little point in summarising and perhaps over-simplifying what is so thoroughly treated by authors whose work is accessible and familiar to primary readers. Three points, however, need to be made in relation to the particular arguments of this present book.

The first is that the 'environment' is inseparable from the devices and constructs we employ for making sense of it: the environment is 'integrated' only if we choose to view it that way and for some the environment might be, equally 'manifestly', not integrated (whatever an 'integrated' environment means, and I confess to having difficulty with the term). This leads to my second point, that the use of the words 'natural' and 'artificial', with their Rousseau-esque resonances, ignores the fact that the concepts and constructs for making sense of the world which the child builds up from the earliest stages and socialisation are rooted in the cultural history of his species. The very language with which he structures and communicates his thoughts is 'artificial' — i.e. man-made. A topic using an undifferentiated, common-sense mode of inquiry is no more 'natural', no less 'artificial' than a history lesson. And the tacitly materialist view of the world in primary ideology, as existing independently of man's thoughts and actions, is no more 'natural' (by which is meant, one suspects, 'incontrovertible' or 'self-evident') than the idealist view that the world is the product of human thinking.

The third point about 'integration' versus 'subjects' is one I wish to develop at greater length since it is pivotal to my argument about the relationship between primary ideology and the professional situation of primary teachers. Following statements such as 'the environment is manifestly an integrated one' one usually hears references to geographical, historical and scientific 'elements' in the environment — 'history is all around us' — as if, again, history/geography/science/social science/art are concrete features of the physical world. For example, a Norman church may be 'history' and a signpost 'geography'. This is a weak and arbitrary use of the subject labels, and represents a very restricted view of the areas of knowledge and understanding connoted. For although the Norman church, being perhaps eight hundred years old, is suggestive of the historian's concern with time past and the signpost of the geographer's concern with location, the church only becomes 'history' once we look at it in a certain way and time past is not the sole prerogative of historians, nor location of geographers. Each can be explored also by mathematicians, scientists and artists as well as by geographers and historians, but in each case the mathematics/science/art/ geography/history resides not intrinsically in these physical features of the external world but in what we do with them, perceptually and conceptually. What makes the church 'history' is if we choose to attempt to build up a picture of its foundation, changing use and situation through an established and highly 'artificial' process, known as 'history', of searching for evidence in the form of primary and secondary sources.

A similar misconception about the nature of subjects is reflected in the NUT assertion in response to the 1978 primary survey's comments on history teaching which we referred to in Chapter 2:

> The passage of time is a very different concept for children of this age to grasp, and the fascination of history for children lies in narrative, atmosphere and the story of people's achievements

(NUT 1979, p. 25)

'History' here is represented as a fixed array of prerequisite concepts, one of which, 'the concept of time', is beyond the young child's cognitive apprehension, and on this basis 'history' must be replaced by 'story'. Of course time is a difficult concept, and not only for pre-formal operational stage children. What adult can really 'conceive' of five hundred years except as a mathematical statement? In any case, is 'time' a single, quasi-psychological conceptual absolute? Are there not in fact many concepts of time? And is it (or are they) concept/s without which the child's exploration and understanding of the past cannot begin? Does the difficulty of the concept of time mean we abandon all historical inquiry with pre-adolescent children in favour of story-telling or the copying out of sections of Unstead?

Such a negative or distorting response to the real or apparent problem of 'the concept of time' is of course not necessary. We can as teachers both convey a sense of excitement about the past and a genuinely 'historical' awareness of how the past is not so much story or textbook fact as a process of re-creation. We can encourage children not only to receive or enjoy other people's versions of history but also to experience at first hand how history is 'made', through, for example, family and local studies using immediately accessible sources like school log-books, family trees, parental and grandparental photographs and other artefacts, parish registers and the like. In such work the child's grasp of a (or the) 'concept of time' is immaterial. On the other hand, a grasp of sequence or seriation is probably essential. In this case, as Blyth (1979) shows, drawing on the work of Jahoda and West, by the age of five the child begins to cope with the ordering of events into earlier and later with respect to the present and immediate past and future, and this can be built upon rapidly during the next few years to establish a basic framework extending from 'long, long ago' to grandparental and parental childhood and 'yesterday'.

The everyday case for integration, therefore, appears to rest first on a distinction between 'natural' and 'artificial' which, shaky at the best of times, becomes untenable in the context of the complex relationships between culture and cognition, man and the physical world; and second on a representation of 'subjects' as collations, of inert and meaningless facts. The case for a differentiated curriculum cannot be said to have been fairly put; and this effectively weakens the arguments for non-differentiation and integration being pressed.

Curriculum conceptions and professional knowledge

The anti-subject view is strongest in relation to the 'beyond the basics' curriculum, particularly in the creative and expressive arts and social/environmental studies: in the 'basics', in contrast, we have seen that there are substantial subject divisions yet, paradoxically, the arguments about 'naturalness'/'artificiality', the 'child's view of the world', 'little boxes' and so on appear not to apply except to some extent as pedagogical rather than epistemological principles (e.g. 'concrete to abstract'). Two further points need to be noted: first, that this 'beyond the basics' area is that most heavily criticised by HMI (DES 1978a and 1982a) for superficiality and lack of progression in learning; and second, that this area receives the least attention in initial teacher training.

HMI's own diagnosis is that professional knowledge in arts and humanities education is insufficient for the task even of non-specialist primary teaching (DES 1978a, 1982a, 1983a). The diagnosis is shared by Sybil Marshall:

> While 'poems' are extracted daily from anyone old enough to hold a pencil, very little poetry is pumped back into them. (The same goes, all too often, for story, drama, music and art). Time is one enemy, but the other is quite often the paucity of the teacher's own knowledge of and liking for poetry.
>
> Marshall (1978, p. 46)

Other writers and reports take a similar view. The Gulbenkian Report (1982) pursues the issue further: the teacher's curriculum knowledge and understanding influences not only the quality of children's learning but the teacher's curriculum values and priorities. Gulbenkian found art frequently perceived as a pleasurable and mildly cathartic, but, in the end, frivolous and inessential activity, given low priority in primary schools (Gulbenkian 1982, p. 49). Like Cockcroft in respect of mathematics, Gulbenkian represents a particular curriculum lobby, but the contrast between that view of arts education and Gulbenkian's claims and justifications is worth pointing up. They see the arts as making six major contributions to general education:

(a) in developing the full variety of human intelligence;
(b) in developing the capacity for creative thought and action;
(c) in the education of feeling and sensibility;
(d) in the exploration of values;
(e) in understanding cultural change and differences;
(f) in developing physical and perceptual skills.

(Gulbenkian 1982, pp. 10–12)

Reflecting a similar anxiety about the inadequacy and caricature in professional as well as popular conceptions of the arts in education, the APU's Aesthetic Development Exploratory Group provide (APU 1983) an admirably succinct rebuttal of the ill-founded dichotomies which pervade such conceptions and influence perceptions of the arts' educational standing: 'objective' versus 'subjective', 'facts' versus 'theories', 'knowledge' versus 'experience', 'reason' versus 'feeling'. Documents like those from the APU and the Gulbenkian Foundation are clearly written and accessible, and it is to be hoped that they have the influence they deserve.

Such recent empirical study as we now have on primary practice cumulatively provokes three related hypotheses:

1. What teachers do not adequately understand they are unlikely to teach well.
2. What teachers do not value they are unlikely to teach well.
3. What teachers do not understand they are unlikely to value.

Together these hypotheses are suggestive of a downward spiral of ignorance or insecurity, low valuation and inadequate practice. On this diagnosis it will be hardly surprising if the qualitative and conceptual divide in primary education between the 'basics' and 'the rest' does not increase, for the differentiation is being reinforced at initial and in-service levels. Teachers' curriculum knowledge in mathematics, reading, written and spoken language, and latterly science, is being strengthened, but increased attention to these areas is frequently at the expense of others.

A final point on this matter: a substantial deficiency in curriculum/professional knowledge effectively negates the primary teacher's claim to be in a position to make valid judgements about priorities in the 'whole curriculum' for which, as a class teacher, he is responsible. Someone who knows little of, say, music, art or moral education, hardly has the right, let alone the competence, to decide what proportion of the child's total curriculum shall be devoted to these areas. Such is the relative freedom enjoyed by the primary head in these matters that he can determine the priorities, goals and structure of his school's curriculum without recourse to that depth of professional knowledge about each of the areas concerned which would seem to be the most basic prerequisite for such decision-making. This is discussed further in Chapters 7 and 8.

'Child, not subject': a hypothesis

If at the individual class teacher level it is possible to argue a relationship between the teacher's curriculum knowledge, the quality of children's learning and the teacher's curriculum priorities, a more general hypothesis relating to 'integration' and 'subjects' becomes available.

Bernstein (1971a) suggests that the breaking down of subject barriers to achieve integration is resisted because it threatens the professional identity on the basis of which the subject specialist's institutional and professional status are secured and legitimised. This hypothesis applies wherever professional expertise is defined in specialist subject terms — secondary schools and higher education for instance. At the primary stage, one can now hypothesise, a similar process operates, but in reverse. Here, the *erection* of subject barriers poses the threat, because in this case the teacher may *lack* the requisite specialist knowledge. On the basis of such generalised curriculum knowledge as he has, the only defensible curriculum is an integrated one with low 'boundaries' or, where subject insecurity is greatest, an undifferentiated one which does not even admit the validity of subjects.

Thus 'we teach children, not subjects' becomes both defence and legitimation of the lack of curriculum knowledge, and an alternative source of professional identity and self-esteem in as far as every professional needs to rest his professional claim on 'expert' knowledge of some sort. The attraction of developmental psychology, which, as we saw in Chapter 2, is widely accepted as the most essential professional knowledge for primary teaching, is that it is self-evidently 'knowledge' in the conventional academic sense, and this makes respectable what might otherwise seem mere romantic assertion. King's 'ideology' (1978) of sequential developmentalism, childhood innocence, play as learning, and individualism, can thus present itself not as ideology but as a legitimate species of expert knowledge, a 'science' of teaching: 'research has proved that this is the way children are'. And, just as King postulates that the 'home/family theory' enables the blame for discrepancies between the idealised and the actual child to be shifted away from the teacher, so the anti-subject element in the ideology enables curriculum deficiencies to be explained away.

Furthermore, the alternative professional knowledge of 'children, not subjects' provides a parallel basis for boundary erection and maintenance to that of secondary subjects. For, as I showed in Chapter 2, developmentalism is strongly structured, both vertically (intellectual, aesthetic, social, physical, moral, emotional, etc.) and, especially, horizontally (ages, stages and 'levels'), so that while at secondary level it is the boundaries of subjects which are maintained, at primary level it is the boundaries of expertise relating to developmental 'levels'. On this basis, King's finding that junior teachers were regarded by infant teachers as strongly deviant is explained, as is the sometimes strong boundary maintenance of infant departments in teacher education institutions: for among staff in such departments, subject knowledge is likely to be thin.

The discrepancy I have noted between the subject characteristics of the 'basics' and the frequently integrated/undifferentiated character of much of the rest of the curriculum does not undermine the hypothesis, but supports it; for, as we have seen, professional knowledge in primary mathematics and language/literacy is relatively substantial (though not necessarily wholly adequate) and is supported by highly structured schemes and materials. Subject boundaries here pose no threat. Although primary teachers have individual curriculum strengths, reflecting interest and educational background, collectively they are best equipped in respect of the basics. Thus, they represent not so much a reversal of the Bernstein hypothesis as a more complex variant upon it: increasingly the primary teacher is both specialist (basics) and generalist (the rest), and the primary curriculum as generally enacted mirrors this exactly (basics as subjects, the rest as mostly undifferentiated or integrated). At the same time both the insecurity in respect of the generalist areas and the overall inconsistency of argument in relation to subjects/integration can be rationalised and legitimised in terms of the claim to professional expertise in children rather than subjects.

This adaptation and extension of Bernstein's idea, it must be stressed, is only a hypothesis, and of course I am employing the device of the 'ideal type' rather than making claims to sustainable across-the-profession generalisation. Yet the idea seems to have more than passing explanatory potential.

CONCLUSION: ONE CURRICULUM OR TWO?

It is time to pull together the various strands in the view of primary curriculum practice and thought that has been set out so far in this chapter. We have identified a number of dimensions whereby the primary curriculum can be analysed: the relative *status* and *priority* of different areas of learning; the associated values and *justifications*, particularly those concerning societal and individual needs; claims and assumptions about the nature of *knowledge* – received/reflexive, rationalist/empiricist; the *organisational characteristics* of given curriculum areas, with particular reference to the extent of subject differentiation, integration or non-differentiation and the degree of *a priori* codification of each area's knowledge and skills; and the recent evidence on the educational *outcomes* of curriculum activities, particularly as reported by HMI. These dimensions are represented below. For the sake of comprehensiveness, other dimensions — *evaluation, pedagogy* and *professional training and resources* — are also included: some of these latter were discussed in Chapter 2, others will be dealt with in Part 2. The dimensions for analysing the primary curriculum are shown in Figure 3.2.

There are two points to make about the use of such a framework. First, the 'dimensions' are not fixed alternatives but are continua represented here by their poles, and in analysing the curriculum as a whole, or areas within it, the possibility of points between the poles should be considered. Second, there is no reason, theoretically, to assume a vertical relationship between the various dimensions.

Despite these provisos, it will by now be clear that it is possible to analyse the primary curriculum, on the basis of both the emerging survey and research material and the extensive prescriptive literature, in terms of what I have called elsewhere the 'two curricula' syndrome (Alexander 1983). In other words it is not merely the

Status/Priority

High   ———— Low
Major time allocation   ———— Minor time allocation
Mandatory   ———— Dispensable

Justification/Ideology

Social relevance   ———— Self-actualisation
Societal   ———— Individual
Utilitarian   ———— Child-centred

View of knowledge

Received   ———— Reflexive
Rationalist   ———— Empiricist
Positive   ———— Negative, anti-knowledge

Organisational characteristics

Subject differentiation   ———— Undifferentiated
Extensive codification of knowledge   ———— Little or no codification
  and skills
Explicit progression of knowledge   ———— Little or no explicit progression
  and skills

Evaluation

Pre-ordinate/'objective'   ———— Responsive/'subjective'

Pedagogy

Teacher-directed   ———— Child-initiated

Outcome

Progressive acquisition of knowledge   ———— Learning experiences random and
  and skills   circular
High level of 'match' between learning ———— Low level of match
  experiences and child's abilities

Professional training and resources

High priority in initial training   ———— Low priority in initial training
Well-developed teacher technology   ———— Limited teacher technology
  of schemes and materials
Relatively high INSET commitment   ———— Relatively low INSET commitment
  by teachers and LEAs   by teachers and LEAs

Figure 3.2   *Dimensions for analysing the primary curriculum*

status/priority of the 'basics' which is different (self-evidently so) from the 'non-basic' areas, but all the remaining dimensions (see Figure 3.3).

It is accepted that the 'two curricula' thesis is an over-simplification, and if used in this polarised form does less than justice to large numbers of primary schools. It is presented, in the same spirit as the set of analytical dimensions, as a model encom-

---

Curriculum I: the 'basics'

High priority, major time allocation, mandatory and consistent treatment.
Social relevance/utilitarian ideology.
Received/rationalist view of knowledge.
Subject characteristics, codified as to structure and progression.
Pre-ordinate, 'objective' evaluation.
Teacher-directed pedagogy.
Progression in knowledge and skills within and between years.
High level of 'match'.
High priority in initial training.
Well developed teacher technology, relatively high INSET commitment.

Curriculum II: the 'other' curriculum

Low priority, minor time allocation, dispensable.
Self-actualisation, child-centred ideology.
Reflexive/empiricist view of knowledge, or anti-knowledge stance.
Relatively undifferentiated, with little codification as to structure and progression.
Responsive, 'subjective' evaluation.
Heuristic, child-initiated pedagogy.
Learning experiences relatively random, with risk of circularity.
Lower level of 'match'.
Low priority in initial training.
Limited teacher technology, low INSET commitment.

Figure 3.3 *One curriculum or two?*

---

passing in extreme form tendencies exhibited to a greater or lesser degree in the system as a whole. Its function is to promote analysis at individual school level. Thus, in general, the polarising of curriculum ideas, practice and expertise may be less common in infant/lower first than upper first/junior schools, partly because the curriculum is narrower in the former and partly because of a traditional emphasis there on the educational centrality of creative, personal and social development. Variation within schools will also occur, usually at the level of individual class teachers; in such cases a key variable is the teacher's curriculum knowledge and expertise which influences not merely the quality of practice but his or her fundamental curriculum value orientation and professional ideology (see below).

I suggested that a vertical relationship between the poles of each dimension is not inevitable. However, in practice what I have noted is that particular characteristics tend to occur together, as shown above, in such a way as to greatly exaggerate and reinforce the differences between high-priority and low-priority curriculum activities. In consequence, in some schools the various non-basics not only receive less time (though note that the time distinction between 'basics' and 'the rest' as broad areas is about even), but the actual quality of professional rationale and practice, and of children's learning, may be markedly inferior. It is the *qualitative* discrepancies in the primary curriculum which are the most serious. The conjunction of prioritisation, values, epistemology, practice and professional knowledge is so marked as to suggest a causal rather than merely contingent relationship.

There is a deeper layer of complication or discrepancy: that concerning ideology and practice. The 'proof' of the child-centred ideology, with its concern for self-actualisation, child-directed learning and a reflexive/empiricist epistemology, is in the classroom practice and its outcomes for the child. Where practice is weakest in the terms analysed in the HMI surveys and the ORACLE reports, it may have in fact the appearance of openness, integration, reflexivity, and exploratory pedagogy, but the reality is a closed, non-negotiable, 'received' curriculum, epitomised in undemanding, stultifying topic work, for instance, where the actual choices available to the child are restricted and mundane. This kind of practice, seemingly all too common in curriculum II represents in operation a model far more profoundly 'closed' than a subject-oriented curriculum, especially when it is associated with the restrictive interpretations of sequential developmentalism which we discussed in Chapter 2.

Similarly, while the professional objection to subjects is that they make the child's curriculum fragmented and incoherent, it would seem that this is a minor problem compared with the substantial cleavage represented by the conflicting characteristics of and within the 'two curricula' at primary level, and in any case, as we have seen, subjects as conventionally defined are a major component of even the most espousedly undifferentiated curriculum. Thus, beyond the rhetoric of 'unity', 'coherence', 'the whole child' and 'the whole curriculum' is the real fragmentation and incoherence of qualitative inconsistency in manifest professional practice and contradictions in educational rationale, all within the one child's curriculum.

However, we must acknowledge equally the many schools whose ideas and practices are, or aspire to be, more coherent, and which seek to avoid the confusion caused by an alliance of the elementary school legacy with ill-understood progressive principles:

1. *Status/priority*. The concept of 'basics' is no longer admitted; there is movement towards a broad 'core' of curriculum experiences, all of which are deemed essential to a complete general education, and backed by comparable human and material resources. No part of this curriculum is seen as dispensable or optional.

2. *Justification/ideology*. 'Social relevance' justifications are increasingly offered in support of, for example, aesthetic, physical and social development; self-actualising potential of all areas are emphasised (e.g. extension of language work into reading for pleasure and varieties of uses of talk).

3. *View of knowledge*. Knowledge claims of all areas are taken seriously, and applied in 'process' approaches to, for example, science and environmental studies; 'reflexive' aspects of all areas are developed (e.g. in imaginative writing, higher-order reading skills, comprehension more open-ended and challenging than sentence-completion, etc.).

4. *Organisational characteristics*. Increasing codification and sequencing of knowledge and skills in all areas especially science, environmental and social studies, art and craft; at the same time, reduction in subject boundaries of language and mathematics.

5. *Evaluation*. Acknowledgement of potential of pre-ordinate as well as responsive evaluation in areas where hitherto the former has been resisted — eg. through itemising artistic skills; greater emphasis on promoting and valuing the unexpected

outcome, especially in writing, classroom discussion and the practical application of mathematical skills to everyday situations and problems.

6. *Pedagogy*. 'Discovery' approaches are less randomly applied, with greater attention to structure and sequence in learning; there is more discriminating and flexible use of individual, group and whole class teaching; more pupil choice and emphasis on exploratory methods in mathematics and language, as well as topics, etc.

7. *Outcome*. There is a net gain for pupils in all areas of higher levels of skill mastery; a greater challenge to cognition and problem-solving abilities; higher levels of 'match' between pupil ability and curriculum experiences.

8. *Professional training and resources*. This remains the anomaly (see Part 2); but one precondition at least for the greater convergence and integration of Curriculum I and II must be more even-handed and serious treatment of the latter in initial training, coupled with stronger resource and INSET support, including the use of teachers' specialist knowledge. (See Chapter 8.)

Implicit in all this discussion, and I believe supported by it, is the assumption that the teacher's professional knowledge is a key factor not only (as HMI argued) in determining the quality of classroom practice, but also in shaping primary ideology and the actual character of the primary curriculum. To understand current primary education, I have suggested, one needs to understand both its past history and the current professional situation of the class teacher. We have examined evidence relating to the class teacher in practice: we turn now to the education and training in which this practice, ostensibly, is grounded. Hopefully, this will make for a more comprehensive analysis, and where there are clear relationships between strengths and weaknesses of training and of practice as we have discussed it, we can postulate ways the class teacher's professional preparation can better serve his professional needs. But it will now be apparent that I am as concerned with the ideational and ideological basis of the primary curriculum as with the observable practices of teachers and children, in as far as the former influence the latter. If anything is (to use an epithet familiar in professional discourse) 'rigid', it is not subjects but primary ideology. Somehow we need: to reduce the divide between the 'basics' and 'the rest'; to generate alternative and culturally more responsive concepts of the 'whole primary curriculum'; to reduce the curriculum insecurity and defensiveness sometimes associated with class teaching; to shift the emphasis in that everyday professional discourse on which school decision-making is based from ideologically closed, non-negotiable recipes to open, autonomous, rational analysis. If the distinction between 'teacher training' and 'teacher education' has any validity, it is in the context of goals such as these.

PART TWO

TRAINING FOR PRIMARY TEACHING

4

The Primary Child and the Teacher's Training

TRAINING AND TEACHING: CAUSALITY OR CORRESPONDENCE?

In this and the two chapters following we shall explore the formal basis of the teacher's knowledge of children, curriculum and pedagogy — the course of initial training — which legitimises the claims about 'the whole child' and 'the whole curriculum' in which primary ideology and practice are grounded and which we examined in Chapters 1 to 3.

I use 'formal' advisedly. Professional groups validate their professional claim by reference to 'expert' knowledge, supposedly hard-won and rigorously tested, but few people are naive enough to believe that in a job as complex as teaching such formal training provides the sole (or even the major) resource for subsequent professional thought and action. Experience plays a substantial (some would argue a decisive) part. 'On the job', teachers develop skills and insights through constant interaction with children; they come to recognise patterns, commonalities and recurrences in behaviours, situations and problems and thereby develop habits of diagnosis and response whose practical effectiveness they can confidently demonstrate. (The quality and validity of their analyses and the educational desirability of their decisions are of course another matter entirely, and one which the assertion that 'being a teacher is the best sort of training' conveniently ignores). Similarly, to an extent perhaps not sufficiently recognised, the teachers draw on their pre-training experience: for, uniquely among professionals, they are engaged in a process with which they have already been involved, continuously and unremittingly, since the age of five or earlier. Their teacher training course is but a brief part of this total, cumulative educational experience and the latter, as much as the specifics of the one to four year training course, shapes the view of the educational process and its purposes within which they operate as teachers. It is a commonplace that many young teachers teach as they were taught in school rather than as they were urged to teach in college (the obvious moral of which all too often eludes teacher educators: they might be more effective if they exemplified rather than prescribed good practice). Significantly too, teachers themselves display ambivalent attitudes towards initial training. In the context of debate and negotiation about salary and status the teacher is a 'trained professional' in possession of expertise denied to all but those who submit themselves to the rigours of Certificate, BEd. or PGCE. But in everyday discourse, good teachers are 'born, not made' and that same expert knowledge may be dismissed as 'irrelevant' theory.

The truth is that it is empirically impossible to isolate initial training from earlier, contemporaneous or subsequent experience for the purposes of demonstrating its precise impact on the way a teacher performs in the classroom. It seems sensible to assume that it does have an impact, but to avoid the extremes of the grandiose strategic claim prepared for negotiation with Burnham (or the CNAA) on the one hand, and the dismissiveness of teacher folklore and staffroom conventional wisdom on the other. Instead, two hypotheses can be supported. One is that by incorporating in its emphasis on certain sorts of knowledge and skill particular views of the teaching role, the nature and needs of young children, the nature of knowledge and the character and purposes of primary education, the initial training course tends to facilitate some lines of subsequent professional development and to discourage others. Second, initial training influences subsequent development as much by what it omits or does badly as by what it treats positively; or, to use for the sake of convenience some mild jargon, a course may 'de-skill' as well as 'skill'. This latter point is particularly apposite in the present context, given that we have seen how primary ideology may relate to professional insecurity. The ideology, it will be recalled, is most strongly focused and most forcibly expressed in relation to those aspects of primary teaching where empirical study shows the greatest weakness.

What we can show, therefore, is not firm evidence of behavioural causality — element x in initial training produces action y in the classroom — so much as a succession of positive and negative correspondences between training and subsequent practice which are sufficiently pervasive and exact as to leave little doubt about a causal relationship of some sort, albeit diluted by the power of experience, circumstance and contingency, and mediated through each individual's unique combination of personality, intellect and worldview.

PRIMARY TEACHER TRAINING: BACKGROUND

To provide a framework for the analysis which follows it is necessary at this point to give a brief resumé of the overall structures and contexts of courses.

There are two main routes into primary teaching, the four year BEd and the one year PGCE (postgraduate certificate in education). The former is a post 'A' level undergraduate course (though also taken by 'mature' students) and the latter, self-evidently, is taken by graduates in subjects which could equally well lead to other careers.

Until recently the BEd and its predecessor the Certificate in Education (or 'Teacher's Certificate') constituted the major routes into teaching, but because since 1972 successive governments have used this route as the tap to regulate teacher supply the BEd/PGCE balance has now shifted. Thus in 1963 19 640 students started teacher's certificate courses, compared with a mere 3840 PGCE students, most of whom were intending secondary teachers. There followed a decade of expansion until by 1972 admissions were 37 381 (certificate and BEd) and 10 365 (PGCE). Thereafter, delayed government panic about the declining birthrate produced the devastating cuts of the 1970s, and the mergers and closures of many colleges, until by 1980, for the first time in the history of initial training, more students entered PGCE than BEd courses (10 830 as compared with 7027). 1984–5 marks the start of a modest expansion of primary training, but one to be secured mainly through the PGCE. However, the BEd will remain for the foreseeable future the majority route into primary teaching. (For a detailed demographic and historical review of recent teacher education, see Alexander, Craft and Lynch 1984.)

More important in the context of this book's analysis, perhaps, is an awareness of the training received by those teachers by now well established in primary schools. Most were products of the 2–3–4 year route, the teacher's certificate and the BEd (the latter was introduced in 1964, but did not take over from the certificate until the 1970s), and it is therefore on this route that we must necessarily concentrate in seeking to identify correspondence between initial training and primary practice.

In the recent history of the 3–4 year route, four overlapping stages are clearly discernible, which are referred to as 'Certificate', 'BEd Mark I', 'BEd Mark II' and 'BEd Mark III' (for a detailed analysis see Alexander 1984).

Firstly, the rise and decline of the teacher's certificate, which expanded from two to three years in 1960, was phased out during the 1970s and enshrined the basic structural elements which have dominated discussion about teacher education ever since. That structure is generally held to be a modified version of that recommended in the McNair Report back in 1944 (Board of Education 1944) which in turn consolidated ideas which went back to the nineteenth century:

1. 'Personal' education: (a) one or more 'academic' or 'main' subjects;
2. 'Professional' education: (b) theory of education;
                             (c) 'curriculum' or 'professional' courses to equip the student with the content and method of the subjects he has to teach;
                             (d) teaching practice.

The second stage we can call BEd Mark I. Following the Robbins Report (DES 1963) BEds were introduced at great speed. These were essentially lengthened and academicised teacher's certificate courses. Because the course was now a degree rather than a certificate, it had to be academically respectable to the validating universities and to be seen to be comparable to their other degree courses. This academic validity was seen to reside in the main subject and education theory, which were greatly strengthened, at the expense, it is now accepted, of professional studies and teaching practice.

Following increasing criticism of this course, the James Report (DES 1972) came up with a radical alternative model, which in pure form was not implemented, but its ideas provided the basis for BEd Mark II. This was 'consecutive' and modular. Deferred student choice and flexibility were major aspirations; this was the era of the 'container revolution', of courses which students put together from a wide selection of units and modules, and which often meant that professional study and work in schools were deferred until the second or even the third of four years.

By the late 1970s, deferred choice, consecutive training and modularity were running into the logistical problems attendant upon contraction, for such courses had to be large to be viable. There were other criticisms, chiefly revolving round the continued lack of sufficient professional emphasis, the perceived divorce of theory and practice and the split between subject and professional study. By now, moreover, the academic status of the BEd was no longer an issue. A large number of institutions had transferred from university to CNAA validation and alternative notions of 'degree-worthiness' had begun to be explored. Mark III BEds lasted the full four years (Mark II were three, with an extra optional honours year), were usually honours only, and included serious attempts to put professional concerns at the centre of the course and at last to break down the barrier between subject and professional study.

But by that time, the early 1980s now, there were countervailing pressures. Successive HMI surveys of primary and secondary schools (DES 1978a, 1979a, 1982a, 1982c) had identified what were regarded as major weaknesses in serving teachers' professional expertise, above all in their curriculum knowledge. First HMI (DES 1983a), then central government (DES 1983b) then ACSET (1983), the teacher education advisory body — less from conviction than recognition of the irresistibility of political dogma backed by landslide election success — and finally the DES again (1983d) proposed that all BEd students, whether primary or secondary, should spend half their course on main subject study in order to remedy these curricular deficiencies. The inadequacy of the models of primary curriculum, primary teaching and initial training thereby encapsulated will be discussed in Chapter 6.

The institutional context

Courses are not disembodied artefacts but events and ideas which acquire their reality from particular institutional contexts. The majority of today's established primary teachers not only trained by the 2–3–4 year route but did so in a distinctive sort of institution, the college of education (or, pre-Robbins, 'training college'), which preserved a culture of remarkable homogeneity and historical persistence until the institutional reorganisations of the 1970s forced many of the surviving colleges into a usually reluctant alliance with mainstream higher education institutions. While the PGCE was located mainly in the universities and — until the rude advent of compulsory initial training, comprehensive schools and mixed ability teaching — prepared its students for grammar and public schools, the 3–4 year course reflected the requirements of a less prestigious tradition, that of secondary modern and primary schools. Thus the two routes embodied and reinforced the mutual exclusiveness of the two central traditions in British education: minority/elitist/academic, and mass/

elementary/utilitarian. Like primary schools, the colleges' origins were humble and impoverished. Like primary schools, they acquired a substantial contrary ideology — idealist, romantic, espousing values of self-actualisation, individualism and student/ child-centredness.

By the 1950s and 1960s, the professionally formative years for the deputy heads, heads and advisers of the 1970s and 1980s, the college ethos was predominantly one, in Taylor's often-quoted words, of 'social and literary romanticism':

> partial rejection of pluralism: suspicion of the intellect and the intellectual; a lack of interest in political and structural change; a stress upon the intuitive and the intangible, upon spontaneity and creativity . . . a hunger for the satisfactions of interpersonal life within the community and the small group, and a flight from rationality.
>
> (Taylor 1969, p. 12)

The extent to which this incorporates caricature is debatable (though the analysis was shared by others, for example Bantock 1969, Skilbeck 1969, McDowell 1971), but when one considers the institutions into which most of the products of these colleges went — primary schools — the correspondence is irresistible. Taylor was writing about a 1950s/1960s college: he could equally have been anticipating some 1970s/1980s primary schools.

Specific manifestations and echoes of these values will continue to emerge from our discussions. We turn now, however, from general background to the first of several specific aspects of initial training: the means whereby it seeks to generate that 'understanding of children' required for primary class teaching and pre-eminent in the class teacher's professional claim.

THE CONTRIBUTION OF PSYCHOLOGY AND SOCIOLOGY OF EDUCATION

In most post-war teacher education courses the intending teacher's capacity to understand and relate to children has been seen as the virtually exclusive concern of two elements:

(a) *academic* — courses in what until the 1960s were termed 'principles of education', subsequently the separate 'disciplines' of psychology and sociology of education, but more recently somewhat disguised within integrated, thematic education/ professional courses;

(b) *experiential* — teaching practice and other school-based activity.

This neat exclusivity of function is characteristic of initial teacher education as a whole. The dominant post-McNair model discussed earlier demarcates not merely 'personal' and 'professional' *aspects* of the training task but personal and professional course *elements*. Little or no overlap of function is envisaged or, in terms of academic territoriality, allowed. There is assumed to be an exact correspondence between professional attribute and course component so that each becomes the 'property' of a particular department or group of staff.

Thus 'understanding of children' is the concern not of anyone with insights to offer, but of just two academic disciplines, psychology and sociology.

The lure of positivism and behavourism

Psychology is relatively well-established in initial teacher education. The McNair Report's 'principles of education' included (Board of Education 1944, paras 45–218): physiology and physical education, psychology, 'great classical writers on education', history of the education system, and appreciation of the 'home circumstances of the pupils'. This approach lasted well into the 1960s: Taylor (1969), Tibble (1971), Browne (1971) and others record the dominance of the 'mother hen' — the education tutor dispensing a mixture of 'method', history of educational ideas and, above all, psychology. The 1960s witnessed the coming of age of the 'four disciplines' of education, but this strengthened the position of psychology in primary training, where the 'child development' course continued to rule supreme.

Despite this relatively long-established pre-eminence in teacher education, it must be recalled that as an academic discipline psychology is young, and sociology younger. Through a combination of empirical research and theory-generation they seek to offer descriptions and explanations of individual and collective human behaviour which must be regarded as tentative, provisional and incomplete. My first major reservation about this means of generating understanding of children is that the required sense of tentativeness and provisionality is too seldom conveyed to students. Theories and models are frequently put forward, or at least received by students, as unassailable truths about the real world, their status as such apparently confirmed by the strong positivistic orientation of a good deal of the research drawn upon and by the convenient tendency of such work to offer quantified findings.

Wilson (1975) showed how the very examination questions BEd and PGCE students were required to answer presumed their tacit acceptance of a wide range of concepts and constructs. That claim is readily substantiated. My own brief survey of examination questions in the psychology of education approved by one validating body in 1982 produced the following not untypical examples:

1. Describe the main types of performance tests of intelligence and indicate their advantages and disadvantages over verbal tests.
2. Outline development during the sensori-motor stage and discuss the importance of any one of the following concepts: object permanence; spatial relationships; causality.
3. What in your view are the important influences in the formation of the self-concept?
4. Compare and contrast any two adjacent stages in Piaget's theory of intellectual development.
5. What are attitudes? How can they be measured?

None of the questions invites critical appraisal: all presume a basic acceptance of ideas, hypotheses and models of sometimes considerable challengeability if not dubiousness — performance tests as means of assessment; Piagetian stage theory; particular definitions of attitudes and the assumption that they can be measured.

Equally unsatisfactory, none of the questions invites application to the task of the teacher. Assuming the intending teachers duly demonstrate that they have committed the various theories, facts and arguments to memory, what then? What are they supposed to *do* with this knowledge? If it is seriously intended that it should inform their thinking about the job of teaching, why is no opportunity given for this capacity to be demonstrated? Or is it more important that they have the knowledge than that they can use it?

Taking their lead from this style of questioning, students' essays are peppered with the catch-phrase 'Research has proved that . . .' without apparent regard for the need for all proof claims to be probed, for the provisionality of scientific findings (or for distinctions to be made between empirical inquiry, speculation and theory-building: if it appears in print it is 'research').

The connection with everyday professional practice is evident. The same formulae re-emerge in much of the published work exemplified in Chapter 1, and in the written and spoken utterances of some serving teachers. Here, however, their linguistic hardness may be duly softened to match the gentler, familial ambience of child-centred discourse, and with the 'authority' now accorded a hushed, parent-surrogate, almost Messianic reverence: 'Piaget has shown us that . . .'.

In both contexts such unconditional deference, by negating the element of natural scepticism combined with informed critique vital to academic study and the proper use of academic research, effectively invalidates the latter's claim: for it is no longer knowledge — open, provisional, challengeable — but dogma.

Conversely, the students are exhorted not to trust their 'mere opinions', to have a higher regard for academic than commonsense modes of analysis and explanation, and to prefer the 'objective' data of the social sciences to their or an experienced teacher's 'subjective' judgement. For example, in one widely used current teacher education text:

> Understanding oneselves and others has probably always been a human preoccupation. Certainly from the time when the first written record was produced we have shown a deep interest in human and animal behaviour. Yet our ideas have been almost entirely un-systematic and unrepresentative. Even now we casually watch others or listen with prejudiced ears to conversation and from this evidence build up distorted rules of thumb about human nature.
>
> (Child 1981, p. 1)

It is of course highly probable that our 'interest in human and animal behaviour' predates written records, but that is to quibble. More problematic, it seems to me, is the implied dismissal of all but the psychologist's way of doing things as 'unsyste-matic', 'unrepresentative', 'casual', 'prejudiced', and 'distorted': clearly not the author's intention, but open to that interpretation by someone new to the discipline.

Thus may be generated or reinforced a basic epistemology to which the polarising of 'objective' and 'subjective', of 'fact' and 'value', of 'truth' and 'falsity', of 'knowledge' and 'belief', are fundamental. If internalised, this simplistic conceptual map is able and likely to provide signposts for a wide range of contexts: the teacher's subsequent response to educational research and theory most obviously, but also other situations in which knowledge claims are significant — record cards and diagnostic or attainment tests for example, and the wide and (for the child) crucial range of claims which teachers make about children, their abilities, their potential, their home background and so on.

The other context where this epistemology bears fruit in a palpable way is the primary curriculum. Its most public and assertive face is the view of curriculum in general and knowledge in particular which we explored in Chapters 1 and 3 — for example the way a view of knowledge as brute 'fact' can be used as a justification for rejecting knowledge in any guise. Less obviously, but perhaps in the end more significant, the framework may influence the way in which different curriculum experiences are presented for the child, and the view of knowledge the child thereby acquires: art at the 'soft', 'subjective', 'value' end of the continuum, science at the 'hard', 'objective', 'fact' end.

Moreover, by according experientially derived insight lower status an initial train-ing course misses an obvious and significant opportunity. Given that it is at the commonsense, intuitive level that the student/teacher is frequently forced to operate once under the pressure of everyday classroom circumstances, it is precisely these sorts of judgements which should be exposed and explored during initial training, with a view to refining them and making them as reliable and reflexive as possible.

However, the psychologist's rejection of such perspectives is the more emphatic for being made on methodological grounds: personal knowledge is counted not so much less significant as inadmissible. Psychology has sought to replace commonsense theories about mental processes with propositions derived from the application to human nature of the methods of the natural sciences. Pre-eminent in this methodology is the charting of observable behaviours. The 'introspective' method which seeks to uncover individuals' private knowledge, beliefs, attitudes and so on by eliciting these by word of mouth, is considered by the behaviourist majority to be inconsistent with the scientific claim. Thus because by the canons of a particular methodology such data is deemed inaccessible, as the object of study it ceases to be of interest.

This raises broader issues concerning the historical development of psychology — its origins in the philosophy of mind, the late 19th century rejection of mind in favour of 'scientific' study of the brain and the central nervous system, the consequent issue of the distinctiveness of psychology vis-à-vis neurology and physiology, and the contin-uity of the behaviourist/introspectionist debates. Such issues are beyond the scope of this book, but what is important for teachers and teacher educators is an awareness of the consequences for the way their task is defined in initial training. For teachers are not neuro-surgeons: their main focus of concern (*pace* the 'whole child' claim) is that elusive entity, which causes psychologists such difficulty, the human mind. Despite this, and paradoxically, psychology is granted a virtual monopoly of the topic and the monopoly is usually exercised by adopting the behaviourist position, which psycho-logists themselves acknowledge to be controversial and challengeable. Alternative perspectives on children which would complement the portrayal of the behaviourist psychologist — from literature, drama, philosophy and, pre-eminently, everyday dis-course — are explicitly rejected.

Apart from its tendency to impoverish the teacher's professional development and classroom thought, this monopoly reveals the extent to which the view of teaching as science has pervaded academic and professional opinion, even including groups — like literature teachers and tutors — who might be expected to be more resistant. Perhaps, as academics so often do, they fail to make the connection between the claim that the arts offer unique and profound insights into the human condition and the obvious fact that teaching itself is nothing if not concerned with that condition.

Three provisos must, however, be expressed, lest it be thought that this chapter's discussion stems basically from an anti-psychology standpoint.

The first is that the teacher education community as a whole, rather than its psychologists alone, have to take responsibility for excluding alternative sources of insight into children in general and into their mental processes in particular. There has been large-scale connivance at this needless impoverishment of the training process.

Second, I am arguing for courses as a whole to include additional perspectives, not for psychologists to do what artists do. Psychology is psychology and literature is literature. Each represents a distinctive way of making sense of our situation. As Hebb, an uncompromising objectivist and behaviourist, himself argues:

> The other way of knowing about human beings is the intuitive artistic insight of the poet, novelist, historian, dramatiser and biographer. This alternative to psychology is a valid and deeply penetrating source of light on man, going directly to the heart of the matter . . . I challenge anyone to cite a scientific psychological analysis of character to match Conrad's study of Lord Jim, or Boswell's study of Johnson, or Johnson's of Savage . . . Trying to make over Science to be simultaneously scientific and humanistic . . . falls between two stools. Science is the servant of humanism, not part of it. Combining the two ruins both.
>
> (Hebb 1977)

The third proviso is that the psychology component of teacher education courses, particularly until, in the mid 1970s, it began to be taught by graduates with a broad psychological training (as opposed to ex-primary teachers who had briefly studied one branch of educational psychology on a diploma or MEd course), may have been singularly unrepresentative of the parent discipline. It may, for example, over-emphasise Skinnerian behaviourism or developmental psychology; it may neglect study of the unconscious mind or of the social dimension of behaviour. It may fail to develop in students a proper consciousness of the extent to which a psychological model is a metaphor for behaviour, not the behaviour itself nor even necessarily a particularly accurate representation of it. Above all it may fail to convey the necessary sense of psychology, as of every discipline, as variegated, contentious and changing.

The dominance of developmental approaches

The extent to which psychology of education courses directly reinforce the 'sequential developmentalism' element in primary ideology, which — drawing on King and others — I discussed in Chapter 2, provides a good example of several of the points above, particularly those concerning distortion in content and methodological oversimplification. The central theme or core of such courses has traditionally been a chronological treatment of child development. Here 'development' is conceived as a matrix with norms for ages and stages providing one axis and various categories of human development — 'intellectual', 'social', 'emotional', 'moral', 'physical' etc. — the other. This developmental matrix, open to fundamental criticism as it is (see Chapter 2), provides a basic, widely accepted structure for primary discourse, curriculum planning and pupil assessment: the firmly fixed reference points on an otherwise shifting and undifferentiated map.

It is usually well understood that the ages attached to stages postulated by Piaget (whose work has come to dominate developmental psychology in primary initial training) are approximate, and that the inevitability of the sequence and the stage-independent processes and mechanisms of cognitive development — equilibration, assimilation, accommodation — are more significant than any inferred chronology. Yet it is notable that in student essays, as in professional discourse and teachers' books and curriculum materials, the stages as such feature more prominently than the stage-independent theory, despite the fact that an understanding of the latter is essential to using the undoubted insights of Piagetian theory to promote or accelerate learning. A Piagetian approach to HMI's concept of 'match', for example, would demand that children encounter learning tasks which are slightly, but not excessively, more complex than their present understanding, and that without this element of 'stretching' the disequilibration necessary for learning will not be produced. Where students or teachers perceive development in terms of stages rather than processes they will tend to wait for learning to occur 'spontaneously' or 'naturally' rather than seek as teachers to advance it, on the grounds that the child has to be 'ready'.

Educational 'failure': the child and the teacher

Just as the dominance of developmentalism in everyday practice is matched by the dominance of the developmental 'matrix' in educational psychology courses, so the traditional fare of sociology of education courses corresponds strongly with another element in professional discourse, the family and home as the prime or even sole causes of the child's difficulties or failures at school. Until the early to mid-1970s (and in some colleges even now) sociology of education courses were dominated by the issue of the effect of family and social-class factors on the child's attainment at school. Early studies of streaming pointed the way to the possibility that the school itself might be a contributory factor in the under-achievement of working-class children, but research on class-related socialisation practices, parental attitudes, language and so on tended to swamp such relatively slender evidence. Only with the 'new' sociology of education, with its two-pronged, ideologically committed concern to explore first the cultural loading of the school and its curriculum in favour of certain groups of pupils and, second, the nature of everyday classroom life, did alternatives to the family/ home deficit model present themselves with much credibility. A substantial literature concerning the effect of teacher expectations on pupil performance, teacher constructs and typifications, classroom interaction and teaching styles, now permits a more balanced appraisal of the relative impact of family and school, parents and teachers, on the child's educational career. Some of this work was referred to in Chapter 2.

The shift, however, is recent, and everyday primary discourse, in as far as it is demarcated and to some extent controlled by senior members of the profession such as heads and advisers, still appears to display fairly unreserved affiliation to family/ home theories; certainly the confident professional assertions about 'good' and 'poor' parents and homes are part of the essential fabric of both staffroom discussion and pupil record cards.

What will be worth monitoring is the extent to which the 'new' sociology of education produces a discernible shift in the way children's learning difficulties or lack of motivation are explained as students of the 1970s gain headships in the 1980s and 1990s and seek to influence their school's 'philosophies'. If, however, the family/ home background theory is such an indispensable element in professional ideology as I have argued — in that, for the weaker teacher in particular, it is fundamental to the preservation of his self-esteem — we can anticipate little movement overall.

Understanding the child, or understanding the teacher?

Theories of child development and educability, it will be apparent, not only have ideological potential but need to be simplified, and perhaps even distorted, to achieve that potential. Thus, as I have suggested, Piagetian theory may be interpreted as confirming a doctrine of 'readiness' rather than as challenging the teacher's ingenuity to provide the child with appropriately structured and sequenced learning experiences. Similarly, the complexity and tentativeness of, say, Bernstein's work on language and social structure may be ignored in preference for gross polarisations of 'restricted' and 'elaborated' codes which may confirm a student's or teacher's existing cultural stereotypes and prejudices. Both theories exemplified can be invoked to justify low expectations of children — on the 'grounds' of age, or of social class. In fact, much of the theoretical material regarded as indispensable in initial training is intrinsically extremely elusive and difficult to understand let alone to apply, and especially so for the 18–21 year old with neither professional experience of schools and children nor a background of introductory study in the social sciences. However, its misinterpretation could be reduced or offset if the typificatory process which it appears to reinforce were itself the object of scrutiny on initial training courses. But it is a characteristic of mainstream education courses in initial training that, more recent sociology and social psychology perspectives apart, they tend to devote little attention to the teacher as such.

This is particularly true of psychology of education courses: an examination of student texts and course syllabuses will reveal that most deal not so much with the psychology of *education* as with the psychology of the *child*, and that child's education is treated only in so far as it can be conceived independently of the person who is its chief architect, the teacher. The child emerges with an identity shaped by a combination of heredity and (home, not school) environment, having characteristics which are given and immutable (even by the age of five). There is little or no psychological analysis of adults in general or teachers in particular; nor of the teacher's contribution to that classroom character of the child which serves as the basis for the teacher's appraisal of him or her (despite the fact, known to all teachers, that the child at home and in school can be two very different people). The child's actions are presented, if only by default, as independent of the teacher's (see King 1978); a conception of the child is encouraged which is somehow independent of the person, the teacher, who does the conceiving.

These tendencies can be illustrated by comparing two recent psychology of education textbooks.

Child's *Psychology and the Teacher* (Child 1981) focuses almost exclusively on the learner: motivation, attention, perception, learning theory, concept formation, language and thought, intelligence, creativity, personality, handicap and so on. Though the analysis is sufficiently comprehensive for it to be applied, sometimes, to teachers as well as to children, that connection is not really made: tacitly, the teacher emerges as well motivated, perceptive, able to learn readily, conceptually advanced, linguistically sophisticated, highly and diversely intelligent, creative and of stable personality. The model is not of the interaction of minds and personalities (a few paragraphs are devoted to 'teacher–pupil interaction'), still less of teaching as dependent on teacher qualities as well as child attributes, but of the operating theatre: the teacher, as complete person and competent professional, works on the child's mind with the detachment of the surgeon working on the anaesthetised body of the patient. Skill is presumed; the sole knowledge required is of the mental anatomy of the child.

Fontana's *Psychology for Teachers* (Fontana 1981) stresses in its introduction that 'no child's behaviour can be fully understood unless we study also the behaviour of others — teachers, parents, school friends — towards him', and subsequently argues that within the context of the school the teacher is the most important influence upon the child. Despite this promising beginning, and the author's reservations elsewhere about traditional psychology of education courses (e.g. Fontana 1977), twelve of the sixteen chapters are devoted to the pupil, only three to interaction and teacher–child relations, and just one to 'teacher personality and characteristics'. The latter is a brief summary of research on the behavioural characteristics of 'effective' teachers, contextualised in an acknowledgement of some of the problems involved in defining teacher effectiveness: about a page each (in a book of 400 pages) on the teacher's emotional security, attitude, styles and classroom talk — all crucial issues but far too briefly dealt with. In addition the chapter 'Knowledge of self', which could provide a basis for the kind of analysis which is needed, though it sets out a set of propositions concerning the self-concept which could apply to all humans, applies these to the issues of self-esteem, personal maturity and identity in the pupil.

These problems are acknowledged in a recent paper by one of the authors referred to (Child 1983). He documents systematically the neglect in educational psychology of teacher practices and classroom processes: in the *British Journal of Educational Psychology*, for example, Child records just six index entries on 'teachers' between 1930 and 1954 and 27 between 1955 and 1980, and even this increase tended to focus upon teachers apart from their classroom role, concentrating instead on supposedly 'determining' factors like personality, social origins, career expectations and so on.

Textbook writers are thus placed in something of a dilemma: they recognise a need but cannot meet it, for it is the essence of the general textbook that it draws on material which is both published and to an acceptable extent established. This is particularly the case in a discipline like psychology which is committed to the search for truths through empirical study and the accumulation of evidence. Authors, then, in doing justice to the field as it stands at the time of writing, may well recognise the omissions and anomalies in terms of what is needed, but beyond speculating on what these are they can do little to remedy them.

Worse, the lecturer and student using these books may be some way removed from the global grasp of the field which gives the writer/researcher this awareness. For them, and particularly the latter, it is what the textbook says rather than what it cannot say which is significant. In turn, this extant material forms the basis for lectures, essays and examination questions (and, in teacher education, for school-based study tasks); it acquires increasing authority through familiarity and use. It comes to determine the very way in which student, lecturer and teacher may conceive of the field in question.

Moreover, in the economic climate of recent years, publishers have been increasingly reluctant to take on other than obviously marketable basic texts and course readers in education. The original or unusual is squeezed out and the second- or third-hand comes to rule supreme. Primary education has suffered particularly from the flood of edited 'readers', many of them drawing repeatedly on the same rather limited pool of 'safe' articles.

Thus, though one must not overstate the case, the public, teachable, examinable face of the educational process is increasingly defined by a combination of academics' personal interests and market forces: the research which, fortuitously, happens to be feasible, interesting, fundable or available, and what publishers and entrepreneurial editors or authors see as likely to sell.

But that is to digress. As I argued earlier, 'understanding children' is an attribute not of the object of that understanding but of the teacher who claims it. The teacher will perceive a child in a particular way not only because of the sort of person that child is but because of the sort of person the teacher is. And in the primary school, we remind ourselves, the class-teacher system ensures that a child is so perceived for educational purposes for a whole year (or longer) by just one person: with that much at stake it seems indefensible for initial training courses to neglect the psychology of the teacher.

Four shifts are indicated therefore. First, the inclusion, as argued, of a substantial focus on teachers and their impact on those various aspects of the learner conventionally treated as independent of them (learning, creativity, motivation and so on).

Second, a deeper exploration of the ways individual behaviour — whether the child's or the teacher's — can be understood in the context of, and sometimes explained as a consequence of, interaction, possibly through the use of transactional analysis techniques applied in industrial psychology and psychotherapy, as well as interaction analysis schedules and theoretical perspectives of social psychology and interactionist/phenomenological sociology. Third, a preparedness to explore the irrationality which frequently characterises human actions and interactions, not least in the classroom; the dominant psychological tradition in teacher education, as we have seen, takes the teacher's total rationality for granted and moreover imposes a sometimes over-tidy, predictive framework on the child. Fourth, just as theoretical study of children in teacher education is required to be supported by work with children in classrooms, so teachers in classrooms and above all students themselves would need to be the object of practical study. If self-exploration is now included in the training of other professional groups whose job involves the management of people and relationships, it can surely be justified in the training of teachers.

UNDERSTANDING CHILDREN THROUGH SCHOOL EXPERIENCE

The second major context a course provides for developing the student's understanding of children is school experience. Again, a historical perspective on this part of the course is helpful because its character and purposes have changed in recent years, though not as radically as some current advocates of 'school-based' courses would have us believe. Forty years ago the McNair Report identified two main types of school experience, 'practical training in schools' and 'continuous teaching practice':

> Practical training in schools . . . To provide the concrete evidence, illustrations and examples to supplement and give point to the theoretical part of the student's training. The schools are his laboratory and the scene of his field studies. School practice of this sort should include . . . comparatively discontinuous periods of teaching and observations in the schools, visits, minor investigations and so on . . .
>
> Continuous teaching practice . . . To provide a situation in which the student can experience what it is to be a teacher, that is, to become as far as possible a member of a school staff.
>
> (Board of Education 1944, paras. 260–1).

In 1979 a major review of school experience/teaching practice in all CNAA-validated BEds distinguished two main types, 'intermittent' and 'block', in almost exactly the same terms as McNair, but found the former a relative novelty in many institutions, something needing further development (McCulloch 1979). It was indeed a novelty. Taylor's 1969 study of teacher education reported as the norm for both Certificate and Mark I BEd courses block practices only, three in total, taking place in years 1, 2 and 3, with students given their final teaching practice grade at the beginning of year 3 (when in the case of the BEd. they were barely half way through the course) and undertaking no more work in schools for a further five terms (Taylor 1969). This may seem, in retrospect, hard to defend but at the time the overriding concern of the universities (who had a monopoly of teacher education course validation until the mid-1970s) — for the BEd's academic respectability — was argument enough. This arrangement ensured that professional work in general and the pressures and anxieties of teaching practice in particular were not allowed to disturb the smooth flow of what was held to matter most in the final two years of the new degree, main subject study and theoretical studies in education.

Thus, despite McNair, the history of developments in this part of the course shows three clear stages:

Stage I. The nineteenth-century 'apprenticeship' model, or what in Britain is called 'sitting by Nellie' by some teacher educators (not, obviously, by serving teachers, who naturally enough see great value in apprenticeship): here the student acquires most of his/her teaching competence through close association with, and imitation of, an experienced practising teacher.

Stage II. The 'teaching practice' model, where students acquire professional knowledge and skill in the training institution, then apply or 'practise' these during extended periods in school, watched over by the experienced teacher whose class they take over, and visited once a week or so by their college/university tutor.

Stage III. The 'school-based study' or 'school experience' model, where the school becomes not only a place to practise teaching, to demonstrate what one can do and to be assessed, but also a place to learn, to observe, to study and to experiment; to carry out specific tasks of observation, working with small groups of children, working alongside experienced teachers, undertaking small-scale inquiries, analysing at first hand how children develop, how they learn, the different styles of teaching used, how children respond to these, their impact on children's learning . . . and so on. The school here is perhaps the central resource and arena for the student's professional education and it follows that the close relationship of theoretical and subject studies with specific school-based activities is essential. What is viewed as the minimum precondition is partnership between teachers and trainers and a mutual exchange of ideas and personnel between schools and training institutions.

The latter is the model most earnestly being explored at present, and to some extent (though tinged with nostalgia for Stage I) with government support: the government at the time of writing want more school experience than hitherto, and a greater involvement by serving teachers in initial training — in selecting students for entry to courses and in assessing their teaching competence (DES 1983a, 1983b, 1983d). But it must be clear that the reality of 'partnership' is less easy than the rhetoric: it requires very fundamental shifts in traditional attitudes towards teacher education by both teachers and trainers, and involves changes in structure and procedures at the institutional level and between schools and colleges/universities.

Clearly, whatever the espoused objectives of school experience, students will gain some view of children simply by virtue of interacting with them. This applies equally when the acquisition of such experiential understanding is explicitly valued (as in Stage III) and when more limited objectives are pursued (as in Stage II): the issue is not so much the teacher educators' intentions as the dynamics of the situation in which the student is placed. The critical questions therefore relate to the treatment of the student's experiential understanding rather than the formal structure of school experience. To what extent and in what ways are the students encouraged to make explicit and explore the views of children and teaching they themselves evolve and encounter (in other teachers) while in schools? What is the relationship between such views and those 'ready-made' characterisations offered in theoretical parts of the course, as discussed above? And what value is accorded to the different views, definitions and perspectives — theoretical and experiential — which the student acquires or meets?

Hitherto, however, even in courses committed to Stage III above, the everyday, experiential perspective has probably counted for less than it might. There are, of course, problems in explicating and communicating these understandings, as we saw in Chapter 2. Being to a considerable extent private and idiosyncratic such knowledge is not readily expressed through the conceptual and linguistic structures currently on offer for public discourse about education. This may be a good example of the pervasive influence of behaviourist psychology on the initial training course as a whole. For although there is no good reason why the distrust of introspective methods should influence a part of the course which makes no claim to psychological status, the urge to assert the 'scientific' character of teaching and teacher training may result in what are perceived as scientific methodological criteria being applied across the board without regard to their appositeness. In terms of such criteria the perspectives of individual teachers could be deemed inadmissible. Moreover, difficulties in articulating and characterising such perspectives make for unflattering comparison with the apparent ease, sophistication and conceptual tidiness of academic modes of discourse. Everyday analysis, haltingly articulated, appears banal and brutish, a telling confirmation of the academic's disdain for 'mere' subjectivity, opinion and intuition.

In reality the reverse may well be the case: a complex, subtle conceptual map not readily amenable to expression in terms of the relatively crude public constructs offered by the existing, monopolistic modes of respectable educational theorising about such matters (the social sciences). Thus, for example, the general concept of 'typification' referred to at various points in Part 1 seems a potent one. What is less convincing is the claim that we can identify, in all their richness, diversity and paradox, exactly what a teacher's typifications and constructs are, using, for example, the relatively simplistic tool of repertory grid technique.

Where, then, lies the true banality: in the thinking and practice of teachers as such, or in the versions thereof offered by researchers and the procedures and models from which such versions are constructed? And what is being valued, depth of insight or sophistication of language? Fortunately, no simple answers to these questions are available: to provide them would be to compound the felony. But it can be suggested that the philosophical uncertainty surrounding the matter of how others' thoughts can be 'known' makes it inappropriate for teacher educators to accord such unequal status to 'academic' and 'everyday' versions of classroom reality. Take, for example, a course with a flexible 'workshop' concept of school experience (Stage III above), on which a student may be required, as now commonly happens, to come to 'understand' children's cognitive development by carrying out Piagetian tests in school. The rationale for this exercise is 'applying theory to practice', or, put another way, demonstrating the validity of the theory, confirming the Piagetian model. However, since in replicating the test the student will also have to replicate the circumstances, the result is predictable. What the replication does is simply to illustrate the hypothesis, not confirm it (see Chapter 2). Indeed, possibly the last thing the psychology tutor concerned may want is genuine testing of the model. We have then, two questionable assumptions endemic to teacher education and exemplified even (or especially) in Stage III 'progressive' models of school/course interaction. First, that the academic model of human behaviour is qualitatively superior to the everyday, less by virtue of its proven veracity than because of the context and manner in which it is generated and the language through which it is expressed. Second, that professional knowledge is acquired by making the idiosyncratically observed and experienced world 'fit' theoretical models of it; or, put another way, by theory verification rather than theory falsification.

Again, it seems to me, the impact of this kind of covert epistemology extends well beyond the immediate circumstances of initial training and will affect or support the everyday predilections of the serving teacher in respect of both his knowledge of the child and his view of the child's knowledge of the world. Despite the teaching profession's public scepticism about educational theory and research, its own characterisations of children and educational processes are heavily dependent upon their conceptual frameworks, but, crucially, simplified, as in the case of children's development and socio-cultural background which we have discussed, and as exemplified in the general tendency to conceive of empirical educational inquiry only in terms of quantification and proof.

ALTERNATIVES

To make use of schools not merely as a context for practising executive skills but as a prime means for developing the student's capacities to observe, understand and relate to children is a *sine qua non* of teacher education. It has to be asked, however, whether the opportunities are fully exploited. This is only partly, as we have seen, a procedural matter; what needs closer attention is the teacher educators' and course validators' view of what this 'understanding' might mean. At present, and certainly during the decade when today's primary teachers and heads trained, the interpretations, explanations and hypotheses of students and serving teachers have been undervalued and therefore insufficiently pursued and tested. And while a somewhat restricted canon of child-related theories has been, in comparison, over-exposed, it has been the exposure of obeisance, rather than critique. Some of the consequences, or correspondences, suggested by this restricted epistemology have been outlined in this chapter and exemplified more fully in Chapters 1 and 2.

There seem to be a number of ways the situation can be improved, of varying degrees of radicalism:

(a) the focus for 'understanding' can be broadened;
(b) better use can be made of existing education disciplines;
(c) additional (academic) sources of insight can be explored;
(d) 'everyday' modes of understanding can be more fully exploited;
(e) different conceptions of professional theory for teaching can be applied.

Broadening the focus

In an obvious sense, by definition, students are the main concern in a course of initial training: the qualities, skills and knowledge which they are deemed to need are the course's raison d'etre. So in arguing that the course needs to focus more explicitly on the student and on the serving teacher I am arguing for a specific kind of attention with which this self-evident concern is not to be confused. Courses are premised on the importance of teachers' mastery of certain executive skills, their manifestation of particular personal qualities and their possession of certain kinds of knowledge.

Pre-eminent among the latter is that academic knowledge about children which we have explored in this chapter, and which they may or may not make significant use of in practice. What, by and large, are neglected are the many layers or facets beyond these generalised propositions which combine to create the particular ways individual students and teachers actually view, or 'understand', the children they teach in particular classroom settings: teachers' actual and tacit, as opposed to preferred or espoused or idealised, knowledge of children, and the biographies which produce this knowledge; their subjective realities, as opposed to the quasi-objective ideas or the educational situation with which they are presented in training.

Merely to offer to the student a set of propositions from psychological/sociological theory or research — 'this is the way children are, this is what they are like, this is the reality to which your decisions must be addressed' — is to ignore, or at least to fail to acknowledge sufficiently, two basic arguments concerning children in classrooms in which much of this book's discussion has been grounded. First, regardless of generalised principles of child development, motivation and so on, children are 'as they are' in classrooms, in part at least, because of the actions of the teacher; they respond, as in interaction all humans respond, to personality, to climate, to tacit or explicit signals, attitudes and expectations from a variety of sources, but chiefly, in the educational context, from the teacher. Second, though individual children are viewed differently by each of those with whom they interact, and their self-concept indeed in part evolves from a consciousness of these various perceptions, in the educational context the teacher's view of them is the most significant. It is the teacher who defines their abilities, their potential, their personality, their attainment and their attitudes, for the purposes of making curricular decisions, evaluations and predictions, and, as we have seen, in a way which is consistent with their ideology. Such is the nature of the educational process, and the classroom power relationship, especially where young children are concerned, that the central assumption in child-centredness, of the child's autonomy, is not only fallacious but dangerously so. It can never be the case that on the one hand we have the child, about whom there is pre-existing objective knowledge, and on the other the teacher, who simply has to acquire that knowledge. The teacher's knowledge of the child is subjective, it is created by the teacher, its character is therefore as strongly conditional on the way the teacher is as the way the child is.

The theme for initial training, which should complement 'understanding children' is 'understanding how teachers "understand" children'. And if it is indeed students' understanding that we wish to promote rather than their capacity merely to parrot the propositions and formulae of others, the source as well as the character of such 'understanding', on the basis of which students and teachers act, needs to be explored; this necessitates attention to the unique individual biographies of each student as well as to the more generalised analysis of the professional, historical and ideological situation of the particular groups of teachers (in this case primary) offered in Part I of this book. The outcome of this process should be to sensitise the student to the possibility of a much wider range of diagnoses and explanations. Traditionally, courses offer a limited range of answers to the teacher's question 'Why is this child like this?' (developmental level, personality 'type', home background etc.). The added dimension stems from the immediate preparedness to ask in addition: 'Why do I view the child in this way?' 'Is there an alternative diagnosis?' 'What is the connection between how I view the child and the sort of person I am?' 'Between the child's behaviour and mine?' 'Which of the child's characteristics seem to be independent of the context within which the child and I operate?' 'What part does my personal history play in formulating my views and actions in the classroom?'

The phrases 'self-analysis', 'self-awareness' or 'self-criticism' only partly encompass what is required because conventionally they are affectivity-oriented, referring primarily to attitudes, motivation and emotional response: self-analysis in the present sense has to include, in addition, attention to one's personal and professional epistemology — the nature of one's knowledge about the children one teaches, its validity, its source, its limitations, its influence, and so on. The fact that introspective methods are unacceptable to some psychologists is worthy of debate in this context but is not grounds for rejecting the perspective I have defined. The course aims to train teachers, not professional psychologists, and if a perspective is helpful it should be included, methodological qualms notwithstanding.

Thus the scope of 'understanding children' in initial training needs to be broadened chiefly by taking in *teachers'* influence on both the children and their 'understanding' of them. Equally important, and more easily enunciated, is the need to allow existing perspectives on children offered by psychology and sociology to be supplemented by alternatives from within those disciplines. In Chapter 2 I tried to show how currently taught models of child development may feed the complacency surrounding primary class teaching while different psychological traditions might provide a basis for a keener appraisal. Clearly, given our discussion of the complementary relationship between ideology, professional theory and practical situation, the introduction of less comfortable psychologies and sociologies might be resisted, but perhaps we can begin to accept that our comfort may well be secured at the expense of the quality of the child's education.

This shift has already begun in the sociology of education: the sociology of knowledge and of classrooms has provided the needed counterbalance to the family/home educability preoccupations of the 1950s and 1960s. We now need a 'new' psychology of education which more fairly represents the richness of mainstream psychology.

The newer perspectives offer both alternative focuses and tools for analysis. Centre-stage are not only classroom processes and the interactions of teachers and children which feature in 'objective' study in the Flanders tradition, but also the meanings which the teachers and children themselves (rather than merely the observer) assign to those processes. The underlying assumption here is that human actions can be properly understood only if one uncovers these meanings, since 'action is forged by the actor out of what he perceives, interprets and judges . . . The "objective" approach holds the danger of the observer substituting his view of the field of action for the view held by the actor' (Blumer 1969).

Equally important, we are presented with an alternative view of the self which might prompt us to look as closely at the child, now, in the classroom, as at supposedly fixed and unalterable attributes like intelligence, personality and home background:

> All human beings are possessed of a self . . . they are reflexive or self-interacting . . . We think about what we are doing, and what goes on inside our heads is a crucial element in how we act. The self is . . . not a fixed structure, frozen by our toilet training or early conditioning, but rather a dynamic, changing process.
>
> (Delamont 1976, p. 23)

This basic perspective influences, to varying degrees and in different ways, most members of the family of the 'new' sociology of education which has emerged since the early 1970s, some of which I have either referred to directly in this and earlier chapters or have allowed to penetrate, albeit loosely, my own analysis. What divides the family is the extent to which action can be studied and interpreted exclusively in terms of actors' meanings. Strictly applied, *social phenomenology* examines events in their own terms and resists explanations in terms of wider social and economic forces. Sharp and Green's (1975) study of a 'progressive' primary school found this an unacceptably purist paradigm and injected a *Marxist* perspective so as to show how primary schooling both reflects and reinforces prevailing societal structures and ideologies. More determinist still, the notion of schooling in general, and curriculum in particular, as mechanisms of social control and cultural reproduction, is prominently represented in the work of Young (1971) and in the collection of papers edited for the Open University by Dale, Esland and MacDonald (1976). Moving back towards phenomenology, but representing in terms of historical origin a parallel rather than a related movement, and not asserting actors' total independence from societal structures and forces, *symbolic interactionism* gives prominence to actors' meanings but focuses especially upon the processes whereby these are arrived at, often through 'negotiation'. Thus, in studying classrooms it becomes important to understand pupils' as well as teachers' 'definitions of the situation' and the extent to which the latter are not autonomous but are influenced by the former; at the same time the power differential in classrooms (particularly at the primary stage) makes the impact of teachers' meanings on children and classroom life considerable. This perspective prominently informs the classic and comprehensive exploration of school interaction by Hargreaves (1972) and specific studies of primary classrooms like that of Berlak et al (1976). The study of infants' classrooms by King (1978), to which I have made frequent reference, is eclectic: it is critical of phenomenological, interactionist and Marxist perspectives (and also the earlier functionalist tradition which these in turn aimed to supplant) yet is also influenced by them. It belongs to the 'family' in so far as it is grounded in close and sustained observation which is interpreted by reference to actors' perceptions and explanations rather than observer preconceptions. At the same time it places these in broader frameworks of ideology and social structure.

These developments are recent: empirical study of primary classrooms, of whatever methodological complexion, is still relatively thin. Nevertheless, in terms of what by this book's analysis seems to be needed — far greater attention to how teachers (as opposed to researchers) 'understand' children and teaching — the growth points are now significant, diverse and rich.

Making better use of 'the disciplines'

The last point notwithstanding, we also need to ask whether the monopoly by psychology and sociology of insights into children and classrooms is to be desired or supported. The other two disciplines in the educational studies pantheon are philosophy and history. Philosophy of education — whether so defined or used thematically in an integrated course — tends to concern itself with broad non-contextualised questions about aims, the nature of knowledge, the justification for particular educational concepts and activities, the ethics of reward and punishment. Frequently it is conceived as a tool for encouraging a sharper, more reflexive and considered mode of analysis than the easy, instant judgement, as a basis for critique of teachers' and students' 'commonsense' statements. This is undoubtedly necessary, but it is also the case that by such means, intentionally or unwittingly, is the status of academic thought preserved, for philosophical analysis ought equally to be applied to the statements, judgments and explanations offered by psychology and sociology of education: conceptual analysis should have no boundaries. Especially, a concern with epistemology ought not to start and finish with the school curriculum, but should encompass the knowledge and truth claims of the teacher training curriculum as well, the ways of making sense of and understanding children, teaching and learning which the initial training course expects the student to internalise and subsequently 'apply' in the classroom. (A fruitful starting point for such analysis might be the assumptions in the quotation on p. 89). In other words, 'ways of knowing' about educational processes should be subjected to the same level of scrutiny as are the ways of knowing which constitute the school curriculum out there in the school. To fail to do this is to miss an opportunity to give the student a working understanding (as opposed to a textbook definition) of epistemological issues (epistemology being about the methods and grounds of claiming to know used by people anywhere and everywhere, not merely in schools); and it could be construed as hypocritical to subject to critique the school curriculum but not that of teacher education.

A similar argument applies in the case of history of education. We saw in Part 1 how usefully an historical awareness of the institutional and ideational background of primary education both illuminates and provides a basis for critique of present-day ideas and practices, particularly in respect of the ways the child is viewed and the curriculum defined in the context of the class-teacher system. We also saw how primary professional discourse with its 'cocoon' imagery and polarising of the child and society, seems resistant to a sense of the interplay of historical events, cultural values and educational ideals. Conventionally, history of education courses have done little to remedy this. Courses in 'the educational system of England and Wales' can still be as normative, functionalist, systemic and superficial as they were in the years following the McNair Report: resumés of the clauses of education acts and the recommendations of major reports, but rarely interpretations or explanation beyond a sort of sub 'O' level 'seven causes of the Boer War' variety, and certainly little real delving into the pedagogy and curriculum experienced by previous generations of children and the justifications offered by teachers and others in support of these. 'Why do we view children like this?' 'Why do we define their educational needs in this way?': these are questions as much historical as psychological, and the desire to ask them (rather than to tacitly, ahistorically, infer 'because this is the way they are') is surely a prerequisite for any teacher in a complex, changing, pluralist society.

Teaching is constituted of ideas as well as action; indeed it is the putting into operation of ideas. These need to be explicated, critically explored and, to be properly understood, need to be culturally and historically located.

Beyond 'the disciplines'

Of course academic monopolies are not fortuitous: the one under discussion reflects aspirations to make teaching a 'science' grounded in a set of empirically derived principles and so to demonstrate the 'expert knowledge' basis of the teacher's professional claim. However, we might try asking afresh, with no preconditions, the open question: 'What is the best way to develop the young adult's capacity to understand other human beings, especially (but not exclusively) pre-adolescent children?' In pursuit of an answer we might attempt to catalogue those ways which humans have learned to understand each other and themselves. On the one hand, and pre-eminently, there is the pervasiveness and potential of insight grounded in individual and collective experience. I return to this below, but if, meanwhile, we concentrate more on academic or public modes of personal and inter-personal exploration, we have to acknowledge, as I argued earlier, that the field can encompass, at least, literature, art, music, drama and religion as well as the social sciences; and that even the latter can extend much further than teacher education has allowed — for example to include social anthropology and social psychology (both, incidentally, very helpful to a more comprehensive view of culture than primary discourse conventionally reveals). The modes of inquiry we actually make available to the student are from one small spectrum of human knowledge, and, as it happens, they are from one of the newest and — to workers in the physical sciences and the arts alike — one of the most suspect in terms of its claims to represent humans as they are.

Putting into operation such extended concepts of 'understanding children and teachers' is not necessarily easy, but the issue needs to be faced. As presently conceived, teacher education courses place arbitrary and unnecessary restrictions on this aspect of the student's development. In the first instance courses could be released from that 'compartmentalisation of function' I referred to earlier and each component could be scrutinised as to its potential for generating insight and skill useful to the intending primary teacher, regardless of academics' claims or territorial anxieties. The most basic reappraisal would concern the academic/professional distinction, and, as a consequence, the common ground between subject studies and education theory as regards each's capacity both to generate professional insight and to meet 'personally educative' functions might be disconcerting.

Rehabilitating the 'everyday'

However, the most substantial and necessary shift in this context is towards the exploration and use in initial training of non-academic, everyday, subjective professional knowledge. The arguments seem inescapable: such knowledge is pervasive, inevitable and influential in everyday practice and therefore requires exploration; it is effective in that it is the basis for teaching of a high quality and therefore may encapsulate ideas worthy of emulation; it is also, conversely, the basis for weak teaching and therefore its limitations as well as its strengths need to be exposed. Where, as in this context, the everyday knowledge in question concerns children, it taps, or may tap, insights stemming from one of the most fundamental of human relationships: it cannot simply be disregarded on the grounds of arbitrary (and, as we have seen, suspect) stipulative definitions of what constitutes 'science' and 'objectivity'.

This is not an argument for rejecting academic inquiry, or for a revival of apprenticeship approaches to teacher education. Rather, the case is made for recognising the strengths and limitations of any mode of understanding pursued in overmuch isolation — particular disciplines, academic study in general, personal, experientially grounded everyday knowledge — and for acknowledging the advantage of using these in combination and juxtaposition, particularly in pursuit of that understanding of ourselves and others which educationists seem happily prepared to lay claim to, despite the fact that the rest of humanity has found it rather more elusive.

Such eclecticism as is argued here would be conditional upon courses sensitising students to the epistemological problems raised. It is not adequate to 'raid the disciplines' (Hirst 1979), or rather to 'raid' all available and potentially productive sources of insight, without also understanding the nature of the truth claim each makes and the limitations thereof. Traditionally courses have tended to treat academic sources as given and experiential sources as suspect or unacceptable: all are problematic, though in different ways.

Reconceptualising professional theory

It will be apparent by now that, in combination, the ideas above require not minor adjustment to the content and pedagogy of initial training courses, but a more fundamental shift. The operational question is 'What kind of professional theory does the intending primary class teacher need in order to understand and relate successfully to and provide valid educational experiences for young children?'

This present chapter has tried to show how the answer to this question involves matters of epistemology as well as content; the related questions are: 'To what extent is teaching a science?' 'Is the attempt so to dignify it appropriate?' 'Exactly what kind of an activity *is* teaching?'

These matters do not concern the particular focus of the present chapter alone, and are therefore discussed in Chapter 6, after the consideration of the training for the curricular requirements of class teaching which follows in Chapter 5.

CONCLUSION

In this chapter we argued the need to seek correspondence between teaching and training, outlined the current systems for training primary teachers, summarised the post-war development of the majority route, the three/four-year course, and compared the culture of the training colleges/colleges of education in which most of today's primary teachers trained with that which prevails in many primary schools.

We then considered the two main sources in the initial training of that 'understanding of children' which dominates primary ideology, and the actual, as opposed to the claimed, characteristics of which we explored in Chapter 2. I drew attention to the following essential characteristics, all of which have distinct resonances in the profession: the normative pull towards naive positivism and the consequent polarising of fact and value, subjective and objective, science and common sense; the restrictedness of the psychological perspectives offered, and in particular the emphasis on chronological development, behaviourism and a segmental model of human attributes (see the 'developmental matrix' in Chapter 2); the prevalence until recently of cultural deficit explanations for educational difficulty, and the restricting of the explanatory framework to family and home; the lack of analysis of teachers comparable to that available of children, of their psychological make-up, motivation, values, perspectives and above all their role in providing the basic definitions of childhood and individual children within which they conceive and implement curriculum. This neglect of the student's and teacher's experiential analyses and understandings I found repeated in that part of the course providing most obvious opportunities for their exploration — teaching practice/school experience. After a brief history of the evolution of this part of the course, I questioned the 'applying theory to practice' function of recent models whereby academic certainties are 'validated' rather than tested or dialectically set against the particularistic, experiential perspectives of the teacher. Finally, I discussed five principles for generating a more comprehensive and reflexive understanding of children: (a) broadening the focus of study, especially to encompass the function of the teacher in shaping the classroom attributes of the child and how these are perceived; (b) extending the modes of academic analysis and in particular, (c) breaking academic monopolies — of the 'four disciplines' as routes to understanding of educational processes and issues, of the social sciences as means to understanding children, of the positivistic, behaviourist and developmental traditions within these; (d) starting to value, explore and exploit the everyday ways of knowing and understanding of the student and the teacher, and setting these in a dialectical relationship to academic modes of analysis; (e) reconceptualising professional theory — as not so much an additional requirement as the extent of change implied by (a) to (d) above.

5

Preparing for the Whole Curriculum

In Chapter 3 we appraised aspects of ideology and practice in the primary curriculum. Many of the strands of this critique are brought together in the conclusion of Chapter 3 though because the 'two curricula' thesis there represented has recourse to ideal types it probably underplays the extent of complexity and indeed contradiction overall which exists: there are likely to be as many inconsistencies within each of the 'two curricula' — as to quality, ideology, justification and so on — as between them.

The main issues to be carried forward into the present chapter — apart from the 'two curricula' thesis — are now briefly rehearsed. 'The curriculum' constitutes the negative pole of primary ideology (contrasted with the positive view of 'the child'), indeed usually and tellingly preceded by the word 'not' itself — 'child not curriculum', 'children not subjects', etc. The positive ideology, the view of what the primary curriculum is supposed to be and to do, has frequently to be reconstructed from statements about what it is *not*, from a rational standpoint an absurd way to proceed, yet in terms of this chapter's focus immensely suggestive of the general defensiveness and insecurity concerning curriculum which I believe recent patterns of teacher education have fuelled, if not directly caused.

Thus, once the rhetoric — of unity and holism, of individual needs being responded to, of integration and coherence, of the paramountcy of individual self-actualisation — is removed, empirical study suggests a somewhat less convincing picture: of inconsistencies, omissions and variation in curriculum provision; of a qualitative fragmentation in children's educational experiences considerably more serious in its consequences than whatever is held to be the harm caused by the fragmentation of subjects; of a narrow, neo-Victorian utilitarianism allowed far more sway than the ideology can safely admit; of areas of learning sufficiently tightly codified to merit the label 'subjects' existing in a context where subjects are strenuously rejected; of mediocre, repetitive, aimless thematic activities, justified on the grounds of openness and self-direction, yet in their arbitrary restrictiveness of progression and challenge in learning far more profoundly 'closed' than the 'subjects' they claim to replace; of progressivism sometimes revealed as a wafer-thin veneer over the solid rock of the unbroken tradition of mass elementary education, especially where older primary children are concerned (in early childhood education the gap between rhetoric and reality tends to be narrower, and practice can be more consistent with claim).

My argument now runs as follows. The inconsistencies and deficiencies discussed in Chapters 1, 2 and 3 are more than the normal qualitative variability one can anticipate in the work of any professional group, be it of doctors, lawyers, architects (or university lecturers). In that event one would expect a wide and random range of aspects of the job to be affected. But in primary education the weaknesses are concentrated in particular areas, while in contrast there are certain other things which primary schools and teachers do supremely well, and with greater consistency than one might expect — pre-eminent among these is their capacity to generate a caring, supportive and physically pleasing environment for young children: a considerable and essential achievement, especially considering the resource limitations and the contrary traditions of much of the rest of the education system. In contrast, curriculum is the recurrent weakness, and the link between the quality of professional practice, the consistency of the child's curriculum experiences, the degree of rigidity and closure of the professional ideology and the sustainability of the educational arguments the ideology purports to advance, seems to be the adequacy of the primary teacher's knowledge of and for the curricular demands of his class-teaching role. Over the years, we can now argue, these demands have been underestimated, both in the profession and in training. We shall take up again the professional standpoint when we look at curriculum decision-making in primary schools in Part 3. In this chapter, meanwhile, we examine how the curricular demands of class teaching are conceived and catered for in initial training.

'CURRICULUM' IN INITIAL TRAINING

The part of the post-McNair initial training course most explicitly identified with the development of the student's knowledge and executive skills in respect of the school curriculum is that part variously termed 'Curriculum Courses' (in the 1950s/1960s certificate and Mark I BEd. in particular), 'Method' (on the PGCE) and more recently in both routes 'Curriculum Studies' or 'Professional Studies'. Traditionally, it was the part which remained once one had extracted academic or subject studies (in the case of the certificate and BEd.), educational theory and teaching practice/school experience. Its 'curriculum' orientation was demonstrated in the nomenclature of its constituent course units, which adopted the titles of areas of the school curriculum —

mathematics, language and literacy, environmental studies and so on. It was the part of the training most clearly concerned with what to teach and how.

I say 'was', and the slightly uncertain tone of the above paragraph reflects a real problem. Whereas the traditional 'curriculum courses' as experienced by most primary teachers now well established as heads and deputies were discrete, instrumental and thus accessible to criticism (e.g. Renshaw's 1971 complaint, frequently echoed elsewhere, that they were 'superficial and intellectually undemanding'), and whereas this accessibility is still maintained in some courses, elsewhere the 'professionalisation' of courses in general, and CNAA-validated courses in particular, since the James Report (DES 1972) has meant that to appraise a course's approach to developing curriculum expertise on the basis of its 'curriculum' elements alone may fail to do justice to its 'integrative' or 'permeative' rationale. Such elements may now be but one part of a comprehensive 'professional studies' component which may also include units in practical teaching skills, multi-cultural education, the curricular needs of the slow learner, the theory of curriculum planning and evaluation, and which may claim an interactive relationship with both practical work in schools and education theory. Moreover, the newer term 'professional studies' is notoriously loosely used: in a recent symposium it was variously defined as the whole of the BEd course; as part of it; as incorporating and integrating both theoretical and practical studies; as being distinct from both of these . . . and so on (Alexander 1979).

However, in four respects the reality may be less confused than the nomenclature. First, the James Report's 1972 concept of a 'professional degree' has produced its dutiful echoes in most subsequent course submissions to the extent that 'professional' has become a word much used, rarely defined, having normative rallying power or talisman status (Scheffler 1971) in initial training not unlike 'child-centred' in primary education.

Second, as we have seen, the basic structure and rationale of initial training courses have proved remarkably resistant to change, and whether a course component is labelled 'curriculum' or 'professional studies', 'teaching studies' or something else, and despite the undoubted efforts at integration of school experience, its structural existence alongside, but distinct from, an education theory component on the one hand and a subject study component on the other reduces its options for being much different from the 'curriculum course' concept it may claim to replace.

Third, course labels diversified most during the decade (the 1970s) when teacher training staff changed least (except to be made redundant or retire prematurely). The new courses were planned and staffed by the same people as before, with the same basic intellectual approaches, the same professional identities, the same interests to protect, prominent among which were, as they had been during the 1960s, the sanctity of the academic subject — there to fulfil a 'personally educative' function and not to be diluted by being 'applied' to the classroom — and the hard-won status of the disciplines of education, that quadrumvirate which alone provided the 'proof' that teaching had at last graduated from mere craft to science.

Finally, though research on the content of teacher education courses is lamentably sparse, a recent analysis of 42 post-James CNAA BEds. (Chambers 1979) identifies a persistence both of the old 'curriculum courses' concept and of the mediocrity and superficiality associated with it. Moreoever, if labels had changed, the overall allocations of time had not:

> Of the 42 submissions approved by CNAA . . . more than 30 have found the constraints of covering the range of professional skills, especially in primary courses, an almost insuperable obstacle to achieving sustained, coherent courses.
>
> (Chambers 1979, p. 42)

This latter point, confirmed by HMI (DES 1979b) and McNamara and Ross (1982), highlights the so-called 'curriculum coverage' problem — that of 'covering', in the limited time available, all the areas of the primary curriculum to be dealt with by the intending class teacher. The problem is perceived very much as one of time, and this perception is partly justified: one of my more recent experiences as a CNAA validating panel member was of a four-year primary BEd. proposal which allocated ten hours of a 2000-hour course to the teaching of religious education, the only curriculum area schools are obliged by law to teach. However, though we start with the matter of time, we shall see that it is but a symptom of a more fundamental failure to think through the training implications of the class teacher's curriculum needs.

'Curriculum coverage'

HMI found (DES 1979b) that curriculum/professional studies was allocated, on average, 225 hours, or 15 per cent of the 'Mark II' three-year concurrent BEd., an allocation comparable to that of the 1960s three-year certificate.

Despite the 'professional' emphasis of the final year of subsequent four-year courses (the 1960s BEd.'s final year was usually divided between subject study and education theory with neither school-based work nor further curriculum study), the overall allocation of time for curriculum was little different.

That 15 per cent for curriculum/professional study compared with 25 per cent on average for education theory and up to 50 per cent for academic subject study. Even allowing for individual variations (and it is better to note overall proportions rather than to attach overmuch significance to the relatively slender evidence about precise figures) the differences were such as to indicate that the future primary teacher's capacity to think and act in respect of the child's curriculum, whose sole agent he was to be for a year at a time, was given comparatively low priority.

It will be noted that the relative weighting of psychology-dominated education theory courses and curriculum courses is consistent with 'child not curriculum', and at the professional level such objections to the balance of studies concerned not these two areas whose relative weighting provoked little comment, but the continued dominance of the academic subject, which was seen by many as serving little purpose to the intending primary teacher (e.g. CNAA 1983a, 1983b) — an assumption which will be questioned in Chapter 6. Writing about pre-1960s courses Eason remarked:

> The need for professional levels of insight among teachers of young children was more readily grasped in relation to psychological development or understanding of social background than in relation to (say) the infant school curriculum.
>
> (Eason 1971, p. 84)

This perception persisted. HMI's 1979 survey of the BEd., while deploring the inadequate treatment of 'non-basics' in curriculum courses, was prepared to argue that while the average of 60 hours for mathematics was rather low, '90 hours . . .

would be reasonable' (DES 1979b, p. 36) — a mere 4.5 per cent of the four-year course to be devoted to an aspect of the child's education which accounts for some 20–25 per cent of timetabled activity in the primary school. More recently, the model advocated by HMI (DES 1983a) and endorsed by central government (DES 1983d) gives language/literacy and mathematics a mere 100 hours each, or just 11 per cent of the total BEd. course, as compared with 900 hours, or 50 per cent, for the 'main' subject.

My view on this matter will by now be clear. Few facts demonstrate so starkly the teacher educators' persistent failure to consider, or attempt to meet with any seriousness the primary class teacher's curriculum-related needs than the distribution of time for curriculum/professional studies relative to that for education theory and academic subject studies, and despite the powerful evidence of the primary and first school surveys (DES 1978a, 1982a) the situation seems unlikely to change.

Time, organisation and treatment within curriculum/professional studies

Of the various ways in which it is possible to conceive of a training for the primary class teacher's curriculum role one has nearly universal acceptance. Its two salient features are: the time available is allocated to a number of discrete units bearing labels corresponding to school curriculum areas; these units are given relative priority in a way which reflects practice in schools, and time is distributed to them accordingly, in proportions which are usually very close to those in schools noted on p. 56.

The rationale for this standard practice is presumably that curriculum studies for the trainee primary teacher must reflect in all respects — rationale, structure, nomenclature, temporal distribution — 'schools as they are'. The correspondence can be very close indeed. Thus the 'basics' tend to be covered by single subject elements — language (with reading sometimes separate, sometimes incorporated) and mathematics. Non-basics vary, from single-subject treatment — PE, science, art, history, etc. — to 'integrated' units in, for example, 'expressive arts' and 'social and environmental studies'. The 'two curricula' distinction is further reflected in the tendency for the basics to be compulsory while some at least of the rest may be optional. Though this may be because of the extreme pressure of time in this part of the course, what become optional (i.e. dispensable) are, naturally enough, those curricular areas which in the HMI curriculum consistency analysis discussed on pp. 56–59 are most likely to be treated as dispensable in schools. The temporal distribution ensures that the task of the curriculum lecturer in non-basic areas — and to some extent in mathematics and language also — is one of extreme compression, distillation and simplification.

This procedure is rarely challenged, presumably because it is deemed unchallengeable. Nevertheless the objections have to be voiced, for nothing in a model of teacher education is self-evident.

First, there is no logical reason why existing curriculum prioritisation in schools should provide the main 'reality' with which professional courses in initial training so strenuously seek to correspond. Not only is 'correspondence' questionable as a principle but it is also capable of different interpretations, though only one is entertained in current patterns of curriculum preparation.

Second, this structural arrangement makes it probable that: (a) students' understanding of one curriculum area will be weaker than their understanding of another; specifically, they will have a deeper grasp of 'basic' than 'non-basic' areas; (b) they will teach one less effectively than another; (c) they will value one less than another — what one does not understand one is unlikely to value.

Third, because such curricular analysis as takes place in these courses does so within pre-established curriculum boundaries and definitions, the trainee teacher's capacity for curriculum planning and implementation in school is likely to be most effective where these boundaries and definitions are preserved. Thus, a 45-hour integrated course in social and environmental studies may help the student to teach in a thematic context (and would doubtless be applauded by many teachers for so doing) but it is unlikely to enable the student to conceive of or enact an approach which enables children to adopt more distinctively 'historical' or 'scientific' means for exploring and understanding their environment. Similarly, a quasi-subject approach to mathematics or to language will encourage a subject approach to these in schools, thus on the one hand preserving the clear separate subject status of maths — desired, perhaps, by mathematicians, but deplored by HMI (DES 1982a) — and on the other militating against the student's capacity to construct programmes for language development across the primary curriculum as commended since Bullock (DES 1975).

Fourth, the initial training course thus takes on the function not so much of reflecting as *confirming* schools (or at least curricula) 'as they are': existing curricular pecking orders, the assumptions of value and utility from which these stem, and the inadequacies of treatment they receive. It is doubtful whether this is an appropriate role for the teacher training course.

Fifth, despite the attempt at correspondence with the school curriculum, the adherence to subject labels ensures that what is corresponded with may in fact be at variance with aspects of practice and indeed of ideology. Thus, for example, such 'integration' as is envisaged in initial training courses tends to be within rather than between areas already 'integrated' for organisational reasons — 'expressive arts', 'environmental studies': primary ideology sets no such boundaries on integration though in practice, as we have seen, this is what tends to happen in schools, with certain areas rarely coming together.

Sixth, the use of the more obvious subject labels ensures that areas for which such labels, and the academic qualifications and staff they generate, do not exist, receive little or no attention. Among these is personal and social education: not only is it claimed to be central to primary education but it also forms, if only as part of the 'hidden' curriculum, a fundamental part of the child's curricular experiences. In the latter context it is doubtful whether a school curriculum pre-packaged for teacher training purposes in conventional subject terms can begin to approach the other 'reality' of curriculum — that experienced by the child.

Finally, this approach conceives of the curriculum in schools not as a whole but as a random sum of parts. Despite the rhetoric of 'schools as they are', therefore, what is corresponded with, except at the most superficial level of labels, is neither primary ideology nor the manifest needs of the class teacher in respect of the totality of the child's curricular experiences that I postulated at the start of Chapter 1. It is rare to find a course which compares and analyses relationships between curricular areas.

Treatment of each is frequently so distinctive and idiosyncratic as to produce not the vaunted unity but fragmentation – as noted, indeed, in the recent BEd. surveys of HMI (DES 1979b) and McNamara and Ross (1982).

It is even more unusual to find a course which explores the 'whole curriculum' both as a counterbalance to the fragmented curriculum produced by course structures and in order to help the future class teacher to put the various curricular elements in some sort of perspective. This perhaps is the most surprising omission of all, because even the most cursory analysis of the job that the class teacher does indicates the necessity for such a whole curriculum perspective.

However, perhaps it is not so surprising after all. For whole-curricular questions are pre-eminently about values and priorities, and the principle of structural/temporal correspondence which informs the organisation of initial training 'curriculum' courses ensures that such questions are in effect pre-empted from the outset since a given set of curriculum priorities and values is already built into the course structure. One can hardly raise questions, in the open way they demand, about the relative importance of the child's mathematical, religious and social education, for example, if mathematics receives a compulsory course of 100 hours, religious education a ten-hour option and social education nothing at all.

Thus the correspondence principle essentially confirms the status quo, both by reinforcing existing values and practices and by denying the intending teacher the chance of developing sufficient understanding in all curriculum areas to weigh fairly the claims and arguments for each or to justify and enact convincing alternatives to current practice. Preparing the student for 'schools as they are', the stated goal of recent teacher education courses, need not (and, arguably, should not) mean 'confirming schools as they are', but the situation outlined above permits no other outcome.

So far the case against the principle of curriculum correspondence, apart from its basic inadequacy in respect of the class teachers' whole curriculum needs, has highlighted the issues of time and organisation. It is, of course, conceded that much also depends on the treatment each curriculum area receives, and that one fifty-hour course on 'primary expressive arts', however severely constrained it may appear to be, may have considerably greater intellectual and professional potency than another course of the same length bearing the same title. But the constraint of time has been so severe that it is hard to see how many such courses could avoid the criticism that

> At their worst, they were called simply 'the teaching of . . .', threw in a bit of basic content and concluded with some anecdotal hints and wrinkles. Their major characteristics were profusion, fragmentation, shortage of time, absence of theory and encapsulation from other parts of the course.
>
> (Chambers 1979, pp. 31–2)

(A characterisation which many of the experienced primary teachers with whom I have shared it find, if anything, too charitable.) For in considering the relative claims of the student's need for immediacy, relevance and a teaching practice 'survival kit' on the one hand, and analysis and evaluation for the longer term on the other, tutors could only opt, in their students' interests, for the former. The temporal constraint is damaging not only because it forces tutors to adopt a concept of curriculum study which sacrifices all to non-reflexive, narrow and short-term utility, but also because it obliges them to differentiate the short and longer term so starkly and inappropriately in the first place.

Although recent years have witnessed a gradual upgrading in the status of curriculum/professional studies (McNamara and Ross 1982, Alexander and Wormald 1979) and a consequent redistribution of time in its favour, the traditional analysis remains all too frequently valid: conservative, superficial, non-analytical, prescriptive and pragmatic ('You'll find this goes down well with eight-year-olds'). Such courses offer pre-packaged learning experiences rather than principles by which learning experiences can be selected. They can induce in the student a sometimes extreme dependence on recipes, and a predictability and repetitiveness in work undertaken in the classroom: how often have the same children been subjected over again to stories like *Where the Wild Things Are* and *The Iron Man*, to musical 'stimuli' like *Mars, The Carnival of the Animals* and the *Peer Gynt Suite* or to a standard, non-progressive sequence of splatter patterns, curve-stitching and topics on transport?

These characteristics are most evident in 'Curriculum II', the 'non-basics' areas, where time is most constrained. A more generous allocation of time permits a more principled and structured approach to language/literacy and mathematics and perhaps a basis for that exercise of intelligent and informed choice about classroom strategies which is essential to all teaching. The correspondence hardly needs pointing out: the student/teacher's capacities are as a consequence least adequate in those curriculum areas which have lowest status in the eyes of teachers, politicians and the public, are least imaginatively and effectively taught in schools, and are currently most at threat at all levels of the education system from primary to higher. A causal relationship is, as I suggested earlier, if not proven then at least strongly indicated.

THE NECESSARY DIMENSIONS OF CURRICULUM PREPARATION

From Chapters 1 to 3 a number of dimensions emerged as essential to an adequate treatment of curriculum in primary schools.

Some emerged by default: the polarising of 'child' and 'society' suggests a dearth of engagement with *cultural* issues beyond those of ostensibly immediate concern like relationships with parents and the local community.

The endemic 'child'/'knowledge' polarity and the assertions about subjects and integration indicate a similar deficiency in *epistemological* understanding.

Others emerged as being undoubtedly prominent but not always sufficiently comprehensively conceived: the *psychological* dimension is, as we have seen, strongly evident in primary discourse, but the psychological models applied may be restricted and restrictive.

A *pedagogical* dimension is clearly central to the business of teaching, yet the polarising of so-called 'formal' and 'informal' approaches and the ideological loading of arguments about individual, group and class methods has made rational discussion of pedagogy virtually impossible in some schools and LEAs, given the power exercised by advisers and heads over the careers of those teachers who dare to question official orthodoxies.

The *planning and evaluation* dimensions of curriculum have been characterised on the one hand, as HMI showed (DES 1978a, 1982a) by inaction or lack of even a modest degree of systematisation and, on the other hand, as Blenkin and Kelly argued (1981, 1983), by unthinking adoption of such models as were available to provide that systematisation, regardless of their appropriateness: examples of the latter include the instructional objectives model for planning and the now ubiquitous checklist for evaluation and record-keeping.

Finally, we have found what one might term *value*-schizophrenia: at once a timorous consciousness of values in as much as 'one mustn't impose one's own values on the children' in obvious areas like religious education, coupled with a neglect of the fact that as a teacher one does this anyway, and a lack of consciousness of the values purveyed by the curriculum as a whole and its constituent parts whereby the hallowed, neo-elementary curriculum of 'basics plus', discussed in Chapter 3, is rarely treated as other than self-evidently the only valid form of education for 5 to 11 year olds.

There are six dimensions to curriculum therefore: culture, values, psychology, epistemology, pedagogy, and planning and evaluation. Their treatment in initial training is the focus for the remainder of the present chapter. However, some basic preliminary points can be made. First, the preceding discussion has shown that courses have traditionally offered a concept of curriculum preparation which has excluded these dimensions, at least in other than a prescriptive capacity, from curriculum/ professional studies. Second, it will no doubt be pointed out that my essential dimensions of curriculum correspond closely to aspects of education theory courses. Thus, obviously, the psychological dimension is the concern of psychology of education, values and epistemology of philosophy of education, culture of history and sociology of education, planning and evaluation of curriculum theory, and pedagogy . . . ?

In a recent review of the development of educational studies Simon pointed to the latter crucial omission:

> As educational studies became more rigorous and inevitably academic, the historic neglect of pedagogy was accentuated.
>
> (Simon 1983, p. 10).

That arbitrary omission is symptomatic of the problem of claiming that the central dimensions of curriculum are or have been 'covered' in education theory courses. For, as I have argued elsewhere, the academicisation of education studies, apparently a prerequisite for upgrading the three-year certificate to a degree, gave it a momentum away from those needs of the intending teacher which had provided its earlier rationale. By the 1960s the content of education courses increasingly reflected the intellectual preoccupations of education theorists and researchers rather than the needs of intending teachers — what was available by way of theory rather than what was required (Alexander 1984). 'The historic neglect of pedagogy' only began to be rectified once researchers turned their attention, for reasons which did not necessarily have anything to do with teacher training, to classroom processes, and Simon's own work (with Galton in the ORACLE project referred to in Chapters 2 and 3) is a particularly pertinent example of empirical study in education which happens, fortuitously, to have important implications for teacher training.

Moreover, the six dimensions that I have listed simply cannot be equated neatly with academic disciplines. I have exemplified the dangers of this equation in Chapter

4, in querying the assumption that because psychology and sociology characteristically focus upon mental and social processes, they offer all the insights about these that a teacher is likely to need.

Again, values as a dimension extends well beyond the conceptual clarification of real or imagined fact/value distinctions offered in philosophy courses. One of the singular failures of education courses in teacher training is their neglect of the value basis of theorising and research in the social sciences, perhaps because of a naive faith in the 'objectivity' of their data and procedures. This in turn indicates a similar necessity for epistemological analysis to be applied here, rather than be confined to discussions about conditions and forms of knowledge in philosophy units.

A similar argument can be presented in respect of all the dimensions: child psychology is as much a philosophical as a psychological issue, while the entire educational studies pantheon is culturally embedded, as sociologists critical of the 'Malet Street school' of conceptual analysis in philosophy courses have pointed out.

As for curriculum planning and evaluation, this is perhaps the most synoptic of all the dimensions. To some extent curriculum theory treats it this way, as I show below, though the 1960s attempts to reduce curriculum planning and evaluation to technology proved quite influential in Britain, and its influence persists at both initial and inservice levels. This demarcation is comparable to that 'principle of correspondence' which, I suggested, informs curriculum courses. There the curriculum 'reality' for which students are prepared is a set of pre-ordained discrete subject labels rather than a coherent, dynamic whole curriculum. The analytical insights which should inform curriculum decision-making are mostly detached and given to similarly discrete education disciplines — children to psychology, values to philosophy, culture to sociology, and so on.

The other scarcely defensible consequence of the compartmentalisation represented by the traditional division of labour between educational theory and curriculum studies is its reinforcement of a dualistic theory/practice polarity, so that while 'thinking about education' involves analysis, empirical study, the marshalling of evidence and so on, 'making curriculum decisions' becomes simply a commonsense matter of what will work. It is the essence of curriculum discourse, planning and action, as the analysis in Chapters 2 and 3 shows, that value, epistemological, cultural, pedagogical, psychological and operational dimensions need to be intrinsic rather than tacked on in order to legitimate decisions and assertions made for other reasons. Post hoc rationalisation is a recurrent feature of primary ideology, chiefly where making educational sense in the 1980s of procedures instituted in the 1870s — such as class teaching — is concerned. The separation of curriculum and educational studies confirms this tendency. It confronts students with confusing and contradictory messages about the proper basis for their executive actions in the classroom; their understandable response is to choose what offers most security — the practical recipes of curriculum courses.

Let us now consider in more detail the treatment of each of the dimensions.

The psychological dimension

The previous chapter examined relationships between the kinds of statements and assumptions about young children which pervade primary education and the means whereby the initial training course seeks to give students a theoretical and experiential 'understanding of children'. In the course of that discussion I commented on the character and role of particular psychologies of education: much of that discussion can be carried over into the present chapter, and there is no point in repeating it. However, the current focus on the teacher's *curriculum* expertise requires some additional comment.

Course compartmentalisation ensures that if psychological theory is prominent in the education components, it can be notably absent from curriculum components. The selection of curriculum experiences demands a synthesis of all six of the dimensions listed above, but there is a particular necessity to bring together knowledge of the child and knowledge of the curriculum possibilities: that, essentially, is what the concept of 'match' boils down to. But, as I have also argued, knowledge of the child has to be curriculum-contextualised to become valid and usable, at least where the child's cognitive development is concerned. 'How the seven-year-old thinks' is a recipe too generalised to be meaningful, whereas 'how the seven-year-old conceives of the causal relationships of physical phenomena (for example, wind and clouds)' might offer psychological propositions of value to the primary teacher planning early curricular experiences in science. Considering how it is a strength of Piaget's work that he particularises the young child's development in this way, it is surprising how rarely a psychological dimension of any depth informs curriculum/professional courses.

The omission is not merely conceptual but structural and institutional: psychology is taught by education theorists, 'curriculum' by subject specialists, often, according to McNamara and Ross (1982) ex-secondary school subject specialists at that, and/or (though less commonly in the 1980s than the 1950s and 1960s) by ex-primary teachers having no great depth of subject understanding but ostensibly 'valid' practical experience to compensate.

The exception here, as always, is in the basics. Thus, the more extensive language courses now available as successors to the 1960s snippets on 'the teaching of reading' may include a careful synthesis of studies in language acquisition and development, language and culture and analysis of current approaches to language teaching. Similarly, current mathematics professional courses usually draw heavily on Piagetian theory of the development of children's mathematical understanding.

In both areas, a 'developmental' curriculum strategy is therefore likely to be encouraged, while this is less common in other areas. It has to be admitted of course that the psychological dimension of the non-basics is considerably less developed, and tends to be somewhat one-dimensional. Since Goldman's (1965) work on the development of children's religious understanding (updated in Peatling 1982) there have been 'Piagetian' studies of children's historical and geographical and particularly of their scientific thinking (as exemplified in the rationale for the Science 5–13 Project). In art the more substantial developmental work of Griffiths (1945), Eisner (1976) and Lowenfeld and Brittain (1982), and the literature on creativity, provide a more extensive basis. But overall in non-basic areas, if the literature as it stands provides the sole resource for psychological insight it is a somewhat limited basis for generating the kind of comparative critique which is needed.

There are two major omissions, then, under this heading: the general lack of a contextualised and specific analysis of children's development and learning in respect of each curriculum area; and the particular lack of such a perspective in 'non-basic' curriculum areas.

The epistemological dimension

> However much children exercise their spontaneous curiosity on life as a whole, their teachers need to know something about the use of the disciplines if they are to give the children the opportunity of extending their interests meaningfully and productively . . . Children out looking at buildings may notice a contrast between two sorts of house. If a teacher recognises that they are of different ages and that this is a clue to the growth of a village or a town . . . then the children's awareness can be much more fully developed. Yet in order to do this, the teacher has to know not only how to classify domestic architecture in relation to other kinds of knowledge, which in turn requires knowing something about history as such. At the same time, the location of the houses, and the way of life and work of the people who live and lived in them, requires also knowing something from geography and the social sciences.
>
> (Blyth et al 1976, pp. 37–8)

Despite the subject-orientation of curriculum/professional courses, distanced analysis of each primary curriculum area as a distinctive way of knowing, or of making sense of or generating experience is as markedly absent from many such courses as is a psychological perspective.

By this I mean a fundamental and necessarily open exploration at three levels. First, an exploration of the essential and paradigmatic features of a curriculum area, its structures, concepts, modes of inquiry, terminology and so on; and of the ways in which it differs in these and in the sorts of insights into experience which it offers.

Second, an exploration of the epistemological claims and characteristics of the area in the primary school, and of the extent to which the above paradigmatic features may or may not be appropriate in the embryonic forms of the subject experienced by the primary child. That is to say, the distinction, if there is any, between 'art' and 'child art', or between 'science' and 'primary science': are they versions of the same basic process, having the kind of continuity argued for earlier (pp. 27–30) or are they fundamentally different activities? (The question is particularly apposite at present as, on the one hand 'process' advocates begin to make some headway into the fastnesses of art and environmental studies, while some mainstream child-centred theorists remain happy to define primary art, for example, as no more than 'making and doing'.)

The third level of exploration concerns the relationship of one curriculum area to another — so obvious a prerequisite for the class teacher's whole curriculum responsibilities that, almost predictably, it is neglected in initial training.

These three levels correspond more or less to those identified by Hirst et al (UCET 1979) as one of the four 'core objectives' for secondary subject teachers. I have argued in Chapter 3 that no amount of anti-subject rhetoric at primary level can disguise the fact that the primary teacher operates within curriculum areas sufficiently distinct to merit the term 'subjects'. In any case, although the primary/secondary split at age 11 (or middle/secondary at 12/13) may represent to the profession a rarely bridged divide between two educational worlds, two ideologies, the child's education is continuous. While the secondary curriculum should, of itself, not determine the character of the primary education which precedes it, primary teachers need to acknowledge that their curriculum provides the basis for that differentiation into distinct subjects which is the characteristic of subsequent stages (Eggleston 1981). However it is organised, the primary curriculum needs to be not only educationally defensible *per se*, but epistemologically valid and consistent in terms of the child's cumulative curriculum experiences.

Moreover, secondary education is characterised by specialisation and the making optional of some areas deemed essential at the primary stage. The choice which forces such narrowing of the curriculum at the ages of 14 and 16 has little validity unless it is informed by some depth of experience in the areas being considered. If, then, it is argued that 'science' or 'history' or 'geography' as distinctive modes of inquiry have no validity in primary or middle schools and all that is necessary is an undifferentiated topic-based 'exploration' or 'discovery' of 'the environment', two to three years (or one year in first-middle-high school systems) of typically crammed, content-heavy secondary science, history or geography are hardly an adequate basis for that crucial choice.

The epistemological dimension to curriculum, for the reasons given above and in Chapter 3, concerns primary teachers no less than their secondary colleagues. Such discussion, however, is unfamiliar in primary curriculum studies. There are several possible explanations for this omission.

Epistemological questions are seen as general and generalisable, as reducible to themes like 'knowledge and the curriculum' or 'integration' which lend themselves to the sort of analysis favoured in philosophy of education courses. The field here is well-worked and challenging but it tends to segregate epistemological questions from specific practical curriculum contexts and make application by the student to primary art, mathematics and so on, somewhat difficult.

In any event, given their academic background subject specialists who teach curriculum studies are unlikely to have encountered this literature and may omit it through ignorance rather than intent. Moreover, being convinced advocates of their subjects they may also be unable or unprepared to distance themselves sufficiently to promote the essentially open exploration needed.

Perhaps immersion in one subject produces only part of the range of insight needed: equally essential, it can be argued, is engagement with others, particularly if there is overlap in methodology or focus. Thus the student may find that the enthusiasm of the convert to sociology provides less insight than the scepticism of the physicist or artist about, respectively, the 'scientific' claims of sociological methods, or the insight into the human condition offered by sociological models and explanations.

The argument applies equally to tutorial staff in other curriculum areas: mathematicians are notoriously unremitting in their advocacy of their subject's place in the school curriculum (successfully so, as it happens) and may see their task in college as converting the student while fighting for an ever-increasing share of the professional studies timetable. Literature tutors may exhibit a somewhat different but even more hubristic version of the same characteristics — a tendency to confuse their art's undeniable engagement with life and life itself.

Arnold suggests that:

> It is quite possible that the student entering teacher training has never been invited to consider his subject as one element in an educational process which should make sense as a whole.

(DES 1981b, p. 9)

Does this apply, *a fortiori*, to the student's tutors?

Finally, the omission of this dimension can be explained in terms of a combination of the constraint of time and the convenient rationalisation available from primary ideology:

1. There is no time to 'go into such depth'.
2. It is not necessary anyway, since experience, not knowledge, is what matters at the primary stage.

The value dimension

That education is about values is a truism; one that is given little acknowledgement, however, in recent HMI/DES statements on curriculum. The primary surveys identify curriculum priorities and needs within each curriculum area, and reassert the 'basics plus' model of the whole, but leave the value basis of these totally unexamined.

In initial training, 'justification' is a familiar theme, but one theoretically rather than practically contextualised, so that the student may acquire the vocabulary for debating, in a generalised and abstract way, matters like 'utility' and 'worthwhileness' but if pressed to justify music or mathematics in the primary school might have difficulty.

In any event, at the macro, whole-curriculum level, the debate about values is to a considerable extent pre-empted by the value prioritisation implicit in the differential time allocations in curriculum studies which we have already discussed. Here, once again, one part of the student's course conveys opposite messages to another: an attempt by, say, philosophers of education, to generate open discussion about the relative merits of mathematics and moral education has little credibility if one has a substantial and compulsory unit and the other a brief option. Whatever the aspirations of education theorists, curriculum/professional studies usually represent, in terms of both structure and treatment, a closed curriculum model from which questions of value have been excluded.

In the same way, primary schools themselves can be all too impervious to a value consciousness at this level. The grand statements that heads are prone to deliver about what they call their 'philosophy' may be strong on assertion but weak on justification. If challenged the response is usually 'society demands it' or 'the children need it' or 'the parents expect it — this is a middle-class area, you know'. The right to determine curriculum aims is strongly defended in British primary education. The legitimacy of the right, however, as Dearden (1976) and White (1982) point out, is suspect. It can only be grounded in a claim to 'expert' knowledge, but since aims are statements of value not fact, the expert knowledge claim is not so much groundless as simply inappropriate, in this particular aspect of the teacher's task at least.

Insensitivity to the value-dimension of the teaching task may be nurtured by the professional climate of schools. This we shall consider in Chapter 7, but at this juncture it is also worth reminding ourselves of Taylor's characterisation of the traditional training college/college of education culture (see p. 87). One of the most pervasive elements in the culture, and one which characterises many other education institutions, is the assumption of value-consensus on key educational and institutional issues, where, even if dissent is not actively suppressed, the civilised rejoinder 'But that's a value question' is not so much a statement of fact, as a device for curtailing discussion before it becomes uncomfortably divergent (Adelman and Alexander 1982, Chapter 5). Enforced consensus was a particularly dominant feature of some of the primary-oriented colleges, where dissent was not so much suppressed as smothered by normativeness of hierarchy, ritual and paternalism.

Such a conformist climate could (or can) be combined for the student with courses which purveyed a 'recipe knowledge' approach to curriculum studies, teaching methods overall which 'encouraged a tendency to passive listening and reliance on the lecturer as the source of knowledge', in which 'students were . . . reluctant to venture their own opinions and support them with argument' and where 'much of their writing was inclined to avoid expressing a reasoned personal viewpoint or making independent critical comment' (DES 1979b, p. 10).

The treatment of values in an educational institution, therefore, is not merely a matter of course content: pedagogy and institutional climate are equally important. In all three respects we need to ask whether teacher education institutions offered during the 1960s/1970s, or offer today, what the intending teacher needs in order to recognise and cope with the value issues central to education in a pluralist society and taking place in a relatively decentralised schooling system according its teachers, for the moment anyway, more autonomy than most.

The culture dimension

Values, as discussed above, are not readily detachable from the cultural circumstances which generate them. Primary teachers educate children from (and they themselves come from) differing and diverse social backgrounds and value orientations; they operate within a state system of education subject to local and national government influence, constraint and control in the context of changing political ideologies; the cultural context of primary education is one of extreme complexity and rapid change for which the monolithic child versus society polarity, or the curriculum apologia 'Society demands it' are wholly inadequate characterisations.

Given these circumstances, one might expect the professional training of the primary teacher to include the following:

(a) awareness of the historical and cultural origins of today's primary schools;
(b) understanding of the different value positions represented by current curriculum patterns and priorities, and the ideological, political and other origins of these;
(c) understanding of the social structure, with particular reference to the diverse political, ethnic, religious and other subcultural elements which bear, actually or potentially, on curriculum purposes and content;

(d) analysis of the processes and forms of social change, with particular reference to those trends and issues which might demand or necessitate a curricular response;

(e) a continuing exploration of the relationship of the child and the adult to the state, of autonomy and obligation, of freedom and control;

(f) analysis of the cultural location, values and beliefs of the student teachers themselves, the origins of these and their influence on the student teachers' educational ideas and practices.

As we have seen, at least some of the areas above feature in sociology and/or philosophy of education courses, and undoubtedly the 'new' sociology of education of the 1970s has made an important contribution to providing tools for scrutiny of the relationships between culture, ideology, social control and curriculum.

There are, however, omissions, notable among which is (f) above. Here I am arguing that primary teachers, as the major agents of the child's curriculum, need self-consciousness about the influence thereon of their own values; in Chapters 2 and 4 we saw that 'understanding of the child' demands knowledge of the person — oneself as a teacher — who claims or seeks that understanding. So far these complementary attributes have received little attention in initial training.

More familiarly, structural compartmentalisation ensures that the kinds of analysis indicated in (a)–(f) above are usually detached from the particulars of curriculum content and planning for primary teaching as treated in the essentially pragmatic curriculum/professional studies. The consequence too is familiar: whatever the quality of the generalised analysis of culture and social change, the character of curriculum courses will effectively neutralise it as a serious consideration in practical curriculum decision-making.

In recent years the issues of multi-ethnicity and multi-culturalism have highlighted this problem. Sometimes such focuses appear as separate course units; occasionally they appear as issues within particular curriculum areas, notably language and religious education. This is an improvement on the earlier tendency to appear to train for cultural uniformity, though examples of surprising insensitivity in this multi-culturally conscious era still exist, as in the case of the college in a multi-ethnic, multi-faith conurbation which built its entire primary religious education curriculum course round its LEA's Anglican 'approved' RE syllabus. But such anomalies apart, the selectivity of the injection of multi-culturalism emphasises its omission elsewhere: if in language and religious education, why not in science, history and mathematics (as demonstrated in Lynch 1981)?

There is a further objection. Multi-culturalism is but one social 'fact' of British society in the late twentieth century which appears to demand an educational response (others were discussed in Chapter 2). Yet multi-culturalism may be the only specific cultural reality or issue to be singled out for special treatment in initial training.

In any event the educational validity of what Keiner (1981) called the 'bolt-on' approach — of adding units covering particular 'issues' to existing course structures as and when external pressure requires it — is extremely dubious. It is possible that existing components will militate, because of their assumed culture-neutrality and consensual ambience, against the cultural commitment of the 'bolted-on' units. The approach also suggests a certain cynicism among course planners: let those who care plan and run an additional unit with the concern prominent in its title, thus satisfying teacher educators' collective conscience.

An alternative, apparently more valid in that it ostensibly reflects a more funda-mental reappraisal, is the 'permeation' approach (Craft 1981) whereby *each* curricu-lum area addresses itself to the chosen issue. However, experience suggests that this too may be less impressive in practice than it seems, for in certain circumstances to claim that multi-cultural concerns 'permeate' the entire course can be tantamount to saying that they are ignored. But in any case neither 'bolt-on' nor 'permeation' approaches resolve the problem of selectivity: why only multi-culturalism — why not also rising unemployment, sex roles, social inequality, environmental degradation, new technology, international tension and so on?

The case of multi-cultural analysis/preparation in teacher education illustrates the ground that has yet to be covered. What needs to 'permeate' is not only treatment of specific issues but a coherent analysis of the cultural ramifications of the curriculum as a whole and its constituent parts in terms, perhaps, of the kinds of models discussed on pp. 31–35.

The climate does appear to be changing on this issue. Summarising the views of a wide cross-section of teacher educators, the 1983 CNAA report on primary BEd. courses commented:

> There was widespread agreement . . . on two priorities: firstly, to develop in students a general capacity to identify and cope with changing needs in *local* contexts; and secondly to develop students' ability to 'read' the changing state of society and to understand that few ostensibly 'fundamental' needs are a-historical or unchanging. These abilities . . . would require a substantial and possibly controversial engagement in teacher education courses with cultural and political analysis (which) would . . . stand in marked contrast to the traditional tendencies towards introversion and political parochialism in the primary teaching profession, legitimated as these are thought to be by a view of 'child-centredness' which puts the 'child' and 'society' on opposite sides of an unbridgeable divide.
>
> (CNAA 1983b, p. 6)

One of the most persistent advocates of cultural analysis in teacher education is Lawton who (1983) provides a useful framework which distinguishes between *cultural invariants* — the 'essential similarities between all societies': their possession of social structure, economic systems, communication systems, rationality systems, technology, moral codes, belief systems and aesthetic traditions — and *cultural variables*, or the essential differences between societies in respect of each of the above invariants. Lawton uses his analysis of the contemporary culture of England as a basis for defining the requirements for curriculum which he sees as a 'selection from culture' informed by psychological and pedagogical considerations. Though in terms of this chapter's discussion Lawton's model is not sufficiently comprehensive and though his approach has been criticised as being insufficiently radical (Whitty 1981) it is an important contribution to the kind of analysis which is needed, and a necessary alternative to the existing dominance in primary discourse of the behaviourist model of curriculum planning allied to the 'cultural cocoon' extreme of child-centredness (see Chapters 1 and 2) which asserts that curriculum planning starts and finishes with a study of the young child.

The pedagogical dimension

Unlike some of the dimensions to curriculum discussed so far, pedagogy has not been omitted from either initial training in general or 'curriculum courses' in particular. Traditionally, 'methods' were dealt with by the various curriculum areas to which they were seen as contingent. Sometimes techniques with no obvious curricular home were extracted and dealt with separately, particularly those relating to the use of material resources in the classroom like blackboards, charts and workcards. More recently, the skills of teaching have become the focus for training procedures such as simulation and microteaching, and the changes in patterns of school experience to which we referred in Chapter 4 are frequently directed towards the systematic and monitored refinement and acquisition of basic teaching skills and ways of organising for learning.

If this is so, can it be presumed that, at least where pedagogy is concerned, the somewhat pessimistic analysis of recent pages is inappropriate? Unfortunately, the fact that 'methods' have always been attended to in initial training has to be squared with the weaknesses in primary methodology revealed by empirical study in schools. On the basis of my earlier analysis, therefore, I want to make two points; one is to try to explain what recent classroom studies show in terms of approaches to 'methods' in primary training courses; the other is to express a reservation about the direction being taken by the new 'science' of pedagogy.

Recent studies of primary teaching methods are consistent in identifying gaps between claims and practice: between the rhetoric of informal/exploratory methods and the reality of a predominance of didactic procedures; between the claims made for individual and group work (and against whole-class teaching) and the reality of the practice and consequences of such methods. How is this explained?

Simple answers are not available, but attention to the *tone* of professional discussion about teaching methods is instructive: assertive, emotive, carrying the unmistakable message that there is one right way to act, that teaching methods can be neatly categorised into formal (bad) and informal (good) with no variations in between either admitted or permitted. In other words a climate of professional discourse, in this area as in so many others, which is strong on the dragooning of opinion, and short on dispassionate analysis. Serving teachers of the decades since Plowden will bear witness to the kinds of pressures to which they could be subjected to organise their teaching in certain ways and to the tacit or even explicit sanctions available if they failed to do so.

Looking again at the treatment of teaching methods in initial training, we can see that it reinforced this climate. Curriculum courses were highly prescriptive in this field, and, in early childhood courses in particular, that cultural smothering that I referred to earlier gave the student no opportunity to question the efficacy of the procedures prescribed, still less to analyse their underlying claims and assumptions. To do so would have been to incur the wrath or wounded pride of the 'mother hen' who, in her tenacious control of the professional development of her brood, more closely resembled a dragon.

Students and serving teachers tended to develop a fatalism in the face of such pressure. Conscious that they had been hoisted onto a bandwagon, they nevertheless offered little resistance and, indeed sooner or later most internalised the norms and willingly hitched their horses: for the destination, for co-operative passengers at least, was promotion.

Something of the cyclic character of fashions in teaching methods comes through from the ORACLE study (Galton and Simon 1980): 69 per cent of the 'individual monitors' were aged under 30, 43 per cent of 'group instructors' were aged 30–39, and 45 per cent of the 'class inquirers' were aged 40–49. The ORACLE observation was undertaken in 1976–7: the majority of 'class inquirers' were thus trained between 1947 and 1956, well before the progressive movement had disturbed the consensus of subject-oriented, 11-plus-geared, whole-class teaching; the 'group instructors' were trained from 1957 to 1965 in the period when the progressive changes commended by Plowden were gathering strength; and the 'individual monitors' were trained in the immediate post-Plowden period, 1967 to 1975 when 'but Plowden says . . . ' curtailed all debate.

The vital missing ingredient was therefore not so much pedagogy as the critical *analysis* of pedagogy (a field poorly treated in Plowden, for example). Simon's reference to 'the historic neglect of pedagogy' is thus correct because he refers to that part of the course — education theory — which claimed to offer analytical perspectives. No such elevated expectation existed in respect of curriculum/professional studies: analysis was reserved for abstract notions like 'aims' and 'autonomy' — in 'curriculum and method' you were told what to do and how to do it.

Assuming that the classroom research of the 1970s has at last generated a basis both for the systematic acquisition of executive classroom skills and for the more generalised analysis of methods of teaching and patterns of classroom interaction and organisation, what reservations can possibly be expressed?

The essential claim of empirical studies of pedagogy like ORACLE is that they *objectify* teaching by observing, recording and classifying behaviours in several classrooms and by subjecting the resulting typologies to rigorous cross-checking and validation, whereas the old 'formal/informal' polarities could mean something different to every teacher. The claim is attractive to teacher educators, because it provides tools whereby they and students can also observe and codify teaching behaviours and whereby those constituent behaviours can be trained for through microteaching and similar techniques.

However, it is clear from the discussion in Chapters 2 and 3 that other dimensions to teaching are also influential. The 'objective' observational studies focus upon the *externals* of pedagogy like frequency of interaction and kinds of verbal utterances. We might term this 'formal' pedagogy and contrast it with the 'hidden' pedagogy of teachers' expectations and conceptualisations of children and teaching which, we have seen, are also powerful determinants of the quality of children's learning. The teacher's actions in the classroom are the consequence of thought: both deserve attention.

The non-analytic, prescriptive treatment of pedagogy in traditional curriculum/method courses divorced the externals of teaching both from their conceptual basis and their ethical justification. It is important that the new 'teaching skills' courses do not do likewise. The apparently sharper tools now available for the analysis of teacher behaviour should not lead us to neglect the extent to which major aspects of teaching have a subtlety and elusiveness which can never be recorded: a behaviourist model of teaching is inevitably incomplete in certain essentials. We need to avoid separating the observable from the elusive, the action from the thought, in the way enshrined in the traditional curriculum studies/education theory split.

In some respect this may seem like a plea to ensure that in the analysis of teaching interactionist and phenomenological perspectives (which use as data actors' subjective meanings) should be given due weight. In response, teacher educators could well argue that a variety of models for the analysis of classroom events has been both available and applied since at least the mid 1970s. Such eclecticism is to be welcomed, though it is possible that it does not go far enough: too often, true to the tradition in education of reducing complexity to mutually exclusive polarities, students may be introduced to 'quantitative' and 'qualitative' paradigms in a way which suggests there are just two possible answers to the question we should all constantly be asking about classrooms: 'What is going on here?'.

Joyce and Weil (1980) provide a usefully multi-faceted framework in response to this challenge; it analyses teaching methods in terms of their underlying models of human behaviour and in terms of four sets of variables: methods and procedures ('syntax'), diagnostic and evaluative principles and processes ('principles of reaction'), pupil and teacher roles and relationships ('social system'), and resources and operational conditions ('support system'). The framework is sufficiently eclectic to accommodate differing approaches, and theoretically conscious enough to facilitate the explication and analysis of underlying assumptions, yet it is also geared to operational realities. The authors argue, as we do here, that the teacher needs a basic repertoire of models and techniques and the diagnostic ability and practical flexibility to determine how and when each can most appropriately be used. Moreover, in a reference highly pertinent to the British class teacher system (the work is from the USA), they argue that these capacities assume critical importance where the teacher 'is responsible for teaching many children in several different curriculum areas'.

A further concern must be expressed on this matter. In initial training the inculcation of pedagogical skills needs to be closely allied to this analysis of classroom events. However, though both are grounded, or ought to be grounded, in theorising and empirical study, there is a tendency for the new 'teaching skills' components to refer only to those studies having the most obvious concern with pedagogy, the Bennett and ORACLE studies of teaching 'styles' for example. Ethnographic, qualitative and interpretative studies are as much concerned with pedagogy even though their terminology is less obviously consistent with the everyday professional constructs represented by words like 'individual', 'group', 'class', 'informal' and 'formal' which those operating within the pre-ordinate tradition tend to use.

Finally, we need to exercise caution about separating teaching skills from specific curriculum contexts. It is true, for example, that recognising different questioning strategies is a skill which can be developed in isolation; but formulating actual questions for classroom use has to have particular children and curriculum contexts in view and to be grounded in minimal levels of curriculum mastery and understanding of the children concerned. Questions have to be to someone, about something.

The planning/evaluation dimension

This final dimension, like pedagogy, has always been prominent in initial training — it is too obvious to be omitted.

There are, however, two quite distinct planning/evaluation traditions. These emerged separately and at different times, coexisted uncomfortably and only occasionally combined.

The earlier tradition is that associated to this day with curriculum/method courses. It is, like so much in these courses, pragmatic and lacking in a coherent theoretical basis, but nevertheless has employed a technology having remarkable consistency and persistence across time and place. I refer, of course, to the dominance of the 'teaching practice file' into which went 'schemes of work' and 'lesson plans'. The latter in their means–ends structure (aims through to evaluation) and their loyalty to the steps of the Herbartian lesson plan, proved increasingly inappropriate to the primary classrooms of the 1960s and 1970s but persisted nevertheless; as much for the benefit of the tutor as the student, one suspects: the former then had something concrete to latch onto when he went, in time-honoured fashion, to observe 'a lesson' and found children engaged in thirty-one different activities and spread across the 'home base' and 'wet area' of an open plan school. This technology imposed a certain apparent order on a planning process (for of course curriculum planning is an activity, not a piece of paper) which may well have been fairly random.

The later tradition was the hybrid curriculum theory, which at various times laid claim to becoming the total integrator for the initial training course (Skilbeck 1970, Whitfield 1970, Chambers 1971) — an objective not yet achieved. Curriculum theory, it must immediately be mentioned, became a branch of educational studies, not an adjunct of 'curriculum' courses. Its methodological roots were in the disciplines of education, mainly psychology in the first instance, and despite the relevance of 'curriculum' in its title it was always remote from 'curriculum' (i.e. what to teach on teaching practice) as understood in that other part of the course. More literally foreign were its concerns and assumptions, for these were imported lock, stock and barrel from the USA in the form of the Tylerian model of curriculum planning with its emphasis on prespecified behavioural objectives and elaborate quantitative evaluation.

Blenkin and Kelly (1981, 1983) argue persuasively that this inappositeness to primary teaching did not prevent the Tyler-Bloom model becoming influential in primary circles. They argue, indeed, that its influence has been generally unhelpful, not to say harmful, in so far as it negates the 'process' model which they see as underpinning the best of current practice. How far this is true is difficult to judge, but there is no doubt that the Tyler-Bloom model, or rather Kerr's (1968) exegesis thereof, has become identified in many teachers' minds as the 'correct' way to plan a curriculum ('First state your objectives . . .') just as the scored test is the 'real' way to evaluate learning. I suspect this is less the influence of the model as such than its consistency with the positivistic tradition in educational inquiry which we discussed in Chapter 4 and which has always seduced teachers by its ready supply of 'proven' 'facts' and to this day provides for many the only valid concept of 'research'.

Further examples of this persistence are emerging from the current LEA responses to the DES Circular 6/81 (which required LEAs to give an account of their curriculum policies within two years). Among the primary curriculum policy documents I have seen there is a tendency to veer between the romantic, aphoristic pose exemplified in Chapter 1 and an uncritical use of the mechanistic terminology of the 1960s curriculum planning models. In one such document, the Bloom categories 'cognitive', 'affective' and 'psychomotor' are used with no obvious consciousness of the questionable 'image of man' they represent. However, it is equally common to find in such documents a repetitive and equally uncritical allegiance to the 'developmental matrix' (ages and stages/aspects of development) which was criticised in Chapter 2. The latter is at least as restrictive as the former, and since the developmental matrix informs not only documents published to keep politicians quiet but also the everyday thought and practice of teachers its influence must be counted more significant than the Bloom/Tyler model. (For a fairly typical example of the uncritical application of both the objectives model and the developmental matrix see the recommendations on how heads should plan the curriculum in Whitaker 1983).

What this tradition fails to do, of course, is to acknowledge most of the dimensions of curriculum with which this chapter deals and which analysis of primary ideology and practice shows are of fundamental importance: dimensions such as culture, values, epistemology and so on. Instead, 'curriculum planning' is reduced to a sequence of technical tasks.

Subsequently, curriculum theory has diversified and curriculum technology is now balanced by curriculum analysis and critique. Nevertheless, the purpose and perspective of these courses are frequently opaque. As a minimum provision distinctions need to be made between theory which is *descriptive*, *prescriptive*, and *speculative*. Which particular 'curriculum' is being theorised about has for long been unclear, despite the inevitable first chapter in curriculum theory textbooks which juxtaposes 57 definitions. Is it the teacher's curriculum as idealised? Or as practised? Is it the child's as intended? Or as received? Is it a generalised, semi-abstract notion of curriculum? Or is it specific curriculum circumstances rooted in actual problems?

Tacitly or overtly there is a tendency for certain emphases implied by these questions to dominate initial training curriculum theory courses. Thus a tidy, rational ideal is preferred to the frequently messy and irrational reality. The limits to the complexity portrayable are fixed by our inability to represent more than three dimensions on paper: cube-shaped models abound, two-dimensional and bipolar continua are even more common (*mea culpa*). The curriculum as perceived, received and made sense of by the child is rarely studied (Blishen's *The School That I'd Like* (Blishen 1969) being regarded as an amiable and non-rigorous curiosity), and there is a high level of generality and abstraction to the concepts.

To a certain extent these tendencies are endemic to academic education theory, and they reflect the circumstances in which the theory is generated: in institutions other than schools, by people other than teachers, even for reasons other than the pursuit of better educational practice.

Certain aspects of curriculum theory display this tendency more strongly than others. Until recently 'curriculum development' meant not something teachers do but the activities of teams based on universities and colleges producing materials for commercial dissemination and supported by Schools Council funds. Similarly, 'evaluation' was not the process whereby a teacher judged the worth and/or effectiveness of his classroom practices but the activities of paid consultants evaluating those same funded projects. Curriculum development, innovation and evaluation remained, apparently, activities which only took place outside school. Until, that is, these same people invented 'school-based curriculum development' and 'self-evaluation', and successfully marketed them to college lecturers who, as before, dutifully crammed them into their curriculum theory syllabuses as yet more recipe knowledge, thus entirely missing their point.

We still await the emergence of a coherent, grounded curriculum theory for primary schools.

This incongruence between curriculum theory and teachers' everyday curriculum concerns has tended to exacerbate the education theory/curriculum and method gap referred to earlier. Both components claimed to provide necessary expertise for the teacher's central tasks of curriculum planning, implementation and evaluation, but the language, constructs and procedures of each were so contradictory that the student sensibly took the line of least resistance and opted for what most helped him to cope on teaching practice, the curriculum/method tutor's hints and prescriptions.

Not the least among the omissions in both approaches to curriculum planning was analysis of the actual processes adopted by the student and by serving teachers (Taylor's 1970 study of primary teachers is an exception, as, most prominently, is the Ford Teaching Project referred to below). For though curriculum lecturers, as we have seen, provided guidelines for teaching practice notes and files, the actual process of planning (as opposed to making its results fit a preconceived framework) — of identifying children's needs, of making choices about content and methods, of exercising practical choices and operationalising personal values — remained extraneous to a course's timetabled concerns. The supervising tutor was there to comment on the *consequences* of planning, not on the planning process itself.

This was also the case with evaluation. Undoubtedly the mode of evaluation in most frequent use in primary classrooms is informal. Grounded in intuition and experience, it is subjective and idiosyncratic. Yet the student's preparation may have included on the one hand (in curriculum theory) an excursion into the world of publicly validated tests and scales, of debates about 'classical' and 'illuminative' approaches, and on the other (curriculum/method) the none-too-tacit advancement of, as criterion, 'Did they behave themselves?' and, as method, 'Was it OK?'. The vital middle ground, which exposes and explores these self-same everyday evaluations of and with teachers and students, and which thereby stands some chance of refining them to a point of greater consistency, reflectiveness and impartiality, was left untrodden.

In the 1960s and 1970s, we saw earlier, curriculum theory was offered as the integrative device that teacher education courses so clearly needed. The mistake was to assume that because its central concerns existed in the worlds of both theory and practice (aims, methods, content, planning, evaluation, etc.) they would provide the bridge. But what was subsumed under those labels was yet another body of theory as far removed from the task of teaching primary children, in the student's eyes, as the syllabuses of the four education disciplines. It might have stood some chance of success had the starting point been the processes of curriculum analysis, planning, implementation and evaluation employed by teachers and students working in primary classrooms.

Perhaps the best-known example of a serious attempt to explicate teachers' understandings of classroom processes and use them as a basis for professional conceptualisation and problem-solving is the Ford Teaching Project which Elliott directed (Elliott and Adelman 1976, Elliott 1980). Here, researchers worked with teachers to elicit the latters' aims for discovery/inquiry teaching; on the basis of this 'action perspective' and its clarification and systematisation into a common language for discourse about classroom events, teachers and researchers moved to the analysis of problems of implementing discovery teaching. The project, in retrospect, is significant less for its particular statements on the teaching strategy in question than for its seminal contribution to the emergent methodology and community of action research (Nixon 1981). Proponents argue that this methodology provides teachers with tools for rational reflection and dialogue about everyday teaching challenges, and liberates them from the hegemony of what they may see as the alien and inapplicable modes of discourse provided by mainstream academic study and research in education.

It is perhaps appropriate to note that there are many routes to rationality, a critical and independent stance towards research, and a shared language for professional discourse and problem-solving (issues, it will be recognised, of concern throughout the present book). What would very much weaken the case for action research, indeed would tend to invalidate some of its fundamental premises, would be any assumption of exclusiveness or a new orthodoxy about its approach: this tendency is now beginning to be evident. In fact, action research in the Ford Project tradition is but one strand of a much larger movement towards school-based and school-focused research, curriculum development and professional development. Examples include the way teachers and researchers have worked together on the development of strategies for evaluating and improving teaching methods as a follow-up to the ORACLE research reported earlier (Galton and Willcocks, 1983, Chapter 11), the work of Harlen and her colleagues which led to the 'Match and Mismatch' primary science materials (Harlen et al 1977), the joint Open University/Schools Council 'Curriculum in Action' project with its materials to aid teacher self-evaluation (Open University/ Schools Council 1980) the Open University's IT-INSET project which brought together student teachers, experienced teachers and teacher trainers within the shared focus of classroom-based curriculum development and evaluation (Ashton et al 1982), the explorations of various concepts of 'school-centredness' in curriculum and professional development by the CUEDIN network (Chambers 1982), and countless unrecorded ventures by individual teachers, schools, colleges and universities which in different ways aim to eliminate the conceptual and institutional boundaries between academic study, research and teaching, and to enhance teachers' capacities and procedures for analysis, appraisal and modification of day-to-day professional ideas and practices.

Our discussion of curriculum in initial training, then, raises much larger issues: of theory/practice, which we examine in the second part of the next chapter; of the intellectual climate needed in schools for ongoing curriculum appraisal and renewal which we discuss in Chapters 7 and 8; and of the language and style of professional discourse generally, which is a major concern throughout this book.

CONCLUSION

At the start of Chapter 4 I suggested that though causal connections between particular patterns of initial training and specific professional practices in schools are hard to demonstrate we can legitimately seek correspondences and, with due caution, draw causal inferences from them. If these are evident when we examine perspectives on children, as we did in Chapter 5, they present themselves even more dramatically when we consider perspectives on curriculum. For if curriculum is the most suspect part of primary professional ideology and the least impressive aspect of practice, the treatment of the primary curriculum is undoubtedly the weakest aspect of the initial training course. And if, as we saw in Chapter 3, professionally the least flattering parts of primary ideology can be explained by reference to the basic curriculum insecurity of the class teacher, it seems not unfair to lay some of the blame for this at the door of the training institution.

We saw how courses appear simply to have failed to understand the intense curricular demands of class teaching, allocating these far less time than either main subject study or education theory, and how with so little of the latter explicitly concerned with curriculum the student's chief resource was the 'curriculum'/'professional' elements.

Though teacher educators generally acknowledged that this created a problem, its conventional analysis as one of 'curriculum coverage' was premised on the validity of what I termed the 'principle of correspondence' — conceiving of preparation for the curricular demands of class teaching in terms merely of a set of discrete components bearing the subject labels and accorded the proportions of time each receives in school. That, we saw, might superficially reflect practice but it was hardly a sufficiently comprehensive preparation for the actual 'whole-curriculum' responsibilities the class teacher faced.

Thus, apart from the fact that by the most obvious definition of teaching competence the time allocated to curriculum studies overall was insufficient to provide more than rudimentary skills in the minority areas, its combination with the correspondence principle effectively confirmed the serious qualitative variation between the 'two curricula' of primary schools which we discussed in Chapter 3. Together, schools and training institutions appeared to be locked in a mutually reinforcing cycle of perpetuating the questionable value assumptions, cultural insularity, epistemological confusion, ideological stridency and variable practice which all too often has characterised the primary curriculum.

For all the 'professionalisation' of initial teacher education since James the old 'curriculum course' traditions have endured. Such courses were frequently superficial and highly prescriptive, offering justifications for practice which rarely went beyond the pragmatic. Taken together they offered little guidance on the curriculum as a whole, or on the relationship of its parts, or on cross-curricular aspects like social and personal education for which no subject labels are available.

The key dimensions of curriculum discourse and action identified on the basis of the analysis in Chapters 1 to 3 were little in evidence in this approach, though they might appear in generalised form in education theory courses. However, the two sorts of courses could convey messages so contradictory — open, dispassionate principled analysis on the one hand, recipes for survival on the other — that students were unlikely to integrate them in the forms they were presented, nor, in the face of practical necessities in schools, to be particularly impressed by the theoretical bases they offered.

Thus, for all the emphasis on child development in education courses, it tended to be generalised, rather than contextualised in practical curriculum decision-making. This, indeed, was the case where all six of the identified dimensions were concerned. The value basis of curriculum decisions was neglected, or rather, pre-empted by priorities built into the course structure, by a conformist, consensual, institutional ethos and by transmission modes of teaching. The relationship between curriculum and culture was left unexplored, save in respect of arbitrarily selected social 'realities' like multi-culturalism. Epistemological analysis of each curriculum area was, despite the prominence of epistemological caricature in the ideology, scant or non-existent. Pedagogy featured prominently, but not the analysis of pedagogy: in place of the careful comparison of the relative justifications and consequences of particular teaching methods, fashion and ideology emerged as the imperatives. Similarly, while curriculum planning could not reasonably be omitted, courses increasingly offered two contrasting and not easily reconcilable approaches: one the pragmatism of teaching practice lesson planning; the other the idealism of US-style behaviourist rationality. Since the theories of planning and evaluation in the latter case were grounded in circumstances quite unlike those facing teachers in primary classrooms, curriculum theory, for all the apparent relevance of its concerns, could not but appear alien. Whatever 'curriculum' was being theorised about, it was not that of primary schools.

This is an unsatisfactory picture and it is hard to know where to lay the blame. College lecturers did the best they could in the limited time available, but many thought the distribution of time and the approach quite just, or were influenced by apparently more pressing imperatives — the low status of professional work relative to academic subject studies and education theory, or the validating bodies' unpreparedness to define the 'degreeworthiness' of courses other than in conventional, safe academic terms. Nor was there much pressure from the teaching profession. The recurrent demand was for less 'irrelevant' theory and more 'practical' guidance of precisely that prescriptive variety curriculum courses already offered, but dealing with generalised classroom skills rather than curriculum understanding as we have defined it. For since the primary profession had inherited both a training and an ideology in which such understanding was deemed unimportant, they could hardly be expected to see as problematic something so fundamental to their professional situation.

However, the climate has now begun to change. Curriculum has become, since the mid-1970s, a national political issue and the two HMI primary surveys have had a catalytic function in primary education. The teacher's curriculum needs are now officially acknowledged, both by the professions (e.g. CNAA 1983b) and by HMI and DES (1983a, 1983b). We are now entering an era when the content of initial training courses is to be more tightly circumscribed than hitherto and all new courses will have to be submitted for approval to an Advisory Council for the Accreditation of Teacher Education (DES 1983d). Curriculum features prominently in the new orthodoxy, though in a way which does little to alleviate the more fundamental weaknesses outlined in this chapter and Chapter 3. Since the new proposals are inseparable from, and perpetuate, two of the most persistent and counterproductive dichotomies in teacher education, personal/professional and theory/practice, we shall discuss them together in the next chapter.

The professional climate, too, is changing — and in a way which provides both hope for a more rigorous approach to curriculum matters in schools and initial training and the necessary counterbalance to creeping centralisation. These changes are represented by the developments in action research, school-centred initial training and in-service development and so on to which I referred earlier. They constitute symptoms of a wider and more variegated shift in climate, yet at the same time many schools and training institutions remain largely insulated from its impact. In the latter settings, central intervention will impoverish even further curriculum thought and practice. Elsewhere, if the school-centred, professional self-determination movement reaches deeper than have most recent educational innovations, its juxtaposition with centrist pressures and requirements might just generate the kind of intellectual energy and commitment which primary curriculum discourse has so seriously lacked in recent decades.

6

A Training for Polarisation

So far our discussion of how primary teachers are trained has concerned itself with specific issues from Chapters 1, 2 and 3 concerning the class teacher, children, curriculum and pedagogy. The discussion is completed in the present chapter by a consideration of two dualities more generally fundamental to recent teacher education: the opposition of 'theory' and 'practice', and, below, the separation of 'personal' from 'professional' education and the part played therein by academic subject study.

Both dualities, I hope to show, are major obstacles to the improvement of initial training; but more than that, in our present context they seem to reinforce or encourage that tendency to deal in mutually exclusive polarities which, as we saw earlier, pervades primary professional discourse and the models of the educative process this reflects.

PERSONAL AND PROFESSIONAL

Marsh's assertion (1973) that 'A basic sensitivity, coupled with a professional competence in ways of getting things done . . . are the [primary] teacher's prime needs' might be regarded, in the light of this book's discussion, as incomplete as a recipe for teacher education. At the same time it carries an emphasis upon the qualities of the teacher as a person which most of us would probably endorse and which, despite HMI/DES adoption of an increasingly utilitarian model of the primary curriculum, is now, if anything, more strongly emphasised in that quarter also.

The 1983 HMI recommendation on the content of initial training reads as follows:

> The personal qualities of teachers, and their ability to form good relationships, are fundamental to teaching success. Training institutions look for a range of personal qualities which include a lively curiosity and attitude to learning; the ability to communicate easily, clearly and with good use of English; the capacity to relate well to other adults as well as to children and to maintain an inner strength in the sometimes lonely nature of the teacher's job.
>
> (DES 1983a, pp. 4–5)

Or, as it was put more succinctly in the 1983 White Paper:

> Personality, character and commitment are as important as the specific knowledge and skills that are used in the day to day tasks of teaching.
>
> (DES 1983b, p. 8)

More tellingly the White Paper reminds us of the findings of the 1982 HMI study of probationary teachers that:

> the personal qualities of the teachers were in many cases the decisive factor in their effectiveness.
>
> (DES 1982c, para. 6.2)

And in turn the above study listed those personal qualities which the schools themselves expected in new teachers:

> energy, enthusiasm, commitment, conscientiousness, confidence, imagination, resourcefulness, good relations with pupils and staff, willingness to seek advice and receptiveness to advice when given.
>
> (DES 1982c, para. 5.5)

So on this issue we find, for once, unanimity. It might be expected, therefore, that the fostering of the personal qualities of the intending teacher would receive high priority in initial training. Looking at the quadripartite post-McNair course structure, however, we find grounds for perplexity. For although academic subject studies have conventionally been justified as the 'personal education' of the student, it is not clear whether the phrase means 'education of the person' (which would necessarily, in any reasonably comprehensive definition, include attention to personal qualities) or 'education according to the personal interests of the student' (as opposed to 'professional education' in the sense of 'education according to what are defined as his or her professional needs, regardless of personal interests'). If the latter definition holds, one then turns to the more exclusively 'professional' part of the course to seek the fostering of the personal qualities which all agree that the student, as professional, will need. But here we find education theorists purveying a body of propositions which, as we have seen, encompass the child and the educational process after a fashion, but extend little if any of this analysis to the psychological and cultural situation of the teacher, and which tend to conceive of pedagogy less in terms of the kind of mix of personal qualities and professional skills exemplified in the quotations above than as generalised, personal non-specific 'styles' or 'methods' definable by their externally observed behaviours. We find professional/curriculum courses which offer pre-packaged solutions to barely analysed classroom problems, recipes for coping rooted in the experience of others but paying scant regard to the unique experiences and personalities of the students themselves. And while on teaching practice both tutors and serving teachers are invariably expected to assess the personal and interpersonal dimension of the student's performance ('Relationships with pupils: very good/good/average/weak/unsatisfactory'), in the same way that they have to assess curriculum planning and classroom management, one usually searches in vain for preparation for the personal dimension to match that offered, however inadequately, for curriculum planning and the other attributes listed in teaching practice assessment schedules.

Where then are the teacher's personal qualities treated? There seem to be three possible answers:

1. Everywhere: that is to say, the 'permeation' argument comes conveniently into operation, as it does in relation to multi-cultural awareness and of course the personal and social development of the child in schools: 'We are concerned for our students as individuals, and aim to foster desirable personal qualities in all our staff-student contacts'. It is certainly true, as we have seen, that the culture of the teacher education institution can be highly normative with respect to attributes and behaviour deemed acceptable in its students: the heyday of both primary progressivism and the training colleges was marked by expectations in the latter institutions of consensus and conformity, enforced, however benevolently, by hierarchical and paternalistic structures and relationships. But this concept of personal education may not be compatible with the respect for personal autonomy which is surely a necessary concomitant if personal qualities are to be internalised. Alongside this basic response we encounter two others which, I suggest, provide the real clues as to the anomalous and elusive nature of this aspect of teacher training.

2. The issue of personal education, it is argued, whether of the child or the teacher, is too value-saturated for anyone to risk putting forward a list of desired personal qualities comparable to the specifications of, say (for the child) mathematical or linguistic concepts and skills or (for the teacher) related professional knowledge. This was the problem encountered by the Assessment of Performance Unit's Exploratory Group on Personal and Social Development. Its report refers to the area as 'sensitive and controversial', involving the risk of 'undesirable encroachment upon privacy and the rights of the individual' (APU 1981). If this is problematic where children in schools are concerned, how much more so with their teachers, it is argued.

3. Personal qualities are inborn, it is asserted, or at least so firmly established by the time the sixth-former or graduate applies for entry to an initial training course, that they are not amenable to treatment as part of the course itself. In other words, as far as this dimension of teaching is concerned, the good teacher is 'born not made'. This view is strongly implicit in recent DES documents. For these commend close attention to personal qualities not during the course but at the point of selection for entry. Indeed the HMI document is quite explicit on this:

   Only those applicants with personal qualities demonstrably fitted for teaching should be allowed to pursue a course of training.

   (DES 1983a, p.5)

The draft criteria from the Secretary of State for the approval of courses confirm this view, though slightly less categorically. Institutions are to assess applicants' personal qualities, looking for a 'blend of awareness, sensitivity, enthusiasm and ease of communication' and thereafter, apparently, giving these qualities little further attention (ACSET 1983).

These arguments are unsatisfactory. The 'permeation' response may well represent, as the APU document infers, the appropriate way to conceive of personal education, in teacher education as in schools, but it too readily serves to rationalise or conceal neglect both of the treatment of personal qualities and of the debate in which such treatment should be grounded.

Similarly, the 'value-loaded' response makes a point which is almost too obvious to need stating, but again uses it as an excuse for inaction. In curriculum planning, precisely because they are so pervasive, the value issues demand most, not least attention. Moreover the entire curriculum is value-saturated, not just that part explicitly concerned with 'personal and social development'. Or do those who dodge this issue genuinely believe that while the identification of desired personal qualities is value-loaded, the selection of content for a science course is value-free?

For students, school experience/teaching practice is where they encounter with most immediacy a set of expectations as to their personal qualities as a teacher. Whatever the extent of their reservations about these, or of discrepancy between these school norms and those tacitly or explicitly promoted in college, they are usually advised to accept them without question, or at least keep their reservations to themselves: 'You are the guest of the school . . . Once in the school the head is boss — what he says goes . . . We depend on the school's goodwill for teaching practice places — you must do nothing to offend them . . .' And that is probably the end of the matter, for they are unlikely to be able to raise these issues back in college: 'The schools accept students on the understanding that they don't go back to college and criticise them . . .' Thus is an opportunity lost of exploring in an open manner not only the particular matter of the personal qualities of the primary teacher but also the central value dimension, in action rather than in theory, of curriculum and pedagogy.

As for the third response above, the DES assumption that the personal qualities needed for teaching are fixed by the time the applicant comes for interview is naively determinist; it places wholly unwarranted faith in the capacity of student selection procedures to both evoke and identify all the required personal qualities; and it is manifestly wrong — people continue to change in respect of these and other personal qualities, and such change can be deliberately fostered in an educational institution. Perhaps the ACSET and DES mandarins, being in or beyond middle age, and of secure world-view and income, forgot how vulnerable the 18 to 22-year-old can be. Perhaps, too, there is a confusion here between the psychologist's concept of personality as 'fixed' and other 'personal qualities' which can change.

The answer to the question of where in initial training the teacher's personal qualities are explored and fostered seems to be, therefore, 'nowhere and everywhere': nowhere as a matter of serious academic and analytic concern, everywhere as a matter of chance, the efforts and value-vagaries of individual tutors and teachers, and, above all, the workings of the hidden curriculum.

Given this extent of anomaly, confusion and evasion, what are we to make of the 'personal/professional' polarity which has been a near-universal feature of post-war 2/3/4-year teacher education courses? At the outset it has to be acknowledged that to discuss this structural division against the background elaborated above may be to compound the confusion.

For the part of the course labelled by common usage 'personal education' (i.e. that portion, up to 50 per cent of the whole, constituting study in depth of one or two subjects) seems to have acquired over the years at least three justifications:

(a) as the chief means whereby the student develops more fully as a person;
(b) as the chief means whereby the claim of the teacher, as an educator of others, to be fully educated rather than merely trained, can be substantiated;
(c) as the means whereby the student acquires the depth of understanding of his or her subject(s) needed for teaching it or them in schools.

Thus, at the same time as 'personal' and 'academic' are each set up in opposition to 'professional', we find one half of the training course justified in terms of all three — personal development, academic study and professional training.

A historical perspective on this matter is helpful. Ross (1973) pointed out that subject study became identified with the personally educative function of teacher training very early. The McNair Report's distinction, in 1944, between 'personal' and 'professional' subjects is credited with perpetuating the conceptual dichotomy, though in fact McNair warned against it (Board of Education 1944, para. 230). Subsequent labelling, however, reinforced the dichotomy and added a status dimension: subject study became 'academic' study, thus implying that other studies were not only 'professional' but non-academically so. And as Eason (1971) pointed out, the label 'main subject', while originally correlative to 'subsidiary subject', increasingly stood in opposition to 'education' as meaning not so much the major of two subject studies as the main area of study in the course as a whole.

Yet in the 1960s it was usually the case that the 'academic' or 'main' subject was also the student's teaching subject. Thus, for example, although the 1965–66 London ATO regulations (quoted in Taylor 1969, pp. 112–13) identified the 'personal' function ('Students will select as a main course . . . one field of study for their own personal development') they also made it clear that the basis for that selection should be professional intention ('The main course must be appropriate to the curriculum of the secondary school'). However, significantly re-loading the justification in favour of the 'personal' they added: 'and the college must provide a professional course in relation to it' (i.e. the main course). Thus, although the subject chosen would be the future secondary teacher's teaching subject, its treatment in college was such as to relegate professional preparation in that subject to a separate 'curriculum'/'method'/'professional' course, which under many ATO regulations governing 1960s certificates and BEd courses was not examined by the university. The messages were unmistakable: that in teacher education learning how to teach one's subject was less important than continuing one's own study in that subject; that there was no necessary connection between such 'personal' study and the kinds of understanding needed for teaching that subject in schools; and that, in Eason's words (1971) 'instead of being perceived as each student's central and deepest engagement with the school curriculum' the 'main' subject was justified in quite different terms.

The move from certificate to BEd strengthened the polarisation of the personal and professional aspects of subject study, for to the various subject specialists in different university departments who were involved in BEd validation the depth study of an academic subject untrammelled by professional methodology provided the only criterion for 'degree worthiness' that they could recognise (or that they were competent to judge: an aspect of university validation much more serious in its implications). College subject staff tended to be happy with this development. To ex-secondary subject teachers the pursuit of subject study to degree level with more mature students constituted a natural and attractive career development, particularly if coupled with 'university recognised teacher' status (Tibble 1966, p. 231).

This polarity was then legitimised in the James Report's endorsement of consecutive training, and despite the subsequent return to concurrence, it has persisted in many courses into the 1980s.

At the same time the DES has held consistently to a view of subject study as providing preparation for subject teaching in schools. In the 1960s it supported the establishment of 'wing' courses in school shortage subjects such as mathematics, science and PE, and more recently, as we see below, its view on this matter has become wholly unequivocal.

The concept of one or two main subjects, whether or not these are divorced from the subjects' professional preparation, is sustainable in respect of secondary teaching. As a preparation for primary teaching, which requires cross-curricular expertise, the model is more problematic and, not surprisingly therefore, primary teachers and lecturers have always been the strongest critics of the dominance of subject study (up to 50 per cent of the Mark I/II BEds, DES 1979b), for with few exceptions, the main/education/ professional studies pattern applied equally to primary and secondary students. This was particularly so in those colleges training both primary and secondary teachers and where (as is the case in many primary/secondary PGCEs) the primary student's preparation for teaching the entire range of primary curriculum subjects had to be accomplished in the same time as the secondary student's subsidiary and/or main subject 'method'.

By 1981, the primary sector's anxiety on this issue had developed to the point where at a national inter-professional conference on primary BEds such advocacy of depth subject study as was offered was overwhelmed by the view that its emphasis had become disproportionate, causing vital aspects of the primary teacher's professional preparation to be neglected or skimped (CNAA 1983b).

Such views were often linked with a questioning of the apparent monopoly by subject study of the epithets 'personal' and 'academic'. The academic standing of a course component is a relatively straightforward matter: the criteria are explicit and widely understood. The professional charge is that they tend to undervalue the kinds of intellectual rigour available in vocational courses but not identifiable in conventional academic (subject) terms. But the exclusive claim of subject study to the 'personally educative' function is rather more mysterious, for, as Renshaw pointed out prior to the James Report:

> The concept of 'personal development' embraces a range of qualities that cannot be realized through the academic study of a main subject alone. Some in fact could not be developed through the curriculum at all, as they are more likely to be the result of social and emotional experiences outside the college or within the student-staff community.
>
> (Renshaw 1971, p.55)

Certificate and BEd courses preserved these assumptions, intact as to their essentials if not in their structural manifestations, into the late 1970s, and many courses still do. By the early 1980s, however, there were signs of a shift towards a more unified concept of professional study in place of the old personal/professional polarity, in which the student's understanding of a subject was to be integral to his capacity to teach it and at the same time to be reconciled with the way children's apprehension of the subject's structure evolved from childhood to adolescence: a reconciliation or synthesis, in other words, of at least two of the necessary dimensions to curriculum discussed at the end of Chapter 5.

Both academic and political influences are discernible in this change. There was an increasing concern in educational theory with epistemological issues, whether from a philosophical standpoint (e.g. Hirst 1965), sociological (e.g. Young 1971) or psychological/pedagogical (Bruner 1963, 1966); this was operationalised in a number of 'process' oriented curriculum projects which had an eager market in teacher education institutions, if not in schools. On the other hand such ideas had been around for quite a long time, and the colleges needed a political nudge before many were prepared to operationalise them. This came in the official re-ascendency of the 'teaching subject' view of subject study consequent upon HMI's identification of weaknesses in secondary subject teaching (DES 1979a, 1981b) as well as in primary teachers' curriculum understanding as suggested by the 1978 and 1982 HMI surveys, for which the 'curriculum consultant' idea foreshadowed in Plowden (CACE 1967, paras. 136, 137) was seen as providing the remedy.

A third factor, more overtly political, was central government's more restricted view of what the teacher's curriculum understanding should entail. Whereas educationists sought a synthesis of insights, DES argued for subject knowledge pure and simple. First HMI, then the 1983 White Paper and ACSET stipulated that all students, primary as well as secondary, should spend two of their four years on subject study (DES 1983a, 1983b). In response to strong criticism of their 1982 draft (e.g. CNAA 1982, TES 1982), especially from the primary sector, HMI softened the proposal somewhat by emphasising the desirability of bringing together 'personal' and 'professional' within subject study and allowing 'subject' to mean for primary students a broad curriculum area, a modification confirmed in the 1983 White Paper and in the DES and ACSET recommendations on course approval criteria (DES 1983b, ACSET 1983, DES 1983d).

This, then, is the 1984 state of that personal/professional polarity which, to its detriment, has informed teacher education discourse for much of the present century. Of the three functions of subject study discussed earlier, the first two (personal education and higher education) have now been made subsidiary to the third, the professional (preparation for teaching one's subject).

In the process, however, the loss of ambiguity over function and the strict 50 per cent subject studies stipulation provide a model of primary teacher training somewhat less flexible than its predecessors. Nominally at least (though the reason may have to do more with administrative tidiness) the justification is the strengthening of the primary class teachers' curriculum expertise: if they cannot do everything, then at least they can do one thing really well. Curriculum consultancy is an attractive notion and well-trained curriculum consultants will undoubtedly prove an asset to many primary schools (provided that certain school staffing and management conditions, to be discussed in

Chapter 8, can be met). But the primary teacher is first and foremost a class teacher and the subject studies model of primary teacher training must be open to a number of criticisms on that score, of which one is fundamental.

Put simply, it is a matter of balance. The consultant/specialist recommendation may well be at the expense of the rest of the intending class teacher's professional expertise. DES recommend the equivalent of two years for the specialist area, including attention to 'the application of the subjects to the learning of young children' and a minimum of twenty weeks' block and intermittent school experience spread over the four years of the BEd. This leaves the equivalent of four terms, or one third of the course, for what DES call 'the wider role of the class teacher' and 'educational and professional studies'.

The earlier papers from HMI and DES put the matter starkly and arithmetically: two years' subject study, one year's school experience, 100 hours each for the teaching of language and mathematics, leaving just 250 hours, or one seventh of the course, for everything else. The model available at the time of going to press (February 1984), which seems likely to be the final version (DES 1983d), preserved proportions but, in response to near-unanimous pressure from teachers, teacher educators and validators, blurred boundaries so as to permit a great deal of flexibility (including the possibility of many courses continuing more or less as before). Subject study became a 'broad area' with a strong 'applied' bias. School experience was reduced from thirty to twenty weeks' minimum (which may not be a sensible concession), and the language/mathematics requirements, while still 100 hours each, now included school experience and private study as well as 'taught time' which allowed so much room for manoeuvre as to make the prescription pointless. But the underlying model remained intact as to what DES regarded as its essentials: subject study for specialism/consultancy 50 per cent, all other aspects of the class teacher role 50 per cent.

Thus, for example, intending primary class teachers who happen not to be preparing to become language/literacy specialists will spend a mere 6 per cent of their training on spoken language, reading and writing — an aspect of the child's education to which, in some form, they will be obliged to give almost continuous attention in the classroom.

The class teacher's task, of course, does not stop at specialism plus language plus mathematics: the remaining 22 per cent or so of the BEd. course (about 400 hours) will have to encompass everything else that a minimal preparation for class teaching requires. The list, which is not mine but DES's own (DES 1983d), includes: all 'relevant' areas of the curriculum . . . adequate mastery of basic professional skills . . . small group and whole class teaching . . . awareness of the structure and administration of the education service . . . the full range of pupils . . . with their diversity of ability, behaviour, social background and ethnic and cultural origins . . . the different ways in which children develop and learn . . . gifted children . . . the more common learning difficulties . . . children with special educational needs . . . teacher–pupil communication . . . assessment and detailed knowledge of appropriate levels of performance to be expected from children of different ages, abilities, aptitude and background . . . class management and control . . . the contribution of new technologies to children's learning . . . staff collaboration and school development . . . the role of parents in their children's education . . . school and the adult world . . . (DES 1983d, Appendix paras. 9–12).

This is an impressive list, but clearly an unrealistic one in view of the pressure created by the specialist requirement. But what is one to make of the way the final clause is then elaborated (. . . 'ways in which children can be helped to acquire knowledge of the economic foundations of a free society')? Some, conscious of the tightening of central government's grip on the curricula of schools and teacher education institutions, may find the hint of indoctrination into the unassailable truths of monetarism and cold war rhetoric somewhat sinister. Others will find it bizarre. Either way, it is hard to take seriously a list having such an inept climax.

The curriculum consultancy idea underpinning the new model of the BEd. (Mark IV in the sequence discussed in Chapter 4) is significant. Our analysis in these chapters suggests that it could well produce substantial improvement in specific aspects of the primary curriculum provided that certain attitudinal and organisational difficulties in schools are overcome. But this condition is fundamental and, as we shall see when we discuss the professional implications of specialisation in Chapter 8, not easily fulfilled. On balance, we shall find, the new model probably requires considerably more from LEAs and school staff than it does from the training institutions, and in this respect for DES to stake so much on consultancy and thereby so distort the training process as a whole may be regarded as irresponsible. For, as to the conception of the expertise needed for class teaching beyond the consultancy function, the new orthodoxy simply perpetuates the worst features of its predecessors which were discussed in Chapters 4 and 5 and which do not therefore need to be repeated here. In fact, far from marking progress in respect of class teaching, the new model shows the same failure to come to terms with the primary teacher's job as did the old.

And as for the personal/professional polarity, that has been replaced by another, equally unsatisfactory. If the new model has eliminated the opposition of 'personal' subject study and professional training it has done nothing to grapple with the problem of how the personal qualities needed for primary teaching might be fostered.

THEORY AND PRACTICE

Starting with the everyday, common-sense viewpoints of students, teachers and teacher educators, how is the 'theory–practice problem' generally diagnosed?

Students frequently display scepticism to the point of frustration (e.g. DES 1979b, Reid, Bernbaum and Patrick 1981) about the 'irrelevance' of much theoretical study to their immediate needs to cope and survive under pressure on teaching practice or in their first full-time post. They may see such theory as representing a body of knowledge which, though it may well be intellectually interesting in itself — particularly if presented in a lively and thought-provoking manner — is largely unusable for their practical purposes. In contrast the most readily usable professional knowledge comes from some of the more instrumental 'curriculum' or 'method' courses, from serving teachers in schools who actually 'know' what will work, from other students who by trial and error have discovered practicable classroom strategies, and from those teaching practice tutors who are sufficiently attuned to the student's anxieties and difficulties and themselves experienced as teachers to be able to offer sound practical advice. By this diagnosis, therefore, the solution to the theory–practice problem is to dispense with much or most of the theory and to put in its place clear, systematic instrumental guidance first on how to cope with typical problem situations like disruptive children, mixed-ability teaching and slow learners, and, second, on what they might do to provide a full and successful five week programme in mathematics, art or whatever.

The serving teacher view in this not wholly fictitious characterisation retains the memory of the above experience but imbues it with a deeper scepticism. If not, as serving teachers are reputed to do, actually urging students undertaking teaching practice in their classrooms to 'forget all that rubbish they tell you on education courses and learn how it's really done here at the chalk-face', less iconoclastic teachers may still, on reflection, dismiss the greater part of the theory they received when in training as not really appropriate to the challenge they now face. At the same time reactions to the teacher educators may range from respect for the manifest conscientiousness of a teaching practice supervisor, particularly if the latter has had the wit to drop into conversation the fact that he actually taught for some years in primary schools, including a spell as head of Gasworks Lane J. & I., 'and you know how tough that is . . .', to contempt for others as 'refugees from the classroom' mingled with envy for the more civilised aspects of their life-style in metaphorical 'ivory towers' atop eighteenth-century mansions set in rolling parkland and serving cream cakes daily. The solution to the problem thus diagnosed is to assert that teaching is above all a practical activity, make the acquisition of the practical skills of teaching central to the course, abolish much or most of the education theory component, abandon academic subject studies as an (albeit enjoyable) luxury, and let students learn how to teach in the place where they will continue to do so until retirement, but initially as apprentices alongside experienced practitioners.

Finally, there is the teacher-educator himself. At the sharp end of the criticism and scorn ('those who can, do; those who can't, teach . . . and those who can't teach, train teachers') yet also at the point of delivery of what is being objected to, his position is somewhat more ambivalent and variable. He may be totally convinced of the necessity for his students to acquire a 'firm theoretical basis' for practice, that basis being pre-eminently whichever one of the four education disciplines he is paid to promote, but be puzzled and even distressed by the students' apparent inability to 'apply' this theory to practice. Or he may indeed be that ex-primary teacher recruited on the strength of his all too rare combination of primary experience and a degree, confident that he has a fund of valuable experience from which students will benefit, but frustrated by the low valuation set on such experiential knowledge by colleagues, course structures and examination requirements, and even more so by the fact that somehow his experience is not that easily transferable. Or he may relapse into cynicism — 'Don't blame me, blame the system: It's the fault of those academics at the university who validate this course . . .' Or he may throw up his hands at the anti-intellectualism of serving teachers and define the problem not as the actual relevance of theory but as teachers' failure to acknowledge such relevance, their preference for strategies grounded in pragmatism rather than principle, and their consequent tendency, deliberately or unwittingly, to sabotage the college's efforts by displaying to the student, and inculcating in him, the attitudes characterised in the previous paragraph. For such people the solutions are various — more theory, less theory, different theory, integrated theory and so on.

Students, teachers and teacher educators will recognise, I hope, the accuracy in each of these characterisations: each contributing perspectives which have to be attended to because each is a vital element in the teacher education enterprise, but together, even in this simplified picture, achieving almost pathological divergence and contradiction. Clearly, there is not one 'theory practice problem' but several, with a meta-problem of why this should be.

In our analysis we take two distinct starting points. The first is the teacher education course — both as the focus for all the concern and as the manifestation of the most serious attempts to solve the problem: for it must at once be acknowledged that 'theory and practice' has vexed no group more acutely than the teacher educators themselves. My second starting point will be what goes on in primary schools, as analysed in this book: this will lead to a very different perception of the problem from that characterised above and from those which are now summarised.

Theory and practice: the teacher educators' response

> I say boldly that what English schoolmasters now stand in need of is *theory*; and further that the universities have special advantages for meeting this need.
> (R.H. Quick, speaking in 1884, quoted by Tibble 1971, p.4)

In the centenary of Quick's pronouncement are we still as bold? The dominant view of theory during the period in which most of today's primary teachers were trained has been of its constituting a set of propositions about children, teachers, educational processes and contexts. Such propositions are seen to be validated by (a) the methodology of the social sciences, particularly the postivistic tradition within that methodological spectrum; (b) their origin, predominantly, in the institutions which define themselves, and are publicly defined, as existing to create and disseminate such propositional knowledge, the universities.

This view, tacitly more often than overtly, has informed much debate about the 'theory–practice problem' in teacher education. The theory was 'given', so the problem was to find ways of making its relevance to students' and teachers' practice understood by them. The implicit analogy, as Jonathan (1981) points out, was with those professional activities whose theory is firmly grounded in the physical sciences — medicine and engineering for example — where previous empirical study would be expected to provide the formulae for the solution of subsequent practical challenges. Jonathan also points out that the view of teaching as an applied science is untenable, partly because of the questionable status — at least as quasi-physical science, of the social sciences, partly because of the infinite complexity, variability and unpredictability of human minds and interactions, by comparison with, say, concrete or metal structures, and partly because of the value-dimension which pervades all educational action.

Yet despite this, generations of students, as we saw in Chapter 4, were encouraged to use as the ultimate criterion of validity for educational propositions not their own or serving teachers' observations and experience — often dismissed as 'mere' 'intuition', 'common sense' or 'subjectivity' — but the apparently incontrovertible 'research has proved that . . . '. They were encouraged to extend this oracular authority to anyone whose views on educational matters had appeared in print — a field which ranged from writers offering profound insight as the result of sustained intellectual effort to the entrepreneurial authors and editors of moneyspinning textbooks and readers.

The earlier eclectic mixture of psychology, 'great educators' and classroom prescription, which was seen to fulfil the need for a general professional theory, was superseded by the more demanding educational studies of the 1960s and 1970s, in response to academic requirements. The emerging disciplines of education rapidly acquired an independent momentum as academic studies in their own right. Segregated from the so-called 'professional' or 'curriculum' components in initial teacher education they indeed met existing criteria of 'degree-worthiness' central to university validation; but the theory–practice gulf became more pronounced. Educational studies and professional theory were treated as synonymous. The problem, as it was perceived, was not whether the former were appropriate to the needs of the intending teacher but how to demonstrate that they were: a second-order problem of *relationship* and *application*, rather than a first-order question of *validity*.

Since 'integrating theory and practice' was the perceived objective, integration became fashionable as a universal panacea. Courses adopted thematic rather than discipline-based approaches so that by using titles like 'The young child' rather than 'Psychology of education' the commitment to focusing on real 'professional' concerns was apparently demonstrated. (The comparison with ideologically committed primary teachers' preference for 'aesthetic development' to 'art', as discussed in Chapter 2, is irresistible.) In addition students might be given 'applied' theoretical tasks to undertake in the newly designated 'school experience' or 'study practice' (successor to McNair's 'group practice' — a term still used in some university departments of education) like undertaking Piagetian replications (a practice we discussed in Chapters 2 and 4). Both strategies — integration and application — were strongly favoured in the 1970s both on BEds (DES 1979b, Alexander and Wormald 1979, McNamara and Ross 1982) and PGCEs (DES 1980, Alexander and Whittaker 1980, Patrick, Bernbaum and Reid 1981).

Assuming the relationship/application analysis to be valid, we have nevertheless to note how incomplete the integrationist solutions were, even in their own terms: integration within education theory, between education theory and school experience, between curriculum/professional studies and school experience, but rarely between education theory and curriculum studies, between — most vitally, as I argued earlier — study of the child and study of the curriculum, or between subject studies and the rest of the course. For integration, as since Bernstein's analysis (1971b) it is a commonplace to acknowledge, is a matter of boundary-maintenance, of the identity and prestige of different groupings of staff and of the relative status of their activities — high for academic studies, fairly high for education theory, and low for curriculum/professional studies (Foss 1975, Alexander 1979), except in the case of the PGCE where of course there was no competing academic or 'main' subject (Patrick, Bernbaum and Reid 1981a, 1981b). However, the basic fallacy in the integrationist solution is the assumption that integrating sections of a course will in fact unify theory and practice. Thus the problem of 'application' persisted. Moreover, the enormity of the intellectual task implied by that somewhat over-clinical word 'application' was perhaps beginning to dawn on teacher educators. As Hirst pointed out:

> Understanding theory and being able to use it in the analysis of practice are two quite different things.
>
> (UCET 1979, p.9)

To this we might add a third task, the one to which, presumably, all these efforts were addressed, that of applying theory to the solution of practical classroom problems: together the tasks represent stages in the development of a highly complex ability. The integrationist devices of the 1970s might achieve understanding, and application in the first sense, but students' approaches to classroom problem-solving seem to have remained as relatively atheoretical as ever.

At some point, therefore, the relationship/application diagnosis has to give way to the possibility that if integrating devices achieve only limited success the actual content or concept of theory might need reappraisal: 'What sort of theory does the intending primary teacher need?'. This can be responded to in at least two ways. Reformists might suggest that there should be, for example, more psychology, less philosophy, or (to take the 'integrated' approach) more on children's development, less on aims: that the fault lies in the existing theoretical mix, not in the overall model of what constitutes a theory for teaching. The more radical response allows for the possibility that this model is inapposite and that we need neither the present arrangement nor alternative mixes of disciplines or themes but a different sort of theory altogether.

By the early 1970s, indeed, the givenness of 'theory' so defined was being questioned:

> The job of theory is to evoke judgment rather than rote obedience. The application of theory to practice is the bringing to bear of critical intelligence upon practical tasks rather than the implementation of good advice.
>
> (Naish and Hartnett 1975, p.14)

Others pointed out that serving teachers could not, or did not, to any fundamental extent 'apply' such theory to the solution of everyday professional tasks. Coming from serving teachers (as such objections had for years) that view was seen if anything as an argument for increasing the theoretical content of courses. But coming from a university researcher (McNamara) doing what teachers had always urged, namely returning to the primary classroom as a teacher, the argument could not be that readily dismissed. As he somewhat irreverently pointed out:

> Developments in glue technology have had a greater impact upon the primary scene than developments in classroom research.
>
> (McNamara 1976)

And as Dunlop argued, after an analysis of 1970s articles on the theory-practice issue:

> These papers show a growing consensus that the 'disciplines' approach to education theory . . . is unsatisfactory, and a realization that the criterion of 'relevance' is not just the 'problem-centred' nature of theory but the question of whether it actually does help the teacher to understand his situation.
>
> (Dunlop 1977)

By the late 1970s, therefore, solutions more fundamental than 'integration' were being explored. The first was the generation of a new professional theory grounded in the close analysis of classroom practice which by then had become a significant strand in educational research and which, indeed, this book has drawn on. But Hirst (1979) and McIntyre (1980) were among those who argued that this aspiration was doomed to failure: 'There is not, and cannot be, any systematic corpus of theoretical knowledge from which prescriptive principles for teaching can be generated' (McIntyre 1980, p.296). Hirst's alternative was eclecticism — 'raiding the disciplines' as he termed it (1979) — in pursuit of whatever insights were available.

By this stage the emergent question is not so much 'What should be the *content* of our theory for teachers?', still less, 'How can we get students to *apply* that content?', but 'What do we mean by a theory for teaching? What do we mean by practice?'. Or as Reid (1978) succinctly put it, the problem is not one of theory and practice but of 'theory' and 'practice'. Neither 'theory' nor 'practice', then, is an absolute, but words given stipulative or programmatic definitions which tend to have stuck. 'Theory' has become whatever ideas paid education theorists create and purvey, while 'practice' is its polar opposite, that which teachers do in classrooms, an activity which, by implication, necessarily excludes theory.

Thus the missing ingredient in the traditional theory-practice analysis is acknowledgement of the extent to which teachers themselves theorise independently of the theories created for their use by academics. Teaching in fact is intensely theoretical: it involves deliberate thought and is grounded in assumptions about children, learning and knowledge and so on. Indeed it is with the characteristics of *this* theory more than academic education theory that I was concerned in Chapters 1–3, for this is what informs and guides everyday practice in primary classrooms. King's teachers (1978) were no less theorists in their day-to-day decisions and judgements, framed and constrained by the overall primary ideology of developmentalism, childhood innocence and so on, than was King himself as the academic who thus theorised about them. Or, in Popper's phrase, all practice is 'theory-soaked', including that most basic of professional tools, the observation of children by their teachers which provides the springboard for the latters' curriculum decisions.

This 'theory in action' is, as we saw, a highly eclectic mixture of experience, professional folklore, the sometimes bowdlerised outcomes of educational research, ideas gleaned from advisers, colleagues and courses, all framed by and merging imperceptibly with the personal beliefs, values, predilections, prejudices, intellectual capacities of the individual teacher — as ordinary, fallible adult, not as teacher. We also saw that academic theory is neither irrelevant nor unused as some teachers would argue, nor is it indispensable to good practice as teacher educators are bound to assert, but instead filters in and out of everyday professional thought and discourse in an elusive manner, though there does seem to be evidence that the academic theories and research findings most explicitly endorsed and referred to are not so much those which, viewed dispassionately, might make for improved teaching, as those which are supportive of primary ideology (or 'espoused theory') and the situation of the primary class teacher.

It is partly the elusiveness and idiosyncracy of this everyday professional theory, and partly its inseparability from the world view of the teacher as a person, with its roots in his unique cultural experience, which account for the difficulty McNamara and Desforges (1978) encountered in their important attempt to explicate and codify what they termed teachers' 'craft knowledge'. Beyond offering truistic tips at the level I termed 'folklore' the teachers concerned found it extremely difficult to explain precisely why they acted as they did.

It is at this point that the earlier polarity, of 'personal' and 'professional' relates to that of 'theory' and 'practice' currently under discussion, for merely by paying close attention to what teachers actually do, and how they actually think, we find that *both* polarities, at least in their current operational definitions, cease to be valid. As I argue elsewhere (Alexander 1980a):

> 'Personal' education is adduced as the opposite of 'professional'; courses are either one or the other but rarely both. The teacher as professional is reduced to someone whose qualities as a person are left at home while he assumes a specific 'professional' persona at school. This dichotomy may be qualified by arguing that professional education is that which is unique to the professional role and of use only within it while personal education has no explicit or intended focus on the task of teaching, and its utility and application are a matter of chance. This is an improvement, but it still invites certain somewhat unsatisfactory conclusions. The one which is the most hazardous and difficult to defend yet most frequently heard is that a professional judgment, based as it is on professional training, professional experience and professional commitment, is by definition somehow qualitatively different, superior even, to a mere 'personal' judgment — the latter being intuitive, subjective, whimsical and in various other respects unreliable. Here again a major problem is concealed by the over-ready recourse to polarities. For there are many sorts of judgment undertaken by the teacher during his work. Some of these are indeed rooted in an identifiable corpus of knowledge backed by research or collective and cumulative experience. But others — especially perhaps not a few of the most telling professional judgments which we make of children and events while under pressure in the classroom — may be personal, intuitive, subjective, unprecedented. They may or may not represent an accurate practical manifestation of a deeper commitment to objectivity, rationality, fairness and an argued justification or standpoint of some sort. Where such judgments *are* backed in this way it seems to me that they are not far from the character of those practical judgments any well-educated person, not necessarily a teacher, might strive to make. Where they have *no* such basis, we still dignify them by the label 'professional judgment', which in this case can mean no more than 'the judgment of a member of profession' — a judgment which may be no less questionable, vulnerable and reliable than that of any 'non-professional'. We may have to admit — and it surely does the job no disservice — that teaching is an activity in which the best of practice is deeply imbued with qualities, insights and knowledge which can as well be called 'personal' as 'professional' and that if some of these are acquired through formal educational processes they can be achieved by many routes — including some which conventionally do not earn the label 'professional education'.

The thrust of such discussion is away from the preoccupation of teacher education in the 1960s and 1970s with 'What theory teachers should know' towards the elucidation of 'how teachers think' and thence 'how beginning teachers might be helped to conceptualise their task'. This indeed is a recent though as yet minority line of inquiry. Its core is a notion of theory as *intellectual process* rather than as *propositional knowledge* or content: 'theorising', or what Reid (1978) termed 'deliberation'. But to achieve this demands a shift from the competitive, individualistic and content-heavy approach intrinsic to mainstream British higher education, towards a more communal, interactive style:

> The core of teacher education should involve students' gradual introduction to effective and detailed debate between practising teachers and those engaged in research on teaching from various perspectives.
>
> (McIntyre 1980, p. 296)

McIntyre's analysis is grounded in a Popperian view of educational research, which contrasts with the explicit (or more often tacit and unrecognised) positivism underpinning the mainstream teacher education view of theory/practice. He argues that learning to teach must be a continual process of hypothesis-testing framed by detailed analysis of the values and practical constraints fundamental to teaching. The 'theory' for teacher education should therefore incorporate (a) speculative theory (b) the findings of empirical research and (c) the everyday knowledge of practising teachers, but none should be presented as having prescriptive implications for practice: instead, students should be encouraged to approach their own practice with the intention of testing hypothetical principles drawn from the consideration of these different types of knowledge. To aid this process researchers will need to shift their emphasis to practitioners' concerns which would be identified on the basis of dialogue, participant observation and action research (Elliot 1980, Nixon 1981).

However, the essential element of juxtaposition and mutual challenging of different sorts of theory/theorising in this model needs emphasising, because it can otherwise easily be used to justify regression to an apprenticeship model in which only the everyday craft knowledge of the serving teacher has validity: another sort of recipe knowledge. In fact, far from being opposing models, 'the disciplines' and 'sitting by Nellie' can be sides of the same coin.

From our initial characterisation of three common-sense views of the theory-practice problem we have moved into an area of extreme conceptual as well as practical complexity. These complexities are not universally acknowledged, and indeed most courses to date are still tacitly premised on a definition of professional theory as 'what paid theorists purvey'. As I argue elsewhere (Alexander 1984, p.155):

> The curriculum of initial training still mainly comprises an epistemology in which the constructs of non-teachers looking in on teaching from the outside carry far more weight than the constructs of those actually engaged in the job for which the students are being prepared.

On this analysis the theory–practice problem is more one of *theory—theory*: concerning the status and uses of, and relationships between, different ways of conceptualising, analysing and evaluating the educational process, and the kinds of experience or inquiries in which it is 'grounded' (Glaser and Strauss 1967). These different theoretical modes include: (a) the everyday, commonsense theorising of teachers, grounded in particular experience but framed by situation-related ideology, which we explored in Chapters 1–3; (b) research-based theorising grounded in systematic empiricial inquiry conforming to publicly agreed criteria for its conduct; (c) normative, descriptive or speculative theorising grounded in broader communities of ideas as well as in the particular empirical conditions of both teacher experience and systematic research.

It is clear that many courses are premised on according legitimacy only to (b) and sometimes (c), and, in support of this partisan definition they may well explicitly reject (a). This stance is not only exclusive and elitist, given its tendency to overrate the capacity of education research to withstand critique of its truth claims, but is also absurdly unrealistic in the face of the ubiquitousness of (a) and its demonstrable capacity to produce well-educated children, even by the standards of (b) itself.

We have, then, two basic dimensions to the problem (Figure 6.1). First, there is the issue of the *source* of professional theory and the status or validity it is accorded: whether it is generated by teachers in schools or by researchers and academics in colleges and universities. Second, there is the *epistemological character* of the theory, its tacit view of knowledge as proven factual propositions, or as hypothetical and speculative, or as a mode of *coming to know* rather than a *final state of knowing*: what one might term a product–process dimension.

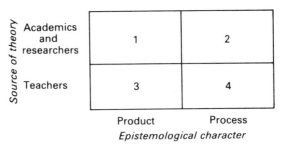

Figure 6.1

Though over-simplified, it is necessary to set the dimensions in this relationship, because it must not be inferred that I am characterising research-based or speculative academic theory as *ipso facto* 'product' nor teacher everyday theory as 'process'. On the contrary, while there is a tendency for some courses to overrate and fail to question the findings of quantitative survey and experimental research, it is equally the case that there is a strong and highly significant tradition of open-ended, creative theorising among academic educationists which has contributed importantly to educational progress — names like Peters, Inglis, Hargreaves and Stenhouse come to mind, as do Bernstein and Piaget: for in the latter cases the problem is not so much the nature of the theory itself, which may be reflexive and tentative, but the way these characteristics can be removed by education lecturers and the theory simplified, distorted and indeed sanitised to provide recipe knowledge. Similarly, teachers, far from having a monopoly of the theorising process, sometimes seem reluctant to engage in it (an issue we take further in Part 3) and instead may display a marked preference, as we saw in Part 1, for recipe knowledge, whether home-spun or academic. Thus the profession does not so much reject as react selectively to academic education theory. Positivistic psychology providing a set of 'facts' about children's development and learning is deemed more 'relevant' than the open-ended exploration of important value-issues on philosophy of education courses: the former provides ready-made solutions and forecloses thought while the latter highlights problems and demands further intellectual effort. Ready-made theory in support of unexamined ideology is preferred to disciplined theorising of the sort which might disturb such ideology. Theory-as-product is preferred to theory-as-process.

This, it must be clear, is at least as much a comment on the *pedagogy* and *culture* of initial training (repeated on many award-bearing in-service courses) as it is on students and teachers. All theory, from whatever source, is by definition challengeable and modifiable, yet this message is not necessarily conveyed in initial training where provisional research findings, a step along the road merely, may be presented as unassailable truths. This — in Wilson's words (1975) — consensual, non-dialectical pedagogic approach does as great a disservice to the intentions of theorists and researchers as it does to the intellectual needs of the intending teacher. The preferred situation is one in which the student is given the capacity and the right to move freely around the intellectual field represented by the matrix above in his search for insights and answers, rather than being restricted to the equivalents of segment 1 in college and segment 3 in school: the complex nature of teaching demands nothing less.

CONCLUSION

In this chapter we have looked at the two perennial polarities of initial teacher education: personal/professional and theory/practice.

We found a number of notions of 'personal education' entangled round the structural separation of 'academic' and 'professional' components of the three/four-year course which serves as the majority route into primary teaching: 'educating the person' in the sense of fostering the personal qualities which everyone accepts are a critical factor in successful teaching; extending the personal education of students in the sense of enabling them to study a subject of their choice in depth; and deepening their personal understanding of the subject(s) they are to teach. One or two or all of these concepts have been adduced by interested parties at different times in the recent history of teacher education to justify the devoting of up to half the three/four-year course, for both primary and secondary students, to academic subject study; a practice which — regardless of the justification — makes sense for intending secondary subject teachers but is more questionable in the case of primary students first because they teach not one or two subjects but a total curriculum, and second because of its undeniably adverse impact on the rest of the course.

We found that the current DES model foregoes the earlier and more questionable claims of subject study — 'personal development' and 'higher education' — in favour of the unambiguous teaching subject argument, reconstructed in the primary context in the light of the Plowden/HMI advocacy of 'curriculum consultancy'. We considered the likely impact of this proposal and concluded that it left the whole curriculum challenge of class teaching largely unresolved. Moreover, while current statements more strongly emphasise the importance of the teacher's personal qualities they omit explication of these qualities and fail to consider their treatment as part of the course. Here again we found different arguments being offered to support this apparent neglect: that of 'permeation' which, at least in its hidden curriculum aspect, seemed not wholly specious; the avoidance of the issue altogether on the grounds of its value-saturation — an argument both naive and disingenuous in its failure to acknowledge the value-saturatedness of all curriculum structures and teaching encounters; and the theory that personal qualities are inborn and immutable, implicit in recent DES/ACSET statements.

'Personal/professional' remains, therefore, a dichotomy at once misconceived and damaging in its consequences for primary training.

We found a similar combination of conceptual confusion and marshalled sectional interests in theory/practice. The commonsense perspectives of student, teacher and teacher educator were sufficiently divergent for the 'theory-practice problem' to be defined in at least three different ways, though the final tally was rather greater. We set the issue in the context of the historical development of what was deemed to be the proper theoretical basis for teaching, academic education theory, and explored the way diagnosis of the theory-practice problem tended initially to be used unconditionally to buttress this concept of theory.

Thus, the problem was seen initially as one of 'relating' or 'applying' this theory to practice, and, typically, different forms of integration were tried. Such devices rarely questioned the validity of the theory as such and failed to take account of the demanding character of the three distinct senses or stages of 'applying theory to practice': (a) understanding theory, (b) applying theory to the analysis of practice (c) applying theory to the solution of practical problems.

Subsequent diagnoses stemmed from more disinterested appraisal of the validity and actual use in classrooms of traditional education theory. Reformists sought a new 'grand theory', while radicals questioned not so much the content of theoretical components as the very concepts of 'theory' and 'practice' in which this content was embedded. They concluded that 'theory' and 'practice' were needlessly polarised, reflected a wholly inappropriate view of theory as fact and ignored the extent of everyday theorising which underpins all teaching.

This led us to suggest that the problem was less 'theory–practice' than 'theory–theory' and to postulate the existence of at least three sorts of theory — everyday, grounded in particular teacher experience, research-based, grounded in empirical inquiry, and descriptive/speculative, grounded in both of these and in wider communities of ideas and discourse — all of which were necessary to the teacher, and which in training should be set in a dialectical relationship.

An alternative model to 'applying theory to practice' was then offered, in which theory had two central dimensions, *source* (academics/researchers and practising teachers) and *epistemological character* (product and process) and it was argued that the ideal outcome of initial training was for the student to be able to move freely around the intellectual field these represented when juxtaposed.

Indeed, 'theory-practice' emerged as multi-dimensional: not merely *procedural* ('applying theory to practice') and *institutional* (school-college cooperation) but in fundamental ways *pedagogical, attitudinal, motivational, political* and, especially, *conceptual*.

So far in this book we have looked at teacher ideology and practice in primary schools and have sought to explain what emerges by reference to the everyday situation of primary class teachers and the way they are trained. Teacher training, whether positively or negatively, seems to contribute significantly to the situation analysed in Chapters 1–3, but clearly the schools and the profession of which the primary teacher is a member for forty years or so after training have an impact at least as deep and without doubt cumulatively more pervasive. It is to primary schools, then, that we return in Part 3.

PART THREE

TEACHER AND SCHOOL

7

Class Teacher and Head: Professional Culture and Professional Autonomy

Newly qualified primary teachers enter a world in which they are part of a strong collective culture, yet at the same time are very much on their own; in which continuities and consistencies across primary schools (and the substantial part of the teaching profession which works in them) contrast with a significant potential for uniqueness and idiosyncracy in individual classrooms.

This apparent contradiction is in part a product of what we have identified as the central salient feature of primary education, the class-teacher system, though the continuities reflect a number of additional factors — primary schools' common roots in elementary education, a not particularly diverse system of teacher education and a high degree of public consensus about the kind of goals primary teachers should seek to achieve. But, as we have seen, the demands of class teaching and the circumstances in which the class teacher operates have given their own considerable impetus to shaping and confining the ideology to which primary teachers subscribe and which supports and justifies their endeavours. At the same time, within this historical, ideological and situational framework, class teachers have considerable room for manoeuvre, they are to some degree autonomous. To what degree, and with what implications, we shall consider later in this chapter.

THE PROFESSIONAL CULTURE OF THE SCHOOL

We are all familiar with the way each primary school has an individual 'feel', consequent perhaps on a mixture of physical properties like the quality of children's work on display, the disposition of furniture and the accessibility and attractiveness of resources, together with less tangible aspects like 'busyness', 'sense of purpose', and above all the personalities and relationships of the children and teachers who work there. We use words like 'ethos', 'climate' and sometimes 'culture' to denote these qualities, but in the remainder of this chapter I want to use the latter term in a more specific sense complementary to my use of 'ideology' in Part 1. *Ideology* is the collection of ideas, values and beliefs which explain and legitimise the actions and situation of particular social groups. *Culture* encompasses both ideology and the social and indeed material structures in which it is embedded, with their attendant behaviour patterns and networks of relationships. In its broadest sense, therefore, 'culture' can include virtually every aspect of what we take being 'human' to entail: it is how we make sense of and cope with our world and how that world makes sense of us. What I want to retain, stipulatively, from this very comprehensive notion, is a sense of the interdependence of ideology and social structure: or, in the specific context of primary teaching, of the relationship between the way primary teachers view children, curriculum and their professional task and their actual situation as class teachers, as members of a profession having certain broad characteristics and as members of a relatively small group of adults existing together with a larger group of children in a bounded institution. In Part 1 we traced aspects of the ideology-structure relationship in respect of the class teacher's classroom activity. In this chapter we pursue the relationship as to the class teacher's situation as a member of a school staff. Thus we are concerned here not with the overall culture of primary education, which would require us to encompass teachers, children, parents, advisers and so on in the manner of Blyth's ambitious study (1965), but with the professional culture of the primary school — just one segment of the broader primary culture admittedly, but one achieving, as I have tried to show, a profound impact on the whole on account of its legitimised power to define the central 'realities' of primary education — the nature of individual children and of childhood in general, the criteria for educational success and failure (and even the criteria for parental success and failure), the nature of knowledge, the character and goals of the curriculum, and so on.

Professional structure

A typical secondary school has a head, one or two deputies, various heads of department and heads of year, and other staff who teach several age-groups and whose dominant affiliation is as a member of a subject department. A typical primary school has a head, a deputy and a number of class teachers, some of whom as 'postholders' also have specific cross-school responsibilities. The essential difference is not so much relative size as the lack of a departmental tier. This gives secondary schools and higher education institutions structural complexity and provides their members with a wider range of options in the areas of professional identity and institutional power. A nursery school's structure is simpler still, mainly as a function of size, but also reflecting the virtual absence of role specialisation. Thus, as Blyth (1965) points out, the older the pupils the more prominent and influential the formal structure within which they and their teachers operate. In as far as all such institutions are hierarchical (they all have heads) and are therefore amenable to representation as pyramids, secondary schools have 'tall' (Figure 7.1) and primary schools 'flat' (Figure 7.2) pyramidal structures (Paisey 1981).

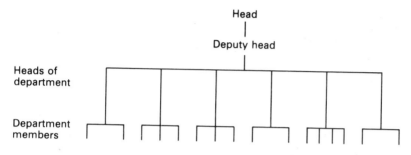

Figure 7.1   *Secondary structure*

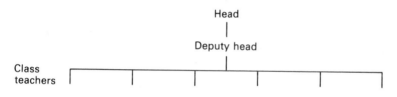

Figure 7.2   *Primary structure*

Since in reality (as we discuss below) the deputy head tier frequently has little significance or impact, the typical primary structure can be represented even more simply, as in Figure 7.3.

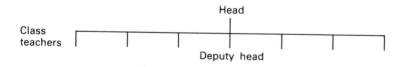

Figure 7.3

However, what this kind of representation fails to make explicit is the way that structure is multi-dimensional: in Paisey's terms (1981) structure represents the distribution of *jobs*, of *positions* and of *authority*, and it is extremely difficult to do justice to these diagrammatically. (Perhaps the terms 'task' and 'status' are more precise than 'job' or 'position'.) Thus in the same eight-teacher primary school the structure might also be represented as in Figure 7.4.

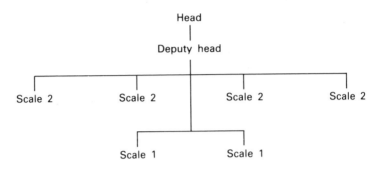

Figure 7.4

This would represent formal seniority, or status, yet it would not do justice either to the actual task undertaken or to the degree of authority exercised by each member. The 'points system', of linking salary scales to school size and age of pupil, effectively ensures the likelihood of substantial anomalies throughout the primary sector whereby teacher AB approaching retirement is at the top of Scale 2 with responsibilities which are purely nominal while Scale 1 teacher CD carries responsibility for, say, language policy and resources because he is competent and ambitious, and has an 'achieved' authority in the school far more substantial than that ascribed to his ostensibly senior colleague (see Figure 7.5). Suspending such diagrammatic endeavours, therefore, what propositions about the professional structure of primary schools might be usefully put forward?

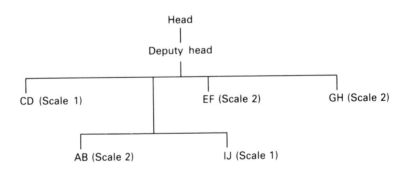

Figure 7.5

First, it seems clear that primary school structures are not only 'flat' in the formal sense indicated above, but are rendered yet more so in practice by the tendency of class teachers to see themselves as a community of equals (Lortie 1969). Each has the considerable responsibility attendant upon being a class teacher — control of the total education of a given number of children for a year or more — and this, rather than the fact that some members of the staff also happen to be on lower or higher salary scales and/or to be responsible for art or boys' games, seems to be the dominant structural reality. There are, in effect, only two professional roles of abiding significance in primary schools, the *head* and the *class teacher*. In other words, there is, as Becher, Eraut and Knight (1981) discovered, a mismatch between a primary school's formal structure and its power reality.

Second, and consequently, this can create substantial difficulty if a head wishes to use staff who are positionally intermediate (i.e. between him or herself and the class teachers) to promote innovation bearing upon the class teacher's day-to-day activities. This issue is of some consequence for a school's capacity to change and to cope with change, and we shall therefore return to it in Chapter 8 when we consider the role of staff with special responsibilities.

Third, the lack of an intermediate (departmental) level enhances the independence, or isolation, or privatisation of the class teacher. The class teacher may in fact prefer this situation and indeed, as we shall see, intense possessiveness about 'my' class is a recurrent feature of primary schools; but equally the class teacher who prefers consultation, who needs a reference point other than the head, may have to accept that these are unattainable. In any event the almost total absence of free periods in primary school timetabling would tend to militate further against such aspirations.

But perhaps the most serious consequences of a structure which, in Coulson's words (1977) encourages professional *independence* rather than *interdependence*, are curricular and, hence, educational. For such fragmentation of professional effort is not readily compatible with the notions of either the 'whole child' or the 'whole curriculum'.

I argued in Part 1 that these holistic claims appear to be less readily achievable than their prominent place in primary ideology would suggest. Thus, teachers' perceptions of their pupils' abilities and potential may not only be restricted in terms of the manifest presumptuousness of the claim that anyone can 'know' another person as a 'whole', but the knowledge they have of the child may also to a greater or lesser extent be distorted or inhibited by the essentially closed and non-negotiable recipe definitions of children and childhood central to primary ideology and to professional discourse in schools, within which teachers may find themselves expected to operate. Similarly, in a number of ways and for a variety of reasons explored in Chapter 3, the curriculum at any one time may lack 'wholeness' by whatever definition of that word one adopts: completeness, coherence, consistency, breadth.

If the whole child and whole curriculum claims can be open to the kinds of reservations I offered in Part 1 in respect of the limited period during which any one teacher has full responsibility for a pupil's education, the claims are even more suspect when one considers the primary phase as a whole. A combination of the school's staffing structure and the privatisation ethic will tend to militate against conceiving of the child's curricular progress through the school as a continuous, coherent and cumulative sequence of learning experiences, and indeed 'lack of progression', 'repetition', and 'lack of coordination' between school years are recurrent and central criticisms in the HMI surveys (DES 1978a, 1982a, 1983c).

Interestingly, the 'whole curriculum' assertions in primary discourse rarely acknowledge what one might term this 'vertical' dimension concentrating almost exclusively on the issue of subject (horizontal) integration. This relative absence of concern, however, is not fortuitous, but can be explained in terms of our analysis in Part 1. For the other side of the familiar 'seamless cloak' claim for horizontal curriculum coherence is 'developmental' boundary maintenance: that alternative 'fragmentation' of levels and stages whose persistence is strongly bound up with professional self-esteem. Thus the neglect of vertical coherence as a professional issue is, if not deliberate, an inevitable and perhaps necessary consequence of the curriculum insecurity produced by the class-teacher system and its related pattern of teacher training. Where curriculum boundaries constitute a threat and must therefore be resisted, developmental boundaries provide security and must therefore be maintained. Professional 'independence' or isolation is not, as Coulson (1977) implies, a consequence of structure alone, but of a combination of structure, ideology, professional knowledge and professional identity. It follows that structural devices alone cannot produce vertical curriculum coherence: the problem reaches far deeper than this, and will only be solved by a massive enhancement, perhaps in the terms discussed in Chapter 6, of the class teacher's curriculum expertise, both during initial training and subsequently. This, as it happens, would also produce a horizontal coherence more in line with the holistic claim than is the qualitative inconsistency within and between the realities of Curricula I and II that we examined in Chapter 3.

Structural issues, it would seem, cannot be divorced from matters of ideology, educational purpose and professional competence — the kinds of concern we pursued in Part 1 — and we shall attempt to bring together these strands in the discussion of professional autonomy at the end of the present chapter.

Structure and milieu

Structural issues cannot be presented as distinct from the behaviour, attitudes, person-alities, values and relationships which combine to give meaning to structure and which constitute what Parlett and Hamilton (1976) called the 'milieu' of an institution. It is to milieu, in fact, rather than structure, that people respond when characterising or appraising a school or classroom, and at the primary stage the simplicity and lack of intrusiveness of structure make milieu that much more significant an element in the teacher's consciousness:

> Sustaining the school milieu is one of the most important aspects of the informal account-ability system which governs teacher behaviour . . . The essential minimum contribution of every teacher is the maintenance of a state of peaceful co-existence . . . A teacher and the pupils . . . should not disturb the peace within the school — they should be reasonably busy . . . A teacher's pupils should not be ill-mannered or have unusual work habits that make them difficult for others to teach . . . A teacher should not threaten the autonomy of other teachers . . . A teacher should not occasion an abnormal number of complaints from parents or other teachers or ancillary staff.
>
> (Becher, Eraut and Knight 1981, p.61)

The concern, they go on to argue, extends to parents:

> Parents usually know when their children are getting on well with a teacher, and this factor can be as important in influencing their judgment as their much hazier notions of whether their children are making adequate progress.
>
> (Ibid.)

The emphasis is probably more prominent in respect of primary than later phases of education: parents want their children to be happy at school but once GCE, CSE and employment prospects begin to loom on the horizon, curriculum and children's progress become much more prominent elements in parental and teacher consciousness.

Despite the importance of milieu, it is framed by structural features, and since it is evident that in primary schools the dominant structural features are the head and the class teacher and that these are also the poles of the informal system, the main agents of milieu and a major focus for expectation and judgement by children, parents and teachers themselves, it is to the situation and influence in the professional culture of the school of the head and the class teacher that we now need to turn.

THE PRIMARY HEAD

The primary head in Britain has a formidable concentration of power which the requirements of the 1980 Education Act concerning the role of governors and the rights of parents have done little to diminish. The Baron and Howell study undertaken in the 1960s and summarised in the Taylor Report found that:

> There was little evidence to show that . . . the standard provision in the articles (of school government) that 'the governors shall have the general direction of the conduct and curriculum of the school' was taken seriously. Heads invariably maintained that they were entirely responsible for deciding what was taught . . . Similarly, the most frequent response from governors was that they felt that the curriculum should be left to the head and his staff.
>
> (DES 1977, para. 2.9)

Notwithstanding recent developments like parental representation on governing bodies, obligatory school prospectuses, LEA curriculum policy documents and other manifestations of the 1970s accountability movement, the reality in the mid 1980s is still very much as characterised above.

It is a power which is considerably more than administrative. 'A head', asserts the 1982 HMI first school survey, 'is responsible for the ethos of a school'.

> This implies . . . planning a suitable curriculum, establishing the organization to implement it and a system for evaluating what is taught . . . maintaining good communications and relations with parents, the local community, the LEA and the heads and teachers of associated schools.
>
> (DES 1982a, para. 3.1)

The survey goes on to highlight good personal relations, the creation of a sense of 'purpose, direction and pride' and the sound use of funds as the hallmarks of a successful head.

The according of massive responsibility and power to the primary head is a constant in all recent writing on primary schools, from those like the old Ministry of Education Handbook (Ministry of Education 1959) and Plowden (CACE 1967) which make the point explicitly, to others like a recent book on primary school management (Jones 1980) where the ascription is tacit yet total, and which almost creates the impression that children, parents and teachers exist chiefly to feed the head's ego.

Other writers point to the close ego-identification of the head with the school (Renshaw 1974, Becher, Eraut and Knight 1981, Coulson 1977) and the tendency of heads to refer to 'my' school and 'my' staff I have found to be a recurrent theme in serving teachers' discussions on primary school management: *l'école, c'est moi*. Many more publications use the possessive form — the head, 'his' school and 'his' staff — without apparent awareness of the questions this raises (e.g. CACE 1967, Ministry of Education 1959, DES 1978a, 1982a).

This personalisation of the senior management function is extensive and of considerable significance. For heads thereby become the 'keepers' not merely of a school's organisational arrangements, but of its entire value-system. The school becomes an extension of their personality and beliefs (or what heads tend to term their 'philosophy'):

> It is the head's personality that . . . creates the climate of feeling . . . and that establishes standards of work and conduct
>
> (Ministry of Education 1959, para.92)

Power as keeper of curriculum, ethos and value-system is reinforced by power as 'gatekeeper and controller of the school's transactions with the outside world' (Becher, Eraut and Knight, 1981, p.74), not merely in the obvious sense that parents, advisers and others are expected to direct their inquiries and concerns to the head rather than the class teacher and the former decides how or if these may be forwarded to the latter, but in that the head can also control teachers' access to the kinds of information and insights which might enhance their professional knowledge and skill. Books, journals, catalogues and information about courses may be made available to all staff, they may get no further than the head's office, or they may be distributed selectively; but it is the head who makes that decision, and any decisions in respect of class teachers' excursions into professional contexts and agencies beyond school (e.g. meetings and courses).

While Musgrove's assertion (1971 p.106) of the head that 'the qualities which gained him promotion have little bearing on his new tasks' may be true in respect of the combination of administrative responsibility and moral authority which the head is accorded, primary headship has also, and always, been inseparable from teaching competence. Many primary heads, not, or not merely, out of sensitivity to the sexist or reactionary connotations of 'headmaster/mistress', prefer to call themselves 'head-teacher' (a term very rarely adopted by their secondary counterparts), and of course in small and medium-sized schools heads do find themselves teaching a class on a part or even full-time basis as a matter of obligation rather than choice. The view of the primary head as 'practised craftsman with his apprentices' (Ministry of Education 1959) is widely shared and primary class teachers would give short shrift to a head whose competence in this respect was in doubt, whatever his qualities as an administrator or a progenitor of 'philosophies'.

Ascribed moral authority, even when combined with proven pedagogic skill, does not necessarily make a good head, however, and the lacuna in the traditional view of primary headship is the extensive and central area of administrative and interpersonal skill, the ability actually to *manage* a school. Indeed 'administration' to many heads is seen as a mere chore, a distraction, extraneous to rather than part of the 'real' tasks of headship. Charisma and common sense, as Coulson remarks (1977), are what seem to be needed, rather than any particular expertise engendered by the role itself. (Matters are changing, however, and management for headship is a current growth point in the education industry. Some of the implications of these developments are explored in the section 'The new managerialism' in Chapter 8, but for the moment we might postulate that an approach to school management which leaves unexplored and unchallenged the traditional assumptions about the head's power, authority and expertise, will solve little.)

The ascription of moral authority appears to be rooted partly in the nineteenth-century 'great headmaster' tradition which is of course in most other respects entirely alien to the elementary and primary world and partly in the earlier view, carried through into elementary schools, of the head as the school's only 'real' teacher — the 'school-master'/'schoolmistress' — with others as apprentices, auxiliaries, pupil-teachers and so on, having neither skill nor authority of their own, but simply 'assisting' the head in the conduct of his duties (Bernbaum 1977). The phrase 'assistant teachers' is still common currency in primary schools and if one were to ask 'Whom do they assist?' the answer could only be 'the head'. Bernbaum shows how state schools imported the public-school 'great headmaster' tradition and used it to enhance this lowlier, more closely circum-scribed model inherited from elementary schools.

Musgrove (1971) contrasts the power and autonomy of primary and secondary heads and shows how the relative freedom from the external constraints of public examina-tions and employment expectations gives the primary head a substantially greater power, which he is more likely to wield without consultation. Indeed, the influential 1959 Ministry handbook (Ministry of Education 1959, p.92) seems to encourage not so much consultation as pseudo-consultation:

> (The head) usually makes his staff feel that their views have had due weight in the decisions taken.

The unwritten final clause here is 'even if he has in fact ignored them'.

The questions of consultation, delegation and participation, and their role in decision-making, will be further discussed in Chapter 8. However, it is clear from both the literature and teachers' discussion that these may frequently be viewed by heads as concessions rather than professional necessities and Renshaw's assertion (1974 p.9) that most primary schools remain 'static, hierarchical and paternalist' with little real collective involvement in decision-making and with staff at the mercy of heads' 'spon-taneous and intuitive' whims probably still holds for many schools, if not so extensively as in the early 1970s.

However, power without legitimation is meaningless. Primary heads, whether autocratic, democratic or bureaucratic, require the acquiescence if not always the total approval of staff. There seems little doubt that legitimation has been readily granted except in the most extreme cases of autocratic and laissez-faire headship. To understand how and why this is so we need to examine the situation in the school's professional structure of the other key element, the class teacher.

Before doing so, however, we need to note, in the light of our discussion so far, a pressing question about the actual as opposed to the ascribed legitimacy of the head's decisions. That being a class teacher and then a deputy head is partly incongruent with the job requirements of headship is generally recognised. However, the incongruence is usually held to be in the field of management and administration — 'teaching a class is no preparation for running a school'. I want to raise the possibility of a more profoundly disturbing incongruence. The head has previously proved himself, by someone's definition, as a sound class teacher, and possibly during his period of deputy headship as a competent organiser of various cross-school activities and an effective occasional substitute when the head is absent. If he goes on a crash management course he may claim additional expertise in this direction. However, given the scope of his responsibilities, is this anywhere near sufficient?

His task has administrative, interpersonal and technical aspects for which he might reasonably claim to be more or less prepared. But defining and prioritising a school's aims, constructing a total pattern of education for children of all ages and abilities between 5 and 11, determining a set of moral and behavioural norms for a complex and variegated community of children and adults — these require competences which are in the first instance *conceptual*, *ethical* and *judgemental*, and which are necessarily rooted in a depth of knowledge and experience well beyond that conventionally held to be appropriate to class teaching. For these the characteristic apprenticeship route to headship is inadequate, especially where the new head has worked in schools where his own head's style has tended towards the autocratic and omnicompetent so that he gained no opportunities to begin to explore such fundamental issues for himself. Nor is experience as a deputy head particularly helpful in this regard, for deputy heads' roles are notoriously diffuse yet restricted, their power considerable in matters like the distribution of stock and the scheduling of playground rotas, but rarely extended significantly into overall school policy.

The office of headship gives the head the authority and right to construct a 'philosophy', to transmit it to staff and to expect them to implement it. The office of headship does not, however, give the head the competence this task requires: the conceptual and intellectual ability to philosophise, the ethical understanding and responsiveness to resolve the value questions at the heart of any educational or curricular policy, the knowledge of alternatives, the judgement to choose between them. I suggested that initial training falls a long way short of the 'whole curriculum' needs of the class teacher; I suggest now that the conventional route to primary headship falls a long way short of meeting the 'whole school' needs of the head. The new courses on school management may make a head a more effective implementer of policy, but they will not necessarily ensure that the policy is educationally sound.

THE CLASS TEACHER

Less needs to be said at this point about the class teacher than the head, since the former provides the main focus for Parts 1 and 2. Our concern here is with one issue, the way the class teacher role as currently conceived is essentially complementary to the head role as discussed above.

Perhaps the key point, as the study of Taylor, Reid, Holley and Exon (1974) showed, is that the school and its individual classrooms are 'separate zones of influence'. Asked to identify major influences within the *school*, teacher respondents saw the head as the strongest by far, with colleagues, pupils, deputy head and formal or informal staff groupings 'definite' but not 'strong'. But in the *classroom* the teacher is the dominant influence, followed by pupils, head, and other staff: the head rules in the school, the teacher in the classroom.

The class teacher's influence, or rather power, within the classroom is reinforced by certain general characteristics of primary schools: the lack of a departmental tier in the staff structure to provide curricular constraints; the absence of externally devised syllabuses such as those by which secondary teachers of pupils aged 14 and beyond are bound; the tendency (Becher, Eraut and Knight 1981) for such accountability pressures as exist to concern milieu rather than curriculum and educational performance; and above all, the class-teacher system itself, which enables the teacher's creation of a world in his or her image to be comprehensive and uninterrupted over time and space. Of course autonomy is not absolute: it never is. But, as the Birmingham study showed:

> There can be little doubt that there is a fair degree of autonomous influence remaining to individuals and groups within the school, and especially to the teacher in the classroom . . .
>
> (Taylor, Reid, Holley and Exon 1974, p.23)

The class becomes the teacher's preoccupation and raison d'etre: complementary to the head's 'my school' and 'my staff' are 'my class' and 'my children', loyally, even jealously and possessively, protected, nurtured and defended against others' interference or criticism. At the same time therefore the school as such becomes very much a subsidiary concern except in so far as it bears on 'my children'. Thus it is not merely that the head is keeper of the school's 'ethos', philosophy and whole curriculum, but that the class teacher may have little interest in contesting that stewardship. The classroom is the physical realisation of the 'cocoon' image we considered in Chapter 1, Froebel's 'garden'; around it the defensive pallisade — no mere metaphor but a tangible reality of judiciously placed children's work on 'display' (over internal doors and windows), bookshelves blocking sightlines from corridors, and, in open-plan schools, closed curtains or aggressively large mobiles.

Privatisation to this extent provides for autonomy and insulation from the kinds of constraints and distractions which can obstruct the achievement of educational goals. Equally, however, privatisation can insulate from positive influence, from productive critique, from ideas, from alternatives. Such privatisation, too, can represent the same assumption of omnicompetence with respect to curriculum and pedagogy as the traditional head's role does with respect to ideology and policy. A recent study of teachers in primary schools holding posts of responsibility (PSRDG 1983) supports this: the introduction of 'experts' can be seen as both a threat to class teacher autonomy and an undermining of the class teacher's professional claim. This claim, however, is not total: that study's class teachers saw themselves as fully competent in the basics and in pedagogy but prepared to accept advice in the non-basics.

> Supporting an infant teacher with reading might be harder than helping a junior teacher with art . . .
>
> (PSRDG 1983, p.21)

This is a response, incidentally, which further buttresses the 'two curricula' thesis in Chapter 3.

This generates an important paradox: privatisation and self-sufficiency are, for teachers, manifestations of their professional competence, their ability to respond effectively to the challenge of class teaching, the hallmarks of the complete professional. Yet rejection of external advice and voluntary insulation from the wider community of educational ideas and practices are also characteristics of the 'restricted professional' (Hoyle 1975), because they inhibit or prevent his or her development.

The introduction of 'experts' into primary schools, already demonstrably problematic (PSRDG 1983), may provoke difficulties even more intractable than those that are loosely termed 'organisational' or 'interpersonal'. Since the use of specialist expertise is an effective way of generating curriculum renewal and professional growth, and since it currently receives strong support at national and local levels, we shall need to explore these kinds of problems further in Chapter 8 when we consider the issue of change in primary schools.

Meanwhile we might tentatively suggest that the line between job satisfaction and mere self-indulgence or even professional irresponsibility, is extremely fine:

> The teacher secures his reward out of what takes place in the classroom and is not greatly concerned about how the school's curriculum is ordered, what its purpose is . . . or whether change in it should take place, so long as he secures to himself a personally manageable and satisfying set of transactions with his pupils.
>
> (Taylor, Reid, Holley and Exon 1974, p.62)

For that curriculum about which he feels little concern is not the school's but the child's.

The head and the class teacher: legitimation through complementarity

The head's considerable power in primary schools is legitimated, it can now be argued, because it is complementary rather than contrary to that of the class teacher. The head rules in the school, the teacher in the classroom. That only works for as long as class teachers are prepared to accept that their professional world is confined to the classroom, and a head who seeks to promote 'extended professionalism' (Hoyle 1975) may thereby undermine a part of his or her authority. One of the roots of the ready acquiescence in this situation, we might suggest, is the imbalance of men and women in primary schools.

In 1981, while 78 per cent of all primary teachers were women and only 22 per cent were men, women were disproportionately concentrated on the lower salary scales: 36 per cent of all women teachers were on Scale I, 77 per cent on Scales I and II. Conversely, men were over-represented in senior posts: 55 per cent of primary heads were men and 50 per cent of all male primary teachers (compared with a mere 16 per cent of women primary teachers) were either heads or deputy heads. The typical staff profile of a 5–11 or a 7–11 school is male head (74 per cent of 5–11 and 84 per cent of 7–11 schools) plus deputy (probably also male) and a number of mostly female class teachers. The exception here, as in other respects, is the 5–7 infants school, where women teachers still have a monopoly (97 per cent of heads and 99 per cent of other staff). The emergence of 5–8 and 5–9 first schools, however, has given men access to early childhood education, though as yet not in large numbers: only 9 per cent of first-school teachers other than heads were men. On the other hand, a disproportionate number of first-school heads (33 per cent) were men, so that in the LEAs concerned the arrival of first schools may have diminished still further women's chances of promotion to senior posts in the primary sector. Nor can women pin their hopes on the continuation of 5–7 infant schools, since they constitute only 18 per cent of primary establishments nationally, though obviously women's chances are better in LEAs with a high proportion of separate infant and junior schools. (All percentages calculated from DES 1982d.)

These figures, whatever their other implications, permit two hypotheses. First, the fact that the overwhelming majority of ordinary class teachers in primary schools are women may generate a climate of more ready acceptance of the head's power than would be likely if the sexes were more evenly represented, even to the point of acquiescence in behaviour verging on the autocratic.

Second, the male head/female staff profile may allow for what one might term a 'familial complementarity' (the family, as it happens, is already a prominent metaphor in primary schools): paternalism complemented by maternalism. The (usually male) head, 'kind but firm', is the school's father figure, head of the household ('my school'); the (usually female) classteacher is mistress of her particular domain ('my class', in effect 'my kitchen') in which the child receives warmth, comfort and even protection from the fiercer excesses of the head/father. This, I realise, is a very Victorian and possibly sexist image, but then the kind of power available to the primary head resembles nothing so much as that of those middle-class Victorian fathers who conceived of and established the elementary schools in which — as Part 1 showed — today's primary practice, more deeply than we may care to admit, is rooted. Is the 1870s household alive and well in the bastions of 1980s progressivism? But is it also the case that this particular model is more appropriate to junior and JI than to infant schools, for the latter, as we said before, are still female preserves? In that event — and this is perhaps as far as the metaphor can be stretched — the fact that infant rather than junior schools have spearheaded those innovations like open-plan teaching which depend for success on an explicit rejection of privatisation may reflect a reduced need for territoriality and competitiveness in the absence of men.

This takes us into the realms of speculation, for empirical study of the professional culture of primary schools is still very sparse. But speculation on these matters should, I think, be encouraged as a part of the process I have urged in this book whereby through an exploration of the kinds of influence to which their thoughts and actions are subject the teachers can achieve detachment, critique and imagination in preference to ideological tunnel vision. Male and female influence on primary professional culture is but one aspect. Parts 1 and 2 offered others — the continuing resonance of the elementary tradition, the historical roots of class teaching, the pivotal concept of ideology and the extent to which it is embedded in, and supportive of, a group's particular circumstances, the relationship between the kinds of knowledge emphasised in initial training and the curriculum knowledge and theorising capacities of the class teacher. In the present case, if nothing else, we might consider a number of questions. Does the male-female imbalance encourage the polarisation yet mutuality of the head and class teacher roles? Does it shield each of them from critique and change? What are the causes of insularity and privatisation among class teachers? To what extent is the expressive (female) culture of primary schools gained at the expense of the kind of societal consciousness argued for in Parts 1 and 2? Are all-female staffs, such as exist in most infant schools, more parochial than mixed? On the other hand might they also be more open, mutually supportive and committed to collective endeavour?

PROFESSIONAL CULTURE, AUTONOMY AND ACCOUNTABILITY

The situation we have explored so far in this chapter is one in which institutional equilibrium is maintained by a number of features: first, and pre-eminently, the ideological consensus we explored in Chapters 1, 2 and 3. Second, a division of labour in which each class teacher has control of the educational programme of a distinct group of pupils for a year or more. There are very few secondary-style timetable constraints or compromises, few juxtapositions of contrasting teacher styles which can so benefit some teachers and disadvantage others, no indelible connection in the pupils' eyes between the status of a subject and that of its teacher. The division of labour among the teaching staff of a primary school is more clear cut and free from complication than at any other stage of education.

Third, there is a comparable division of labour between a school's class teachers and its head, to the extent, as we have seen, that the considerable power of the latter is blunted yet also preserved from fundamental challenge by the fact that in the classroom at least the class teacher reigns supreme.

Finally, the head/class teacher equilibrium in turn appears to be maintained by a complementarity of roles which goes beyond division of labour in the obvious (executive) sense and includes deeper (though perhaps traditional or stereotypical) familial and sex-role aspects: paternalism complemented by maternalism, authority by acquiescence, dominance by submissiveness, empire by home, action and the material world by a concern for relationships.

Of course, such characterisation is very much of the order of an 'ideal type' and all realities are inevitably less tidy. But there is one significant constant, and that is the degree of executive *autonomy* for the head and the class teacher which is permitted by this professional equilibrium, and the structure and culture from which it stems.

Mention of teacher autonomy generally provokes strong reactions. Many teachers point to the constraints within which they operate and refer to a 'myth of autonomy' (e.g. Jones 1980) which they feel has fed a view of the profession as doing what it pleases. The latter charge gathered strength in the wake of the Plowden Report, was fuelled by the Black Papers and the William Tyndale affair, and to some extent was defused by the two primary surveys which gave a picture a long way removed from the wilder libertarian excesses portrayed elsewhere. At the same time, although on the state of the 'basics' such reports could offer reassurance (particularly as it was largely about the basics that critics were concerned) the considerable national inconsistencies in the rest of the primary curriculum must indicate, *inter alia*, the exercise of a professional freedom over the kinds of decisions concerning what to teach and how which is greater than exists in most other countries.

Other commentators, therefore, e.g. Taylor, Reid, Holley and Exon (1974), while being careful to note that autonomy is a relative not an absolute concept and that in primary teaching freedom goes hand in hand with constraint, still tend to question the extent of autonomy enjoyed by primary heads and teachers (White 1982). White argued that the primary teacher is in fact a 'servant of the state' and that though 'she should be indeed an authority on what teaching methods and detailed content she should use in specific situations', the general framework of curricular goals ought to be determined elsewhere. His analogy is with senior civil servants in so far as both teachers and senior civil servants translate political policy into practical courses of action.

It is important, then, to establish in what areas the teacher is currently in a position to act autonomously and what degree of freedom he or she actually has in such circumstances. Lawton (1983) offers a simplified model for determining the extent of professional control and/or autonomy, covering three areas of professional activity (curriculum, pedagogy and evaluation) and five levels of control (individual, departmental, institutional, regional and national): see Figure 7.6 (Lawton 1983, p.120).

Level ＼ Aspect	Curriculum	Pedagogy	Evaluation
1. National			
2. Regional			
3. Institutional			
4. Departmental			
5. Individual			

Figure 7.6

Lawton suggests that in a totalitarian regime curriculum, pedagogy and evaluation are centrally determined and controlled at level 1, but argues that in fact even in such a situation pedagogy is difficult to circumscribe in this way. He then goes on to cite recent developments in secondary school curriculum and examinations as evidence for creeping centralisation.

It is hard to know how to characterise primary schools in these terms since, other considerations apart, the distinctions between 'curriculum', 'pedagogy' and 'evaluation' would first need to be elucidated. Even assuming 'curriculum' to mean 'subjects' (a narrow view not espoused in this book) the only subject in the primary curriculum required by law is religious education and, as every teacher knows, this does not deter some heads from ignoring the religious education requirement altogether. But if one takes 'curriculum' in its more comprehensive sense of 'the totality of experiences provided by the school in pursuit of its educational goals' then, centralisation notwithstanding, the British primary teacher looks to have considerable autonomy, not least as a consequence of being a class teacher rather than a subject specialist. If this is the case in curriculum, how much more so in pedagogy and evaluation, which are largely private dimensions of teaching and which, as we saw in earlier chapters, are hard to disentangle from the teacher's unique personal attributes, beliefs and values?

This would seem to accord with the findings of Becher, Eraut and Knight (1981) who contrasted the autocracy of the head over administrative matters with the class teacher's autonomy over pedagogy. But they also emphasise that any such generalisation needs to be conditional upon an understanding of the complex nature of primary schools and of the extent to which teacher behaviour is in fact influenced by a range of institutional and interpersonal factors, not the least of which is the kind of ideological or professional framework which we explored in Chapters 1, 2 and 3 and whose power is evident from the high degree of similarity between primary schools in a number of basic respects. It is my contention, essentially, that the primary profession is sometimes not so much gently constrained from abusing its executive freedom by ideology as imprisoned by it.

What emerges here, then, is the need to distinguish between *executive* and *intellectual* autonomy. The areas in which the primary head and class teacher have relative freedom to act as they wish can be delineated without too much difficulty, but their actual capacity to take full advantage of that freedom is only partly determined by the kinds of obvious constraints on which teachers tend to focus when discussing this issue: physical limitations such as buildings, facilities and equipment; child/family limitations such as 'home background', children's abilities, number of children in the class; national/local policy constraints; staffing constraints (Taylor, Reid, Holley and Exon 1974). At least as important, it seems to me, are the constraints which the teachers themselves impose by virtue of the sort of people they are, what they believe, how they perceive children and so on. The problem in exploring these other constraints empirically is that they are relatively inaccessible to available research techniques and recognition of them in oneself demands a predisposition to introspection and a high degree of honesty and self-awareness. This problem is well exemplified in the Birmingham study of power and constraints in primary schools to which we referred above. Teachers, when asked to identify and rank constraints on achieving their aims, tended to highlight 'number of children in the class', 'children's home environment' (the deficit model of educational failure again), 'size of classroom', 'availability of resources' and so on. 'Teacher's level of competence' and 'level of professional training' were rated extremely low, among 'uncommon constraints', a view which contrasts starkly with the conclusions of subsequent studies that teacher ability is a major factor in the achievement of educational goals. This study therefore exemplifies a further problem — that of attempting to discover the 'reality' of school life from questionnaires to teachers. The major studies of the later 1970s and early 1980s referred to in Part 1 were observational, but, from the Birmingham study one can really only draw one conclusion: that it provides data on what teachers *say* most influences and constrains them.

On the other hand, in so far as it suggested an unwillingness by those surveyed to acknowledge their own part in constraining the achievement of educational aims, the Birmingham study does remind us that professional autonomy, however defined, raises questions of accountability and culpability.

The East Sussex Accountability Project (1979) identified three types of accountability — *moral* (accountability to one's clients), *professional* (accountability to oneself or one's colleagues), and *contractual* (accountability to one's employers or political masters) — and two main areas of professional action in which accountability of some sort might be expected: *maintenance* and *problem-solving*. This provides a grid in which one can locate procedures for meeting the various accountability needs and expectations, and it is a considerable improvement on the treatment of accountability on a monolithic basis as something one either accepts or rejects (a reaction not uncommon, unfortunately, in some professional circles). The East Sussex model enables one to consider the central questions facing any professional: '*To whom* am I accountable?', '*For what* am I accountable to each of these groups or individuals?' and '*By what means* can I account to such people for the various aspects of my professional performance?'.

However, just as it is important to discriminate between the different audiences, focuses and means of accountability, so we should heed Elliott's warning that a person can only reasonably be called to account for those activities, decisions or outcomes over which he exercises a substantial measure of control (Elliott 1978). His concerns in this field stemmed from what he saw as the emergence in the 1970s of 'crude and unjust ideas about teacher accountability' which tended to presume the culpability of the teacher for everything that happened in the school or could be attributed to it, and he argued instead for the development of 'self-monitoring' procedures — that is to say for an emphasis, in the East Sussex project's terms, on professional accountability not so much as an alternative to contractual accountability as the most equitable means of demonstrating it.

Elliott's argument was well justified: education became during the 1970s one of the main scapegoats in the debate about the causes of economic and industrial decline, and in the 1980s 'value for money' has become the overt justification for imposing major cuts on the education service. Many others shared this concern and the late 1970s/early 1980s has been a period characterised by a proliferation of teacher self-assessment and institutional self-evaluation procedures and strategies (Elliott 1980, Adelman and Alexander 1982) some of which we shall consider in Chapter 8.

Nevertheless it is also important to acknowledge that 'professional accountability', if it remains an essentially closed activity, may do little to allay the anxieties of those such as parents who can make a legitimate and powerful claim for teachers to demonstrate both moral and contractual accountability in respect of their children, and may well be used to dignify actions in which there is an element neither of professionality nor of accountability. The long tradition in Britain of professional groups — doctors and the police, for example — undertaking their own private inquiries when things go wrong has tended to fuel the suspicion that 'professional accountability' is at best a device to excuse inaction, at worst the public face of a 'cover-up'.

Moreover, we have to acknowledge that public accountability may well be a not unreasonable return for professional autonomy, and that to argue both for autonomy and for freedom from public accounting obligations, begins to sound like excessive licence. Accountability presupposes some degree of autonomy, but autonomy presupposes both a considerable degree of responsibility as well as a preparedness to acknowledge accountability demands. Thus the following two assertions, a few pages apart in the NUT's response to the 1978 primary survey, are difficult to square:

> The class teacher . . . has the knowledge and professional judgment necessary to decide on the appropriate curriculum content, organization and methods best suited to individual children.

If teachers have come to work in this way it is because these methods were commended to them by their training college lecturers and LEA advisers.

(NUT 1979, pp.35 and 21)

The teacher is at one and the same time a knowledgeable professional and, in respect of that knowledge, a victim of indoctrination. The teacher knows best and should be left to get on with the job without interference, yet at the same time is absolved from responsibility for his or her actions. This kind of contradiction, and the refusal to face up to the consequences of claiming a high degree of executive freedom which it reveals, do the profession little credit.

Autonomy: executive and intellectual

Our excursion into this issue was prompted by our consideration of the extent to which the primary head and class teacher, as complementary agents in the educational enterprise, have executive autonomy. However one might qualify autonomy as 'relative', or 'in pedagogy rather than administration or curriculum', or (see Chapter 3) 'in Curriculum II, but not Curriculum I', the fact remains that executive autonomy in primary schools is extensive. I argued that such autonomy raises questions of accountability and the need to determine the extent to which the teacher can reasonably be deemed culpable for classroom events and their outcomes. The other question raised is the even more vexed matter of the kinds of competence required by someone accorded this degree of freedom. For it would seem to be a minimum condition for executive freedom that it should be accompanied by a commensurate knowledge to meet the various needs and exigencies in which that freedom will be exercised: that is to say, those situations where a choice has to be made among alternative values, alternative diagnoses and alternative solutions. Thus executive autonomy presupposes intellectual autonomy; freedom of action presupposes freedom of mind.

Such intellectual autonomy, it must immediately be emphasised, is as non-absolute as executive autonomy: we can never be free of our culture, and there must be limits to the range of meanings expressible through language. Autonomy is an aspiration rather than an achievement then, but recognition of that fact at least serves to underscore the degree of effort it ought to entail. Being as an absolute state unachievable, autonomy is less a static entity than a condition of constant intellectual striving, a preparedness to engage the mind in a certain sort of way, a moral commitment to the search for truth.

Thus autonomy in this sense is a commitment to rationality; a preparedness always to question 'authoritative' pronouncements, never to accept them at face value; a search for intellectual independence through an awareness of and an ability to evaluate alternative propositions; and thus a commitment to knowledge; yet at the same time a consciousness that knowledge itself is provisional, modifiable, infinite and cumulative, so that 'knowing' itself is also an aspiration rather than an achievement.

Being a commitment of this seriousness autonomy is as much a moral as an intellectual condition; it entails the operation of conscience, not merely in the more obviously ethical contexts which raise questions of right and wrong, justice and humanity, but in application to ideas as well. It resists unreasonableness in argument with the same vigour as it resists unreasonableness in action.

This view of autonomy as an intellectual condition combining rationality and morality happens also to be central to mainstream philosophy of education in Britain (e.g. Dearden 1968, Dearden, Hirst and Peters 1972, Wilson 1977, Bailey 1980), and so is not unfamiliar to teachers from their initial training courses. It is a mark of the sad failure of many such courses that an issue of such profound importance starts and ends in the training institution. The failure is threefold. First, autonomy is presented as a goal of the *child's* education, with the implication that the *teacher* is already educated and, therefore, autonomous: the relationship between the pursuit of autonomy as an educational goal and the attributes the teacher needs in such a venture is rarely or never explored. Second, the issue remains entirely academic, a stock theme for essays and examinations requiring no more than a certain degree of verbal dexterity, gained by assiduous notetaking: autonomy becomes something one is told about, rather than a condition one witnesses and explores in others, aspires to in oneself and therefore begins to comprehend. Third, therefore, the failure is one of total contradiction; for if it is a minimum condition of autonomous thought and action that it questions authoritative pronouncements, then an approach to the topic of autonomy in initial training which offers recipe definitions thereof for student consumption is invalid. That of course raises the conundrum of whether to accept the assertion that the autonomous person questions authoritative pronouncements is to demonstrate lack of autonomy — everything, by this definition, must be questioned, not least definitions of autonomy. But this level of difficulty in fact serves to reinforce the primacy of rationality and questioning and the minimal view of autonomy as characterised, if by nothing else, then by intellectual effort. Possibly, too, it reflects another tendency, that of those who argue with facility about these issues to assume they have the answer. This, it seems to me, is one danger inherent in the kind of emphasis on autonomy as the achievement of *independence* from the ideas, prescriptions and actions of others which writers like Bailey (1980) offer. For there must come a point when independence becomes insulation, isolation or rejection, and as Wilson (1977) asks, is the person who listens to and accepts advice less or more autonomous than the 'autonomous' individual who does not?

So autonomy requires independence coupled with receptiveness and adaptability, and an acceptance of the desirability of a particular mode of thinking combined with a scepticism towards certainties. Autonomy is thus not an easy notion, complicated as it is by tentativeness and paradox.

Nevertheless, it should be clear by now that the autonomous teacher in this view is a long way removed from the one favoured in union or school discussions of teacher autonomy, who is simply someone who resists the influence of parents, employers and other invaders of Kirby's neo-Froebelian garden. Such a teacher, in his unpreparedness to acknowledge, seriously contemplate or be influenced by the views of others, is anything but autonomous.

Thus it is the teacher's commitment to rationality and intellectual liberation which makes him autonomous, not the fact of being a teacher. Professional autonomy in this sense is gained by effort, not by certification.

The particular case of the primary teacher is more complex than this, however. Class teachers are total educators; they are the agents of a set of experiences which espouse comprehensiveness and breadth, which claim to educate the 'whole' person — a 'general' or 'liberal' education, a 'whole curriculum'. They themselves need autonomy not only as to their habitual ways of approaching the teaching task and of dealing with children, but also as to the curriculum. They need to have not one pre-packaged and unassailable view of what constitutes a general education but an awareness of alternatives, a sufficient knowledge of all that is available to make an autonomous and defensible choice, an understanding of the kinds of arguments that can be, and are, marshalled in support of particular conceptions of a whole primary curriculum, and sufficient alertness to value and cultural realities to distinguish educational arguments from ideological assertions. They need the ability to distance themselves from professional habits and certainties.

This view of professional autonomy contrasts in obvious ways with the 'freedom from interference' view. But there is one commonality. The professional, by the latter view, grounds his claim to that sort of executive autonomy in distinctive, esoteric knowledge acquired through a period of rigorous training, and knowledge is a central element in the view I have just set out. So we can fairly test the extent to which the claim is justified by asking questions about the adequacy of the knowledge base of primary teaching. The answers, as we saw in Part 2, are none too convincing. By whatever definition of knowledge one adopts, knowledge is inadequate or simply unavailable in initial training in respect of major aspects of the class teacher's task, most notably where whole curriculum issues and the non-'basic' part of that curriculum are concerned, but more fundamentally in respect of the various central dimensions of curriculum which we examined in Chapters 3 and 5 — psychological, cultural, value, epistemological, pedagogical, planning and evaluation. The gaps in professional knowledge — whether it concerns curriculum, the child or pedagogy — are adumbrated in Part 2 and to repeat them here is unnecessary. Nor do we need again to emphasise the extent to which such knowledge as is offered, being purveyed largely as recipes, precludes in training the kind of intellectual inquiry required by the view of autonomy characterised above, and militates against the teacher's ability to operate in such a way subsequently. The basic point to make here is simply that by whatever view of knowledge one adopts, whether 'product' or 'process', the knowledge base of primary teaching as reflected in initial training is inadequate.

That it is inadequate for the task is also demonstrated in Part 1's examination of evidence relating to primary teachers' understanding of children, the problem of matching learning experiences to children's needs, the challenge of the whole curriculum and so on: in obvious ways teachers are to a greater or lesser extent underequipped by their training for the tasks they have to perform (and are the first to acknowledge this). And in any case we saw how the kind of knowledge encountered in initial training can be far removed from the knowledge of children, curriculum and learning which the teacher actually uses as a basis for classroom decisions.

Beyond this comparison of training reality with the profession's 'expert knowledge' claim, there is a more basic point, an essential contradiction. For the justification offered in support of professional (executive) autonomy is a view of knowledge as static, fixed, closed, unchallengeable; a set of propositions handed from trainers to teachers, exclusive to them and unavailable to others, in the manner of a password; a view of knowledge, in other words, which is the antithesis of the view of knowledge required by professional (intellectual) autonomy.

So much for the 'expert knowledge' base of professional autonomy: it falls short of whichever aspect of autonomy one emphasises — executive or intellectual. Primary teaching fares little better in relation to our other criteria for autonomy, for we saw in Part 1 how discourse can tend towards emotive sloganising and assertion rather than rationality; towards excessive deference towards the pronouncements of 'authorities', especially those who appear to legitimise primary ideology; towards over-ready acceptance of fashion and dogma relating to children and teaching methods; towards irrational rejection of alternative viewpoints, particularly concerning knowledge and the curriculum; even towards an overriding contempt for knowledge itself as somehow incompatible with education.

Dominant tendencies in professional discourse, then, seem incompatible with the claim to professional autonomy. So too do characteristics of the professional culture of some primary schools as considered earlier in this chapter: the closed structure; the isolation from peer challenge and influence; the determining of answers to the complex questions involved in the notion of a 'whole curriculum' by the simple expedient of imposing one person's (the head's) beliefs and calling it 'the school's philosophy'; the denial of plurality and debate in any but relatively trivial matters; the exclusion of external influences, or at least their filtration by the head; the reinforcement of a restricted professionalism which rules out the kind of open theorising on which autonomy depends; and so on.

Thus we have certain general tendencies in primary discourse and the internal culture of the school which are incompatible with, or inimical to, an adequate notion of professional autonomy. But there is a further contradiction, between such circumstances and the espoused goals of primary education. Among these the growth towards autonomy of the child is pre-eminent:

> The ability to make reasoned judgments and choices . . . a critical and discriminating attitude towards his experiences . . . inventiveness and creativity . . . a questioning attitude towards his environment . . . adaptable to changing circumstances . . .
> (Ashton, Kneen and Davies 1975, pp. 17–23.)

Renshaw (1974, p.9) argues, however, that:

> the supposed curricular aim of personal autonomy could never be attained within the closed social and organizational structure

and that in fact far from fostering autonomy:

> a liberal, open structure and flexible curriculum only mask a more subtle way of manipulating the child into the teacher's prespecified conception of reality.
> (Renshaw 1974, p.10)

An argument comparable to that of Sharp and Green (1975) that child-centredness is less intellectual than situational: a characteristic of the more readily observed social relations and procedures in the school and classroom, but not of learning.

The contradiction is twofold. It concerns first the mismatch between the autonomy goal and the ways children and teachers work. And it concerns, secondly, a mismatch between the autonomy goal and the wider institutional context of decision-making, from much of which, Renshaw argues, class teachers, let alone children, are excluded: the 'open' school may be in reality closed and paternalistic.

The double charge that primary discourse generally and the culture of primary schools in particular may be in fundamental opposition to the pursuit of both the child's and the teacher's autonomy is serious. I put it foward not with total conviction — in any case I have stressed that we are exploring tendencies, not universals — but as a hypothesis capable of being sustained by examination of what goes on in primary schools, though needing to be examined critically. (And autonomously: out-of-hand rejection of the idea — 'schools aren't like that . . . what a monstrous slander on the integrity of the teaching profession . . . etc.' — would in fact demonstrate fairly convincingly that the argument had merit since as a response it would be irrational and thus non-autonomous.)

It should also be emphasised that this kind of double incongruence between educational goals, educational processes, and institutional procedures is not unique to primary education. Stenhouse found secondary schools to be singularly inappropriate environments for the handling of sensitive and controversial issues with adolescent pupils, since inherent assumptions about the teacher's absolute authority were at odds with the acknowledgement of plurality and disagreement necessarily implied by the notion of a 'controversial issue' (Stenhouse 1975, Ruddock 1976). Adelman and Alexander charted similar tendencies in higher education institutions. Citing the handling of a dispute at one university they showed that:

> the supposed hallmark of a university, intellectual curiosity and vitality, was acceptable only so long as it was directed away from the ideas and practices of the university itself as an organization.
>
> (Adelman and Alexander, 1982, p.186)

And summarising the contradictions inherent in two colleges' approaches to curriculum development and evaluation they listed several recurrent areas of inconsistency:

> Between the vision and claim of 'democracy' and the suppression of dissent in practice . . . Between the espoused emphasis on pluralism and the normative pressure towards consensus . . . Between the claim of maximum participation and the reality of minority rule . . . Between the tradition of individual autonomy and the pressure to achieve uniformity and display collective commitment and cohesiveness . . . Between a view of educational decisions as rooted in deeper, open and value-laden questions of educational desirability, and a view of such decision-making as essentially concerned with utility and feasibility.
>
> (Adelman and Alexander 1982, p.160)

Autonomy and democracy are grand words which trip easily off the tongue: they are less readily achieved in practice, and primary schools are no worse than other educational institutions in displaying such contradictions and inconsistencies. On the other hand, their small size, close-knit character and high regard for community and the quality of personal relationships may make them *potentially* more successful in this regard than secondary schools, colleges and universities.

CONCLUSION

This chapter has opened the final section of the consideration of the professional situation of primary teachers.

From an examination of primary ideology and classroom practice in Part 1 and a critical consideration of primary professional training in Part 2 we have now moved back into the school to explore the professional structure and culture which provides the framework for the teacher's career and for his everyday professional thought and action. As in previous chapters we have speculated on connections, causal or otherwise, between ideology, the strengths and weaknesses of classroom practice, the ways primary teachers are trained and the environment within which they work.

We considered typical school structures and the way these might militate against the 'whole curriculum' concerns prominent in primary ideology and essential consequences of the class teacher role. Such structures and their associated divisions of labour tended if anything to encourage extreme privatisation rather than the interdependence and collective endeavour a 'whole curriculum' requires.

We looked at the respective situations of the chief figures in schools' professional culture — the head and the class teacher. We explored some of the background to the considerable power of the primary head, and its current manifestations in some heads' ego-identification with their schools: 'my' school, 'my philosophy', and 'my' staff. Heads emerged as 'keepers' of the whole curriculum and 'gatekeepers' of transactions with the outside world, yet also, whatever their personal qualities and teaching ability, as by no means prepared by their training and previous experience for their substantial conceptual, ethical and judgemental responsibilities. The power of the head in the school was to some extent offset by the power of the class teacher in the classroom — 'my school', but 'my class' — and the former was legitimated by the considerable complementarity (rather than conflict) of the two functions. This complementarity seemed to be more than an operational division of labour and reflected also a deeper equilibrium of instrumental and expressive roles for which the Victorian family analogy was not inappropriate, especially given the dominance of male heads and female class teachers.

The constant in this analysis was the high degree of autonomy of head and class teacher, an issue which raised the question of accountability. After exploring different kinds of accountability we tackled the contingent questions of the degree to which primary teachers can be held to be culpable for classroom processes and outcomes and the kinds of teacher competence which have to be assumed in order to validate the self-evaluation, or professional accountability, which many currently argue is the proper response to public accountability demands.

The key competence, essentially, was an *intellectual* autonomy commensurate with the degree of *executive* autonomy granted — freedom of action presupposed freedom of mind. We explored what autonomy in this sense might mean: rationality, questioning, scepticism towards authority, commitment to knowledge. Such prescriptions generated problems, even paradoxes, but, if nothing else, autonomy in this sense implied a moral commitment to intellectual effort. This view contrasted markedly with the 'freedom from interference' view of autonomy usually offered by professional groups. At the same time, common to both definitions was a commitment to knowledge in some form, and this we explored next.

We found the knowledge claim of primary teaching to be highly problematic. In senses elaborated in earlier chapters both initial training and everyday professional practice fell short, and in any event what the juxtaposition of the two definitions of autonomy highlighted was two very different views of knowledge: the 'freedom from interference' definition of autonomy was premised on a closed, static, product view of knowledge which was the antithesis of that required for intellectual autonomy.

In other respects we found that practice and discourse can fall short in terms of the criteria for autonomy postulated and we referred back to Part 1 to show to what extent ideology can imprison rather than liberate the teacher.

We also found other sorts of mismatch — between the espoused educational goal of enabling primary children to achieve autonomy as persons and the ways classrooms and schools may be organised; and between the autonomy goal and teacher culture, particularly as a consequence of the power of the head and the privatisation of the class teacher. On the other hand, primary schools were probably no more anomalous in such matters than other educational institutions. Contradiction and inconsistency in espoused goals, classroom practice and institutional culture would seem to be endemic.

Nevertheless, nobody can be sanguine about the combination of executive freedom and power, particularly if these are allied to intellectual limitation and ideological imprisonment. Since it is change — initiating change or responding to it — which provides one of the severer tests of professional autonomy, both executive and intellectual, and since change is very much the condition of the present time and the foreseeable future, it is to strategies for coping with change in primary schools that we must now turn.

8

Change and the Primary School

This chapter considers just two aspects of the complex issue of social and educational change: to what extent are primary schools able to respond to external changes, and what is their capacity to change their own practices? The broader question of how far schools do, or should, initiate, influence or merely mirror social change is beyond our scope here though we should remind ourselves of the somewhat banal observation that the school-society relationship is interactive.

The competence to respond to external events and influences presupposes the ability to understand, analyse and make judgements about them. For this reason the ideological polarisation of 'child' and 'society' can have serious practical consequences, not least in producing tendencies to resist the pre-emptive analysis which is needed and to react merely to those events and pressures which become irresistible.

As an example of the latter tendency we might consider the fate of two recent reports dealing with different areas of the curriculum.

The Cockcroft report on school mathematics (DES 1982b) and the Gulbenkian report on the arts in schools (Gulbenkian 1982) both made powerful cases for their respective curriculum areas in terms of both social utility and the child's educational needs. A rational observer might expect the two reports to be treated with equal seriousness: indeed, if anything, the case made for the arts as a central 'core' element of the curriculum was the more powerfully made. In fact, as might have been anticipated, not only have the reports had unequal impact at school level but many teachers appear not even to have heard of Gulbenkian. Cockcroft was commissioned by the Secretary of State; Gulbenkian by an independent foundation. Cockcroft dealt with an area of existing priority; Gulbenkian did not. Cockcroft has become the new orthodoxy for initial and in-service courses and indeed for the everyday professional vocabulary ('As Plowden says . . . As Cockcroft says . . . '). By such means the 'reactive' approach to educational change tends to confirm rather than question established curriculum assumptions and priorities.

Other examples are perhaps more familiar. 'Individualised' and 'group' teaching instituted, apparently, with more attention to external appearances than the quality of learning; informal methods, vaguely and variously defined; the rise and fall of primary French; the uses and abuses of structural apparatus in primary mathematics; varieties of writing all bearing the label 'creative' but rarely evincing creativity; and now micro-computers in every school but for purposes as yet undefined.

This scenario, illustrating the reactive approach to change, comes about partly for reasons to do with the extent of that intellectual autonomy which we defined and explored in Chapter 7. For, though it is true that in respect of all 'swings of the pendulum' the problem for many teachers has been partly institutional or political — pressure, real or perceived, from a head, an adviser, parents or something termed vaguely 'society' — it is also the case that such pressure was the more successful for not being counterbalanced by critical appraisal. Not all these pressures and changes were irresistible or inevitable; in many instances teachers had the freedom to reject them, but executive without intellectual autonomy is, and was shown to be, hardly autonomy at all.

We have explored some of the characteristics and causes of this situation in earlier chapters — the dominance of ideology over rationality; the appeal to individual intuition rather than empirical study or collective experience; the prevailing climate of anti-intellectualism: the narrow knowledge base of primary teaching and the failure of initial training in respect of both this and the generation of the ability to theorise; the enforcement of class teacher isolation and parochialism by the school culture and by the prevailing model of headship which removes all but day-to-day operational matters from the class teacher's shoulders; and the unremitting pressure of class teaching.

Circumstances, then — the norms of professional discourse, initial training, the organisation and culture of the school — combine both to discourage a constant and critical perspective on change and to deny access to the requisite knowledge and skills. This is certainly not to say that such capabilities do not exist, but rather that the many teachers who seek and gain such a perspective do so often in the face of considerable contrary norms and constraints. Their resources are personal rather than situational, and their insistence upon swimming against the tide and valuing reading, theorising, ideas and argument can cause them acute problems in certain school settings where, perhaps, they risk the charge of 'airy-fairy' indulgence or of encroaching on the territory of the head as the school's resident and sole philosophiser.

Handling change within schools depends on comparable abilities — the teacher needs to be able to analyse situations, diagnose needs, conceptualise and appraise alternative strategies and solutions, and evaluate their implementation. The organisational and interpersonal skills of 'making things happen' are central, a *sine qua non*, but have no role without a framework of educational justification.

We shall need to bear this last point in mind as we consider now various emergent mechanisms whereby schools are being encouraged to cope with change — mandatory management courses for heads and deputy heads, the enhancement of posts of responsibility, the rehabilitation of curriculum schemes and guidelines, and the proliferation of procedures for evaluation and self-evaluation, for example. In respect of each such strategy we shall need to consider not only its practical efficacy but its conceptual and ethical basis and the kinds of intellectual as well as organisational demands it places on the teachers concerned.

THE HEAD'S LEADERSHIP

To say that primary heads have substantial power is not to say that all primary heads are autocratic, still less that the power is abused. It is a concomitant of the possession of power that its holders can choose to exercise it in different ways, to the point, indeed, of introducing widespread delegation and power-sharing. But it is also a function of power that the choice in this matter is the head's alone, and he has no formal obligation to account to a school's staff for the way he decides to conduct the decision-making process.

Thus the pivotal point in the matter of how a school copes with change is the *leadership* provided by the head. Studies of leadership tend to use two or three 'ideal types'. Lewin's early typology — 'autocratic', 'democratic', and 'laissez-faire' — has proved durable and influential, though, as Nias (1980) points out, such terms are capable of many interpretations and are rendered particularly problematic by their evaluative connotations. Thus 'autocratic', in a society whose leaders constantly invoke their 'democratic' credentials, soon acquires dictatorial overtones. Similarly, 'democratic' can sustain many different interpretations, from 'popular power in the majority interest' to 'representative democracy conditional upon open elections' (Williams 1976). In turn both such poles have variants; witness (in the latter case) the arguments about proportional representation. So a stipulative and neutral definition of such terms is needed if they are to be useful. We also used the terms 'instrumental' and 'expressive' (in the context of explaining the role-complementarity of head and class teacher in Chapter 7). These terms can also be applied to leadership, as indeed they were by Etzioni (1964).

Commenting on the various studies and the problems they raise, Nias suggests that quite apart from the value-connotations, such 'ideal-type' approaches have tended to be rather one-dimensional. She offers instead these three dimensions:

(a) initiating structure: the degree to which a head defines and structures his or her own role and that of his or her subordinates towards goal attainment;
(b) consideration: the degree to which a leader acts in a warm and supportive manner and shows concern and respect for his or her subordinates;
(c) decision-centralisation: the degree of leader influence over group decisions.

Where earlier 'ideal types' like 'autocratic', 'democratic' and 'laissez-faire' were presented as mutually exclusive, these are interdependent dimensions of leadership.

The particular way they combine produces a head's dominant leadership characteristics, and Nias found that though, naturally, there is infinite variety in leadership styles as in all aspects of human behaviour, there was a tendency for behaviours to cluster in ways amenable to representation as three leadership 'types', which she termed 'passive', 'bourbon' and 'positive' (Nias 1980, p.260):

1. The 'passive' head: (a) sets a low professional standard; has a low level of personal involvement in the school; does not monitor the standard of teachers; has an inefficient administration; (b) is not easy to talk to and does not support individual teachers; (c) has no perceived aims. This type of head was not favoured by Nias's teacher respondents.
2. The 'bourbon' head: (a) has an inefficient administration; (b) treats individual teachers as inferiors; (c) does not allow participation in goal-setting or decision-making. This type of head was not favoured by Nias's respondents.
3. The 'positive' head, whom Nias's respondents preferred: (a) sets a high professional standard; has a high level of personal involvement in the school; (b) is readily available, especially for discussion; is interested in individual teachers' development, (c) gives a lead in establishing aims for the school; encourages participation in goal-setting and decision-making.

In other words, a head can be both 'instrumental' and 'expressive'; can provide firm leadership (see 'autocratic') and involve staff in decision-making (see 'democratic'). Indeed it is the reconciliation of the explicit exercise of power with a high degree of staff involvement and a 'caring' climate which gains most teacher approval and seems to provide a context which permits both job-satisfaction and goal achievement.

A similar point is made by Whitaker (1983) when he identifies 'concern for people' and 'concern for task' as the two central dimensions of leadership and by the use of a grid argues that the optimum position is for a head to score high on both dimensions rather than pursue tasks at the expense of people (or vice versa).

This juxtaposition of positive leadership and involvement is a useful antidote to the kind of argument which equates school democracy with purposeless chat or even anarchy, a sort of leaderless confusion. This characterisation is popular among 'bourbon' heads anxious to resist participation. In fact it is a characterisation not of democratic but of laissez-faire regimes.

The few people who have written analytically about primary headship tend to conclude that since something approaching Nias's 'positive' leadership both works in practice and is preferred by teachers, it provides the best basis for development. HMI in the middle-school survey link the head's positive leadership, high expectations and exemplary teaching with 'higher standards' (DES 1983c, para 3.2). Coulson (1977), Nias (1980) and the Schools Council (1983) all argue, for example, for 'collegiality': the head as chairman of a school board (essentially the staff), to which all, including the head, are accountable for the various and specific responsibilities they exercise. The head would become a chief executive, but the right single-handedly to determine or dominate policy and decision-making would cease.

On the face of it this may seem a sane and civilised development, but in fact transition is fraught with difficulty, attitudinal as well as procedural, and for the staff as much as the head. For while collegiality requires that a head treats the staff as

'professionals' rather than 'employees', it also necessitates that staff too see themselves as — in Hoyle's terms (1975) — 'extended' rather than 'restricted' professionals, concerned with the school as a whole rather than their own classroom only.
And while the kind of paternal/maternal role complementarity we explored in
Chapter 7 may discourage the development of true intellectual autonomy, it could be
argued that at least, after a fashion, it works. To argue that collegiality is desirable is
thus to miss the point that some class teachers themselves — rather than, exclusively,
the head — may prefer paternalism as long as it is reasonable and benevolent, since it
absolves them of responsibilities over and above that of running their class. That this
point does not emerge from Nias's study may reflect atypicality of her respondents. They were young PGCE-trained graduates, whose educational background, it
seems fair to assume, would tend to predispose them towards intellectualist views of
teaching and school decision-making. It could also be argued that as a distinct, and
privileged, minority, PGCE-trained teachers might feel this made them 'different' to
the point, perhaps, of tending to reject the dominant professional culture which they
might perceive as parochial, complacent and anti-intellectual. In turn they might be
perceived by other staff — whether they were or not — as stand-offish or 'superior'.
Consciousness of this perception would compound the difficulty.

Three points of some importance emerge from the discussion so far. The first is that
positive leadership, participation and individual autonomy are not — as they are often
held to be — mutually exclusive: on the contrary, each seems to be an essential
ingredient if a school is to continue to grow and to cope with changes. Second, the
matter of leadership is not merely one of style, still less of mere procedures (staff
meetings, curriculum documents, job specifications, etc.), but revolves fundamentally
round the question of attitudes to and perceptions of the respective roles of a head and
a class teacher, and to/of the characteristics of a community of professionals. Third,
that though the head's leadership is pivotal, the attitudes on such matters held by class
teachers are as significant for the 'health' and effectiveness of the school as those of
the head.

Apart from matters of practical strategy, which we will not neglect, such questions
tend to highlight two central issues — accountability within the school, and teacher
expertise.

INTERNAL ACCOUNTABILITY: A FRAMEWORK

It is noted elsewhere (Alexander 1980b, Adelman and Alexander 1982) that discussion of accountability tends to focus on extra-institutional relationships, on the 'public'
accountability of whole institutions to the outside bodies who have a claim to know
how they are performing. In the present political climate such concern is understandable, but it rather detracts from the equally pressing matter of a school's internal
accountability relations and procedures. Collegiality, participation, 'positive', 'passive'
and 'bourbon' leadership all generate a fundamental question concerning the extent
to, and manner in, which head and staff should or should not be accountable to each

other. Bearing in mind the Sussex project's distinction (see p.170) between 'moral', 'professional' and 'contractual' accountability, the answer is clear for as long as one defines accountability solely in contractual terms. The class teacher, like the head, is contractually accountable to the LEA, but the class teacher accounts in the first instance to the head whereas the latter is accountable directly. Viewed in this way, therefore, accountability is straightforward and hierarchical: this, essentially is the argument invoked by heads in support of autocratic leadership.

We have established, however, that so one-dimensional a view of professional relationships is inadequate because teaching is complex and value-saturated, and happens to involve children and parents as well as employers. Acknowledging these complexities, therefore, we might consider not one mode of accountability ('managerial' below, 'contractual' in the Sussex project's terms) but five.

Professional accountability within the school: five 'ideal types'

1. *Managerial*. This reflects the assumption that individual teachers are exclusively accountable to those who administer and control the school and who allocate human and other resources to their work. What goes on in their classroom, therefore, is of legitimate concern to such 'managers' and to them alone.
2. *Consultative*. This reflects the view that, as professionals, teachers in a school hierarchy have a right to be involved in discussions about their work but that the form of such involvement and the control of decisions still rests with the head. It is the version of 'democratic' decision-making operated in many educational institutions and is a familiar response at local and national government levels to pressure for public 'participation' in decision-making.
3. *Autonomous*. This reflects the assumption that what goes on in a particular school or classroom is the sole responsibility of the professional most immediately concerned. It rests on a view of individuals — whether teachers, or heads — as professionally competent over the full range of activities they undertake, and this competence includes the necessary knowledge and skills to make or seek insightful and valid appraisals of their work and to act on those appraisals. Their status as 'professional' is a guarantee of the integrity of their work. The teachers, or heads, then, are accountable chiefly to themselves.
4. *Mutual*. This reflects the view that education has to be conceived as a collective enterprise, so that all who participate directly in a particular educational activity have a legitimate interest in its quality and progress; that such quality and progress being the result of the particular contribution which each participating individual makes, participants should account to each other for their various contributions. Being the most public and open form it is some distance from 'autonomous accountability' at the individual teacher level, though in fact it is essentially a model for professional autonomy at the whole profession level. It does not necessarily incorporate any particular structural view of school decision-making (e.g. 'open' or 'participatory' in the sense of non-hierarchical): it allows for continued role and status-differentiation, such as is probably inevitable in schools. It is egalitarian only in the sense that it requires that all participants, regardless of role or status, see

themselves as equally accountable to each other for their particular contributions to the educational process.

5. *Proletarian.* This is the exact reverse of managerial accountability in that the accounting relationship is downward from those given managerial responsibility to the 'workers'. At the same time it is neither an 'autonomous' model (since it is collectivist rather than individualist) nor 'mutual accountability' (since the accountability is one-way only). This, since it implies grass-roots staff (or even pupil) control is the least likely in the British educational context, but it is a theoretical possibility, and of course, like all the other models it has its counterpart, as a working out of the relationship of the individual to the state, in national political systems.

(Adapted from Adelman and Alexander 1982, pp. 25–27)

To summarise: 'managerial' and 'consultative' accountability assume accounting upwards only; 'proletarian' assumes downwards only; 'autonomous' denies accountability, other than contractual, to others; and 'mutual' assumes omni-directional obligations. These are 'ideal types' for heuristic and analytic purposes, but some bear ready comparison with situational realities explored in this book. 'Autonomous' is that privatisation most prevalent in primary classrooms and university departments. While it may not necessarily include the kind of intellectual autonomy needed to justify the extent of executive freedom claimed, it is on intellectual autonomy that the claim rests. Strict 'managerial' and its perhaps commonest variant 'consultative' accountability are the traditional models for primary headship. 'Proletarian' is there as a theoretical possibility, but rarely emerges in practice — some of the 1960s/1970s 'free schools' may be the nearest.

This leaves 'mutual' accountability. If one were to rehearse the arguments of earlier chapters it would be seen that the case for mutual accountability in primary schools is strong. Strict 'managerial' accountability can alienate staff in the way explored earlier, and deskill them in terms of the kinds of cultural and educational awareness the class teacher needs. The privatisation of 'autonomous' accountability may offer the freedom which creative teaching needs, but in so extreme a form may feed the curriculum incoherence and inconsistency as between teachers and classes which emerges from recent surveys. A 'whole curriculum' as we have considered it (i.e. as having a vertical dimension as well as the horizontal coherence claimed in the ideology) can exist only in a climate of mutuality, with openness, the sharing and comparing of ideas, and the dovetailing of schemes and practices. And if primary schools are serious in their commitment to educational goals for the child like co-operation, the development of empathy, inter-personal skills and so on, they need to acknowledge the force of the hidden curriculum in such matters whereby the behaviour of adults in the school towards each other is as significant a learning resource as, say, group work in the classroom. The espousal of curricular goals for the child of holism and social interdependence is not compatible with either autocratic management or teacher privatisation (Renshaw 1974).

The 'ideal types' of accountability above are a framework. The required exercise for each school is to ask the following questions:

1. What accountability relationships do existing management and decision-making procedures embody?
2. Are these appropriate in a professional community?
3. Are these compatible with the school's educational goals?
4. Might alternatives be considered?

EXPERTISE: SPECIALISTS IN A GENERALIST CULTURE

Mutuality and collegiality both imply, among other institutional conditions and qualities, that each teacher has — in addition to a shared commitment to the pursuit of the school's collective goals — unique individual knowledge, skills and perspectives. The school gains both when these are pooled and when the teacher applies them to the solution of problems which he or she is uniquely qualified to tackle. Individual expertise and respect for individual expertise are concomitants of the views of leadership, accountability and management towards which these two chapters have moved.

However, the issue of expertise is already firmly on the agenda for primary schools for other reasons: teachers' lack of mastery in specific curriculum areas was seen by HMI to be a direct cause of poor teaching and low levels of 'match'. Conversely, HMI argued, where teachers with specialist knowledge were able to influence others:

> this was very strongly associated with good match for all ages and all abilities . . . particularly . . . in the case of the most able children.
>
> (DES 1978a, para. 7.3b)

and, in the case of middle schools, even more succinctly:

> There was a statistically significant association between a greater degree of subject teaching and better standards of work.
>
> (DES 1983c, para. 2.23)

HMI's view on this matter was quite unequivocal: the full range of curricular demands of class teaching is beyond the scope of most teachers; specific curricular weakness and inconsistency are direct consequences of inadequate teacher knowledge; the only realistic solution is to ensure that every class teacher acquires a specialist strength in training and so to manage primary schools that this strength can be used to the best advantage of all staff, and even to consider starting fully specialist training before the end of the primary stage. This last recommendation came in the middle-school survey (DES 1983c, para.8.22) whose findings on class and subject teaching HMI felt had implications for the final two years of primary schools. My own analysis accorded to some extent with HMI's in as far as we found that the weakest aspects of the curriculum in schools were those given least attention in initial training. However, we also subjected HMI's analysis to critical examination, not least because their definitions of 'curriculum' and 'curriculum knowledge' seemed far too restricted. Such reservations are not my concern here: the issue is simply the inescapable reality that as a result of HMI pressure the development and application of specialist expertise in primary schools has become a priority for initial training, INSET, LEA advisory effort and school policy. It is a shift whose implications are more far-reaching than appears as yet to have been acknowledged.

The formal acknowledgement of specialist expertise in primary schools is recent. Prior to 1948 assistant teachers were on a single salary scale, though individual strengths and enthusiasms have of course always been capitalised on. From 1948 additional salary scales enabled schools to recognise responsibilities by 'graded posts', and the current points system allows heads — within a rather meagre framework which particularly disadvantages medium-sized and small schools — to allocate scale I/II/III posts in response to their analysis of management needs.

The way posts were allocated, until recent interest forced a more rational approach, is an essential part of primary professional folklore. Alongside relatively supportable functions like 'boys' games' and 'library' were a motley collection of odd jobs of an almost sub-monitorial character like 'playground duty rota', 'stock cupboard', 'bottom corridor'[1] and the ubiquitous and highly suggestive 'display'. Though all such jobs were undoubtedly essential to the smooth running of a school, the expertise they required, unlike that needed for the curricular functions which sometimes went unrewarded, was hardly 'specialist' in any sense that a self-respecting profession might want to use the word.

This state of affairs was criticised a decade before the first HMI primary survey by Plowden (CACE 1967, para. 936), though HMI provided the first thorough documentation. In the 1978 and 1982 surveys they identified two main areas of responsibility, *organisational* and *curricular*:

Percentage of primary schools having teachers with organizational responsibilities

Library	54	
Infant department	41	(67[a])
Remedial work	38	
Resources	28	
Year group leader	16	
Junior department	14	(20[a])
Liaison with other schools	13	
Team leader	13	
Home/school liaison	12	
Nursery unit	12	
Needs of the very able	2	
Other	41	

[a] percentage for combined infant/junior and first/middle schools   (DES 1978a, p. 16)

Percentage of primary schools having teachers with special curricular responsibilities

Music	70
Language	51
Games	48
Mathematics	45
Craft	35
Swimming	32
Art	31
Gymnastics	25
Religious education	19
Science	17
Environmental studies	17
Drama	14
French	14
Dance	13

(DES 1978a, p. 39)

[1] My thanks to John Rawlinson, of Leeds LEA Advisory Service, for this one.

Percentage of first schools having teachers with organizational responsibilities

Library	71
Reception	57
Remedial work	39
New teachers	36
Audio-visual	35
Team leader	33
Year leader	30
Liaison with other schools	26
Home/school liaison	22
Resources	20
Supervision of students	19
Needs of the very able	3
Nursery	3
Other	98

(Adapted from DES 1982a, p. 75)

The allocation of curricular responsibilities within 80 first schools (numbers of posts, not percentage of schools)

Music	53
Languages	51
Mathematics	37
Art and craft	34
Physical education	21
General studies	17
Science	10
Drama	9
Health education	3
Religious education	3
Other	60

(Adapted from DES 1982a, p. 74)

These figures prompt a number of comments. First, adopting the perhaps essential procedure of turning all such figures on their heads, we might note the percentages of schools which did *not* have members of staff responsible for major areas of work. For example (1978/1982 percentages): Language 49/49 per cent; mathematics 55/63 per cent; Art 69/66 per cent; remedial work 62/61 per cent; needs of the very able 98/97 per cent. (All the percentages bear reflecting upon individually.)

Second, the high percentage for 'other' organisational responsibilities (41/98 per cent) undoubtedly indicates the persistence of the 'odd job' approach referred to earlier. Third, HMI's survey procedure prevents us from gaining a profile of individual schools, (even in the 1982 report which purports to study schools in depth), so that we do not know to what extent some schools allocated their posts predominantly for organisational or for curricular roles, or for a balance of the two, or distributed them largely or wholly for monitorial 'odd jobs'. Fourth, the allocations depended on school size, smaller schools, because of the points system, having fewer posts to allocate (though obviously the scope of their educational and curricular tasks is comparable to that of large schools); nevertheless, music, language, mathematics and games remained the most frequent areas covered in this way, though in small schools library gave way to age-range responsibilities (e.g. for infants) and PE/games was more prominent in primary than first schools, presumably because of the prevalence of team games among older juniors.

The final point prompted by these figures arises from the anomaly of music. For while the perceived demands of primary music cause heads to give it highest priority when allocating responsibility posts, as an aspect of children's education it has very low priority indeed among teachers (Ashton, Kneen, Davies and Holley 1975). The anomaly occurs for several reasons. One is that music is perceived as a special case, whose teaching requires performance skills ('ability to play the piano essential'). This assumption is significant, because it supports our earlier analysis of how curriculum knowledge is perceived in the primary sector: as skill in providing experiences more than as the kind of epistemological and psychological mastery we explored in Chapters 3 and 5. Moreover, thinking of those curricular areas in which class teachers spend most of their time, language and mathematics, it is perhaps partly *because* these are curriculum priorities and the concern of every class teacher that half the nation's primary schools, apparently, do not deem them worthy of responsibility posts; for to support them in this way might be construed as an imputation that in some of its most fundamental aspects the teacher's professional apparatus is deficient. In contrast, since the child's musical development and awareness are seen as outside the defined zone of competence of the class teacher, to allocate posts of responsibility for music, as for 'display' or 'stock', threatens nobody's professional self-esteem.

Looking dispassionately at the nature of the demands on the class teacher and the kinds of knowledge and understanding needed in order to appraise children's abilities and select appropriate curriculum experiences, this approach might seem almost farcically illogical. We might assume that the rational course would be to allocate posts of responsibility to support teachers in those areas where most is demanded of them (i.e. language and mathematics). But this would be to ignore the extent to which — as we have seen at various points in this book — professional ideology and an associated defensiveness on the vital matter of expertise get in the way of the rational exploration of educational needs.

However, this is a nettle that HMI only partly grasped. They were able to show in both surveys what they took to be a clear causal relationship between the existence of posts of responsibility and the levels of 'match' achieved in the curriculum areas covered. On this basis they proceeded to argue strongly for the rational distribution of posts of responsibility to reflect, above all, curricular need. The 1982 survey extended the analysis and offered a list of roles for the 'curriculum consultant':

— drawing up schemes;
— giving guidance and support to other teachers;
— assisting in teaching where necessary;
— having responsibility for resources;
— assessing the effectiveness of their support by visiting classes to observe work in progress.

(DES 1982a, para. 8.46)

The 1982 survey also argued that those undertaking these responsibilities would need training, and that such training should include:

— up-to-date subject knowledge;
— knowledge of materials and approaches;
— knowledge of ways children learn;
— interpersonal skills for leading other teachers;

   — skill in establishing a progression of work with others;
   — skill in making the best use of teachers' strengths;
   — ability to make best use of 'intuitive and gifted' teachers.

(DES 1982a, paras. 8.62–8.64)

The lead given by HMI in this matter is unusually firm: this, they argue, is the direction in which primary schools must move. But while training may provide a post-holder with certain knowledge and skills, it does not guarantee success. For the nettle HMI failed to grasp was that curriculum consultancy demands as much from the head and other staff as from the consultant. Their own assertion can be shown to be strongly conditional in this regard: 'where a teacher with a special responsibility is knowledgeable *and able to give a strong lead* in planning and carrying out a programme of work, this is effective in influencing the work of other teachers in the school' (DES 1978a, paras. 7.36–7.37, my italics).

What, then, are the school conditions in which the post-holder can provide this leadership, and what sorts of problems and constraints might he encounter? At the time of writing only one study deals directly with this topic, (PSRDG 1983) but since it does so on the basis of the experiences and perceptions of the teachers concerned it probably provides more clues as to how HMI's proposals might be implemented than either of their surveys. The Birmingham study, however, is not immune to criticism: its findings are confusingly presented; it follows what appears to be a Birmingham tradition of conducting research into primary education on the basis of what teachers say outside the classroom rather than what they do within it. Nevertheless, it extends HMI's line of inquiry in several useful directions. One is to remind us that the recent emphasis on curriculum posts superimposes itself upon (rather than replaces) the 'odd jobs' approach, so that teachers may frequently find themselves responsible for 'mathematics *and* resources', 'art/craft *and* display', 'environmental studies *and* first aid', 'language *and* library'. Multiple responsibility posts were also a (criticised) feature of middle schools in the 9–13 HMI survey (DES 1983c, para.2.27). In these circumstances the post-holder's most obvious problem is lack of time, for devising, implementing and evaluating a language policy across the curriculum and the school and reorganising the school library are additional to the job of being a class teacher from 9 a.m. to 3.45 p.m. with no free periods. In a sense, then, a major part of HMI's prescription is rendered unworkable from the outset, for although the postholder can find time after school and during the holidays, this can only be used for those aspects of the role able to be pursued in isolation: but a major part, by definition, entails the postholder working with other teachers 'on the job'.

Lack of time is accompanied by lack of power. Becher, Eraut and Knight (1981) found primary post holders in East Sussex given tasks but denied the necessary authority to implement them — a common theme in the Birmingham study also.

The chief cause of this powerlessness would seem to be the posture adopted by the head vis-a-vis such posts. Post-holders frequently felt themselves to be:

   . . . instruments of the head; to do his bidding, to realize his vision. Theirs is not to be responsible in any but a limited sense.

(PSRDG 1983, p.39)

This constraint operated most strongly in respect of *curriculum* responsibilities: 'as far as the curriculum was concerned, he had decided what it was and that was that . . . '

(PSRDG 1983, p.11). In such circumstances, then, the definition of 'specialist expertise' was extremely narrow: the ability to draw up schemes and guidelines or to marshall resources, but not to conceptualise the curriculum area that these served. The latter, consistent with the tradition we examined in Chapter 7, was the head's concern, and the head's alone. The curriculum consultancy role was simply grafted onto the established model: whereas formerly the head devised 'philosophy' and 'curriculum' and staff implemented them, now post-holders were introduced to ensure that these were implemented that much more effectively.

The posture may be partly defensive. Bernbaum (1977) shows how departmentalisation in secondary schools reduces the power of the head and diffuses it among staff; responsibility posts in primary schools are departments in embryo, a management tier whose existence is premised upon an acknowledgement that neither the class teacher nor the head can be omnicompetent and that the nature of the task demands a degree of specialisation from which both must benefit. The HMI survey came to specialisation through a consideration of the adequacy of class teachers' curriculum expertise. They failed to remind themselves that in primary schools the heads, as creators of the philosophy and keepers of the whole curriculum, may regard themselves as the supreme exemplars of such expertise, and thus the only true curriculum 'consultants'. To argue that class teachers' curriculum needs should be met by other class teachers is thus a fairly considerable threat to heads cast in this mould. They may be able to accommodate curriculum specialisation only by tightly confining it to narrow instrumental functions so as to prevent the emergence of rival 'philosophies' to their own. Hence the use, deliberately or unwittingly, of classic power-constraining devices like keeping the post-holder largely in the dark about the true nature of his responsibilities: the lack of negotiated job-specifications is a common cause for complaint (PSRDG 1983, DES 1982a).

This aspect of specialisation tends to receive less attention than the specialist/class teacher relationship, but I suspect that in the longer term we may find that the greater impact is upon the traditional concept of primary headship and that if anything the position of the class teacher is strengthened, first by being buttressed by colleague support so as to make him or her less vulnerable to external criticism, and second by being linked with a more obviously marketable notion of 'expertise'.

Be that as it may, at this early stage in the rationalisation of responsibility posts, the specialist/class teacher relationship is sometimes problematic: it is bound to be so, considering for how long class teachers have been forced to regard themselves, whatever their private anxieties, as experts in the total education of young children. The Birmingham study exemplifies some of the difficulties, but also shows how this professional self-image is qualified in certain respects. The teachers surveyed saw themselves as 'fully competent' in only two areas, mathematics and language ('Curriculum I' in Chapter 3) and — significantly in terms of my earlier discussion about the anomaly of music responsibility posts — as not needing to be competent in music and religious education. Thus music was one area where advice would happily be received, but so, with one group of teachers surveyed, were mathematics and language. At the same time it is acknowledged elsewhere that some teachers might resist support in these areas because of the implied threat to their self-esteem.

The Birmingham study throws up teacher reactions whose contradictory nature makes neat summary and analysis difficult, but which seem all the more significant for that reason. For it suggests nothing so strongly as ambivalence and the role insecurity we explored in Part 1: defending class-teacher autonomy but acknowledging that the class-teacher role is highly demanding and can benefit from others' help; claiming expertise in those curriculum areas (the basics) which are fundamental to professional and public perceptions of the central business of primary education, while having to admit that to be an expert even in only two curriculum areas simultaneously, especially given the recent diversification of primary mathematics and language, is in practice very hard.

No such ambivalence clouds the situation of 'Curriculum II'. In areas like art and craft, environmental studies and so on, the Birmingham teachers saw themselves as partially competent; yet despite that they were less, not more, inclined to seek advice in those areas than in language and mathematics. This gives a further twist to the 'downward spiral' (see Chapter 3) to which 'Curriculum II' is increasingly subject: only 'partial competence' admitted, but no more than partial competence considered necessary; while Curriculum I needs 'real' expertise, Curriculum II is a matter of getting by.

The strengthening of specialist roles tests both the whole professional culture of primary education and the power structure of individual schools to an extent not envisaged by HMI (publicly, at least). There are obvious logistical problems. How do you ensure specialist coverage of all curriculum areas in a school with only two or three scale II/III posts available? How is coverage achieved in the two- or three-teacher school? Given the current lack of career mobility and the arbitrary manner in which staff may be appointed or redeployed is it not more a matter of chance than policy if a school happens to have specialist coverage of most or all curriculum areas? Then there are problems for the specialist: time, resources, authority, legitimation, credibility. There are problems for fellow-teachers: the intrusion into strongly defended privacy, the need to acknowledge insecurity in aspects of the professional task where such an acknowledgement might previously have seemed tantamount to admitting professional incompetence. And there are problems for the head: the need to relinquish, or at least share, keepership of the school's 'philosophy' and view of the curriculum; the need to reconceptualise his approach to school management in a way which acknowledges the existence of a middle tier having specialist functions and deserving the degree of respect and relative freedom of action that a 'specialist' needs in order to make the term a practical reality; the need, therefore, to review the balance of power, responsibility and accountability within the school.

In effect, therefore, a developed concept of specialisation, even one falling some way short of specialist teaching as such, challenges the long-established culture of the primary school, and especially that head-class teacher equilibrium at its core.

The school which accommodates most easily to specialisation, it can be suggested, is one with certain pre-existing characteristics: a tradition of discourse which demonstrates and nurtures *intellectual autonomy* as discussed in Chapter 7 — receptivity to new ideas, scepticism towards authoritative pronouncements, yet preparedness to admit the limits of one's own knowledge, a commitment to intellectual engagement, and so on; a climate of *mutual accountability* as considered earlier in this chapter; and a leadership style which combines the positive with the supportive, and initiative with participation. Specialisation, in the context of the primary class-teacher system and the notions of 'whole child' and 'whole curriculum' which that system sustains and is justified by, presumes a professional culture which is collegial rather than privatised or autocratic. For the one 'specialist' ability ignored in the HMI formula and subsequent debate is that to engage in informed, intelligent and constructive debate and planning relating to the curriculum as a whole. If it is presumed that the whole curriculum remains the head's personal territory, then not only does this deny a major part of the competence of staff with individual specialisms but it also dooms primary schools to parochialism and ossification. We have seen that no one person can possess the range of understanding and insight which whole curriculum discourse requires, still less the capacity to acknowledge and reconcile the varied and competing value positions which whole curriculum discourse in a pluralist culture generates. The nearest that a school can approach the expertise which is needed is to bring to bear upon the issue the minds, values and experiences of all its staff. The whole curriculum has to become a collective matter and it is for this reason as much as others discussed earlier that I argue that if any threat to the existing order of primary schools is implied by our discussion it is to the absolute rule of the head rather than the self-esteem of the class teacher.

GUIDELINES, MEETINGS AND EVALUATION CHECKLISTS: A NOTE ON STRATEGY

The 1978 and 1982 HMI surveys acknowledge that the expertise of the specialist should encompass more than curriculum knowledge, however defined. Even with the essential resources of time and the head's support success for the consultant role is not guaranteed.

The specialist (and the head) in the context of educational and social change are 'change agents' requiring, in Hoyle's words (1975) 'behavioural' as well as curriculum knowledge (though Hoyle perceives the change agent as an outside 'expert' rather than a member of the school's staff): interpersonal skills; the capacity to support and advise a colleague without threat to his self-esteem; the ability to reconcile what the consultant as expert feels is needed with the class teacher's own perceptions of need, which may be narrower and more instrumental; and an understanding of a range of change strategies.

Three such strategies now in increasingly common use deserve comment: curriculum schemes and guidelines, staff meetings, and evaluation/self-evaluation checklists.

Curriculum schemes and guidelines

Both the 1978 and 1982 HMI surveys link curriculum quality with a school's use of schemes and guidelines as well as with responsibility posts; indeed the former are presented as the latter's chief tool. 'Schemes' were once universal in primary schools: the head presented the teachers with a set covering all or most aspects of the curriculum, and expected them to teach to its prescriptions. The weekly record-book or forecast enabled the head to monitor the teachers' adherence to the schemes. Such devices were viewed as inconsistent with the openness and flexibility required by 1960s progressivism, and indeed in many schools planning in any form became anathema. Record-books listing intentions were replaced by retrospective diaries of events, and schemes fell into disuse, though rarely completely so in the case of mathematics and reading. The 1982 survey found most schools using 'guidelines' of some sort for language and mathematics, but the former tended to be restricted to reading, and perhaps writing, and to ignore spoken language, literature, poetry and drama. In other areas of the curriculum the situation was variable, and more than half the schools visited had no guidelines at all in areas other than mathematics, language, physical and religious education. Where schools had guidelines these were rarely exemplary in HMI's terms, but tended to contain merely lists of items to be taught and to offer little on ways of organising learning experiences. HMI viewed the connection between guidelines which were ill thought-out or absent altogether and curriculum superficiality, unevenness and inconsistency as a causal one.

The situation may not be that clear cut, not least because the absence, presence, or quality of curriculum guidelines can be viewed equally as a symptom rather than a cause of a school's outlook on a number of issues: the desirability of forward planning; the extent needed of such planning; the balance between individual class-teacher freedom and collective adherence to common procedures. It is thus important to avoid naive overestimation of the impact of guidelines. They are only written words after all, a 'paper curriculum' rather than a curriculum in action, and the relative privacy enjoyed by primary teachers permits the possibility of a substantial gulf between words and deeds, even if the guidelines do not actively suffer the fate noted by teacher folklorists of 'gathering dust in the stock cupboard'.

This would suggest that if guidelines are to have any value they should be constructed on the basis of attention to strategies for their use as well as to their content. HMI seem to imply that quality of content is sufficient guarantee of success. I would suggest that the question of strategy be considered before the guidelines are written, not, as commonly happens, afterwards, since the character of guidelines must obviously be consistent with their intended manner of use.

The central question is 'How can a written document influence class teacher practice?'. The usual answer is 'By being as comprehensive and as prescriptive as possible' and armed with this precept post-holders produce immaculate documents which may or may not have the impact they seek.

We are bound to consider the possibilities: (a) that a scheme may be partly or even wholly unworkable for a particular teacher; (b) that, specialist expertise notwithstanding, a document may not be perfect; (c) that the more comprehensive it is, the more it may be seen to cast doubts upon the class teacher's competence.

Even if these are possibilities rather than actualities, they could suggest that the imposition of a 'definitive' scheme upon a group of teachers is an unwise strategy. In any event, apart from the practical, interpersonal and political objections, such an approach runs counter to the view of teacher autonomy postulated in this book which requires close intellectual engagement by the teacher in all activities relevant to his task, and to the notion of a dynamic and responsive curriculum. A curriculum can never be 'definitive': nor therefore can a curriculum document.

It would seem that it may be more sensible to consider an alternative strategy whereby no scheme produced by one individual has more than 'working paper' or 'draft' status, and the nearest a school comes to a definitive statement is a document which is the product of substantial collective discussion and is subjected to regular review and modification in the light of both the experience of implementing it and of changing circumstances. It is worth noting that HMI views on this matter in the latest of the succession of phase surveys, that on 9–13 middle schools, shifted towards a greater concern with strategy. They too now argued for 'working documents' rather than polished 'schemes' (DES 1983c, para.6.4).

This is not to argue that the content of a curriculum scheme should be vague or meagre. On the contrary, provided its status is understood, the more detail it offers the higher the level of debate it can provoke. In this respect HMI are right to castigate those schemes which provide subject-matter checklists and give no attention to pedagogy.

Equally, however, we must be alive to the conceptual and ideological dimensions of curriculum documents: they embody views of the children and the educational process. All such views are inherently challengeable (which suggests that a guidelines strategy should incorporate opportunity for debate as a fundamental prerequisite rather than a stategic option). Thus when HMI argue that schemes should include

> basic aims and specific objectives, clearly defined indicators of progression and detailed suggestions as to how the work might be developed
>
> (DES 1982a, para. 3.6)

we should recognise that this essentially means-ends view of learning is not the only one available and, at the very least, it must cause us to ask, along with the critics of behavioural objectives, whether it is either desirable or possible to specify learning objectives and strategies in advance in this way for all pupils and for all areas of the curriculum. I do not wish to dwell on the debate about behavioural objectives, 'expressive' objectives and 'principles of procedure': it is a field well covered in the curriculum literature. But it must be said that the writing of a scheme by a post-holder, and the discussion of a scheme by fellow-teachers ought to be undertaken with some sensitivity to these issues. Blenkin and Kelly (1981) rightly point out that such sensitivity is as yet in short supply in as far as one particular model of curriculum planning, the Tyler-Bloom objectives model, tacitly underpins many of the curriculum documents and packages of recent years. I have already identified this tendency in initial training courses (see Chapter 5): readers can discover for themselves the same tendency in the many curriculum policy documents emerging from LEAs in the wake of DES circular 6/81 as well as in school schemes.

Thus, if there is to be prescription as to what a curriculum document should include it should be self-conscious and open-ended: a rationale for a curriculum area, which may or may not include specific aims and objectives; a statement of the possible content or subject-matter to be encountered rather than, necessarily, a list of concepts to be 'covered'; indicators as to alternative teaching and learning strategies — which focus teachers' attention on the decisions to be taken in matters like childrens' groupings, the uses of individual, group and class work, the use of resources, but do not pre-empt those decisions; and suggestions as to criteria, means and purposes of evaluating children's learning which do not necessarily presuppose testing and allow for the appraisal of learning processes as well as outcomes.

A curriculum working paper, then, might best be conceived as incorporating what Stenhouse terms 'principles of procedure' whereby decisions may be taken and justified with respect to intentions, the selection of content, the development of a teaching strategy, the sequencing of learning, the diagnosis of individual children's needs, strengths and weaknesses (Stenhouse 1975, p.5).

Such an approach, I suggest, is some way from the definitive and authoritarian uses of guidelines implied in the two HMI primary surveys.

Meetings: random chat, bureaucratised discourse or 'deliberation'?

Staff meetings, whether in connection with curriculum documents or for other purposes, are another current growth point. The relative intimacy of primary schools has sometimes served to justify heads' avoidance of formal staff meetings: HMI (DES 1982a, para. 3.2) criticised the heavy reliance on 'informal gatherings at break or lunch times'. But formal meetings may have been resisted by heads for other reasons, to do less with school size than the assumption that curriculum and policy matters were not open to debate and that residual matters — like arrangements for Christmas parties, sports days and playground supervision — could be dealt with either informally or by the issuing of directives and notes (delivered by that familiar professional auxiliary, the fourth-year junior pupil). HMI, however, clearly regarded formal meetings as an essential ingredient of curriculum planning, consistent with their view that teachers should play a greater part in the formulation of school policy.

As with schemes and guidelines the issues here are both practical and conceptual. Staff meetings can engender a sense of collective commitment; they can help teachers towards an understanding of and involvement in whole school concerns; open up the individual teacher to alternative arguments and ideas; stimulate intellectual engagement; minimise curriculum incoherence and inconsistency: in short, staff meetings are potentially one way of realising both the concept of a 'whole curriculum' as discussed in these pages and the notion of the (intellectually) autonomous teacher. Equally, staff meetings can consist of headteacher monologues, aimless and trivial anecdote-swapping or opinion-parading, frustrating to staff and head alike.

This kind of scenario prompts some to emphasise efficiency and instrumentality in respect of staff meetings: the need for a clearly defined and realistic agenda, circulated in advance; the need for input to meetings, to avoid off-the-top-of-the-head discussion, in the form of previously circulated discussion or working papers; the need for meetings to be firmly chaired so as to ensure progress through the agenda, to enable all staff to contribute and achieve a tangible outcome; the need for decisions to be ratified and minuted.

Such procedural aspects are undoubtedly important. At the same time, the act of formalising professional discourse politicises the process to an extent which those steeped in the relatively informal primary tradition may not apprehend. Procedures facilitate manipulation of the direction of discussion and decisions. They promote the stronger divergence of the two levels of discourse and meaning to some extent present in most human interaction — the spoken and the unspoken, the text and the subtext.

They provide fertile ground for rhetoric and populism, for what Bailey (1983) in his anthropological study of committees, calls 'The tactical uses of passion'. The formal meeting adopts par excellence the trappings of rationality, but it feeds and legitimises irrationality, cynicism, insincerity and manipulation. It requires polite consensus. Yet it may deal with issues on which consensus is unachievable: in which case votes have to be taken and dissent to the tune of 49.9 per cent can remain as an unresolved embarrassment, a reminder not so much that the decision was 'right', or had 'majority support', as that the issue was of such complexity or controversy that to force a vote was the least appropriate way to deal with it: a vote 'for' or 'against' implies the existence of only two points of view.

Such consequences of bureaucratising human interaction are especially marked in large institutions where an added complexity is that the few individuals gathered together may represent or claim to represent many others, so that the committee or board manifests the manoeuvring of sectional interests, the problem of the real or claimed mandate from absent constituents, and the heightening of the power and game-playing dimensions of the whole process.

Committees in this characterisation are an overwhelmingly male preserve. That being so, many women teachers may be instinctively less comfortable in such circumstances than men, who may actually revel in the ritualised aggression and sometimes bogus instrumentality. They may feel themselves disadvantaged by the style of the procedure to an extent which they would not in a less circumscribed situation, and therefore unable to make the kind of contribution of which they are capable.

There are further, conceptual, grounds for questioning this approach however: is it compatible with the nature of curriculum and curriculum issues as we have defined them in this book?

We have characterised curriculum issues (Chapters 3 and 5) as having several dimensions: cultural, epistemological, psychological, pedagogical, planning and evaluation, and value. It will perhaps be acknowledged by now that the last (rather than the third) is the most fundamental and pervasive in that value-issues underpin all the others. This is a diagnosis shared by Reid (1978) who sees curriculum problems as predominantly *practical*, yet in a *moral* rather than a *technical* sense, so that few of them yield ready certainties. He criticises mainstream curriculum theory for its pursuit of rationalism at the expense of proper exploration of the moral dimension, and bureaucratic decision-making for forcing curriculum debate into a mould where 'procedure, majority votes and authoritative pronouncements have . . . usurped the place of appreciation, deliberation and judgment' (Reid 1978, p.60). Each of these latter three words is used carefully: *appreciation* of a problem demands analysis of its many facets and possibly a variety of 'expert' perspectives to elucidate these; *judgement* invokes both a practical capacity and a sense of and discrimination among differing values; *deliberation* is used in preference to 'debate' because the latter presumes the existence of final and correct answers. One might add that 'debate' also suggests a contest between a maximum of two viewpoints, one usually the antithesis of the other. Deliberation, in contrast, is a multi-faceted collective process of seeking to understand complexity; its practical essence is informality and the absence of threat so that members will be prepared both to risk and contest assertions. Deliberation, I would suggest, is the collective pursuit of that 'theorising' which I argued (in Chapter

6) should come to replace 'recipe theory' in both initial teacher training and everyday teacher discourse.

Reid's notion of 'deliberation' is consistent with the approach to curriculum this book has taken, to an extent that bureaucratised discourse is not. On the other hand 'deliberation' is vastly more disciplined and informed than that which highly formalised staff meetings seek to replace, namely random, anecdotal chat. There has to be a middle ground between inhibiting structure and debilitating flaccidity.

Equally pertinent is Reid's suggestion that the optimum group number for deliberation is ten or twelve people in that it enables different sources of expertise to be represented without the tendency to excessive formality associated with larger groups. A medium-sized primary school has that number of staff, and it could be argued in any case that the size and cultural tradition of primary schools makes them less vulnerable to the bureaucratic excesses of, for example, higher education institutions (Adelman and Alexander 1982).

Difficulties arise, however, in relation to the view that deliberation requires a range of expertise. For as long as primary teachers define themselves as experts only on primary children this diversity may be unavailable. But the gradual legitimation of specialists, in the wake of the 1978 HMI survey, may make for conditions in which the specialist contribution to policy is accepted and indeed fostered, provided — as we saw earlier — that the threat potential to head and class teacher can be neutralised.

In that event, primary schools could claim to have available two main categories of specialist expertise — relating to *curriculum areas* (mathematics, language, art, environmental studies, physical education and so on) and to *children* (younger/older, less able/more able). Comprehensive though this might seem to be, it is some way short of what, by this book's analysis, is needed: it could be argued that though like mathematics, language and so on the six curriculum dimensions discussed in Chapters 3 and 5 (epistemological, psychological, etc.) ought to be part of the intellectual apparatus of every teacher, equally, as in the case of the curriculum areas, the complexity of each dimension requires the understanding consequent upon sustained specialist study.

Perhaps, therefore, in the allocation of responsibility posts schools should attend to four rather than two types of responsibility. First, the curriculum areas, second, a particular age-range of children, third, one of the central dimensions of curriculum analysis and planning, and fourth, the various school odd jobs (which have to be done and are therefore not to be despised). Thus, through selective study and experience an individual teacher might claim general proficiency as a class teacher together with specialist expertise in, for example, environmental studies, the education of 7–9-year-olds, and curriculum evaluation; or in mathematics, the education of 9–11-year-olds, and pedagogy/classroom organisation. The 'odd jobs' can surely be fairly distributed on the basis of choice or rotation: 'notice boards' hardly requires a course of advanced study.

This line of speculation is one which schools might profitably pursue: in any case it could be argued that, regardless of the meetings/deliberation issue, the concept of 'specialist' adduced by HMI should not be accepted at face value since it is very narrowly premised. The nature of primary teaching requires professional specialisation in areas additional to the conventional subjects:

to conceive of 'curriculum', as HMI appear to, in conventional subject terms, will tend to produce a notion of specialism which excludes *cross-curricular* concerns . . . A more comprehensive concept of specialisation — 'professional' rather than merely 'subject' — is . . . to be preferred.

(CNAA 1983b, p.8)

Evaluation: beyond checklists

A further strategy to achieve prominence in recent years is formal evaluation. Two uses or justifications are generally cited: public accountability and staff/school development. Thus on the one hand we have increasingly elaborate documentary procedures for providing information about pupils, teachers and curriculum to heads, LEAs, parents and other schools; and, on the other, procedures for generating individual or collective review of teaching, curriculum and policy as a basis for change and development. One responds to external demand, the other to what are seen as fundamental professional imperatives; one provides information for consumption outside the school, the other is an internal matter.

Despite these essentially different purposes and requirements the two activities are frequently treated as necessitating identical or similar procedures. The commonest such procedure is the checklist, which in recent years has become such an ubiquitous feature of the educational scene that many find it hard to accept that it is neither necessarily the only nor the best way of meeting accountability requirements, let alone of promoting professional development. Checklists are now constructed by LEAs and schools as a basis for three sorts of evaluation: of pupils, of teachers and of schools. Their essence is a set of questions or items requiring answers or scores; sometimes, as in the case of pupil records, in the form of ticks or literal/numerical grades/scores; elsewhere, as with some of the school self-evaluation checklists, they are more agenda for discussion.

Thus, while most LEAs have record cards, Rochdale LEA (1978) has a book for each pupil which has to be completed for each school year in respect of detailed lists of concepts, skills and qualities. Inner London LEA, one of the pioneers of school self-evaluation, has its now widely used document 'Keeping the school under review' which offers an extended list of questions about children, parental involvement, curriculum, organisation, staffing and staff roles 'to assist a school to examine its organisation, its resources, its standards of achievement and its relationships' (ILEA 1977). Another pioneering LEA, Salford, shifted from an overt accountability approach, with a detailed primary school self-evaluation booklet requesting the transmission to 'the office' of regular detailed information on facets of school life from the state of the buildings to curriculum areas, resources, community relations and management, to a version which combined accounting to the LEA with school self-assessment 'as a contribution to staff development . . . and . . . curricular and organizational developments' (Salford 1977, 1982).

Detailed analysis of the contents and procedural implications of such documents is now available elsewhere; the most extensive are by Elliott (1980), and by Clift, Weiner and Wilson (1981). Much of the discussion is concerned with technical aspects — format, categories of questions, intended mode of use, problems of clarity, ambiguity, time required for completing checklists and record cards/books, and so on. Because checklists and elaborated record-keeping systems are now a fact of school life it is inevitable that such factors should weigh heavily, for above all these procedures are time-consuming.

Becher, Eraut and Knight (1981), dealing specifically with these practices as used in primary schools, are among the commentators who draw attention to some rather more fundamental problems of this approach. One is the checklist or record card's implicit view of whatever is being reviewed — children's language, teachers' use of resources, schools' relationships with parents, for example. By asking, or giving priority to, some questions rather than others, the head or LEA responsible implies a preferred model. Thus, as we saw in Part 1, LEAs like Avon expect teachers to rate children's writing in terms of the Bullock Report's categories of 'transactional', 'expressive' and 'poetic' and to appraise children's use of language (oral) in terms of Joan Tough's categories (Tough 1976, 1977) of 'self-maintaining', 'directing', 'reporting', 'reasoning', 'predicting', 'projecting' and so on. Apart from the fact that these are indeed only models of language (as their creators would be the first to argue), it appears to be tacitly assumed that teachers completing the cards have the requisite understanding of what such categories mean.

In this regard the danger in such approaches is their apparent but often spurious objectivity. Putting a tick or a number against a word like 'predicting' may seem to some teachers to be more objective than writing an opinion in an empty box. In fact, both activities are heavily value-laden, the latter in an obvious way, the former more profoundly so because the vagaries of personal opinion are compounded by another person's values and by problems of interpretation, meaning and judgement.

In contrast some such devices are so obviously tendentious as to be ludicrous and therefore, paradoxically, less dangerous in use. An example is the checklist sent to me in place of the more usual invitation to write a reference on a teacher. This required ratings on a five-point scale on such items as: 'skill in putting into practice good principles of teaching, judged largely by results; energetic, even-tempered; pleasing, attractive, appropriately dressed, wholesome influence; success in making social contacts; aggressiveness and initiative; intellectual alertness — native mental endowment as distinguished from acquired abilities; freedom from social indiscretions . . . '. No further comment is needed.

The second problem is the lack of attention in some such documents to strategy. As Becher, Eraut and Knight remark:

> To the outside world, checklists appear to offer an interesting compromise between external guidance and authority and internal choice and responsibility. But within the school itself their strong management-orientation can seem to belie their declared purpose of guiding self-evaluation.
>
> (Becher, Eraut and Knight 1981, p.89)

This dilemma is not necessarily resolved by stressing the development function while elaborating the preferred strategy. The strength of the Schools Council/Bristol University 'GRIDS' approach (Bristol University 1983) is that it provides detailed guidance on school self-review strategy as a cyclic process and specifies the various steps and tasks to be undertaken. This contrasts with the more familiar LEA approach of merely sending the school a list of questions to be answered. The GRIDS booklet also emphasises the importance of grounding strategy in key principles or commitments in areas like consultation and staff involvement. In this respect it is comparable to this author's development of an evaluation 'constitution' for a Manchester college (Adelman and Alexander 1982), though the latter was considerably more detailed and covered issues like confidentiality, dissemination and the vital matter of who controls the various decisions which an evaluation requires. Where GRIDS fails to escape the dilemma is its tacit vesting of such control with the head, so that although there is consultation about topics for review and the implications of review for development these are firmly circumscribed by the head's decisions over who should be involved and in precisely what capacity.

Formalised self-evaluation then, is not simply a matter of asking and answering questions, completing forms and cards: it requires elucidation of more fundamental matters concerning schools' and teachers' value-systems in respect of children, curriculum and teaching on the one hand, and school decision-making, and professional relationships and responsibilities on the other.

The external accountability functions of evaluation procedures can be reduced in favour of 'development', but the internal accountability dimension remains pervasive. Formalised evaluation is pre-eminently a management tool and underpinning every style of management (as we saw earlier) is a view of the accountability relations and obligations of the institution whose members and affairs are being managed.

Thus we could, and should, extend our list of the dimensions of formalised evaluation, by analysing the kinds of decisions which all such evaluation necessarily entails.

Formal evaluation: the main decisions

1. Decisions about the *aims* of evaluation. What is it for (information for LEA, parents, head, etc.; school development, teacher development)?
2. Decisions about the *focus* of evaluation. What aspects of school life are to be evaluated (e.g. pupil performance, teacher performance, curriculum goals and content, teaching methods, organisation, resources, processes, outcomes)?
3. Decisions about the *criteria* for evaluation. What will be the nature of the criteria for judging the worth and/or effectiveness of the aspects of school life to be studied? (How will children's artistic progress be judged 'good'? How will teacher *x* be deemed 'efficient'?)
4. Decisions about the *methods* of evaluation to be used. Evaluation is a judgement based on evidence. What will be the character and source of the evidence (e.g. children's written work, behaviour, attitudes; teachers' co-operation, classroom display etc.)? Who will make the judgement (e.g. teacher, head, child)?
5. Decisions about *organisation*. How will the evaluation be conducted (e.g. through tests, checklists, appraisal interviews, profiles; yearly, termly, monthly, weekly; individually, collectively etc.)?
6. Decisions about *dissemination*. What means for recording and reporting evaluation judgements will be used? To whom will they be available? What will be the extent of confidentiality?

7. Decisions about *application*. To what uses will evaluations be put, and how will they be enabled to inform decision-making (e.g. through circulated papers, through discussion, through working group activity etc.)?
8. Decisions about *control* and *accountability*. This is the overriding decision because it determines the direction of the answers to all the other questions. Who, then, decides? Head, individual teachers, teachers collectively, or LEA advisers?

(Adapted from Adelman and Alexander 1982)

These questions provide the kind of framework needed if formalised evaluation is to establish some degree of methodological, educational and institutional legitimacy. They also imply a further prerequisite, that of subjecting the whole matter of evaluation strategy to discussion within the school. Evaluation is about values and valuing: for the head to ask and answer the above questions without reference to colleagues is to imply the paramountcy or superiority of his values. Yet most of the questions by their nature can only properly be approached through open discussion. Other evaluation decisions demand diverse sorts of expertise — in curriculum areas, in children's development and learning, in evaluation techniques — which in respect of the scope of primary education no one teacher or head can possess. Evaluation is pre-eminently an issue for which the 'deliberation' we discussed in the previous section is a necessity. Viewed in this more comprehensive manner, the managerialist/technicist approach through improved checklists gives added cause for anxiety.

Formal and informal evaluation: barking up the wrong tree?

The development of procedures for formal evaluation, we have seen, may all too frequently neglect the central issues discussed above, but, even more fundamentally, it may tend to imply two questionable assumptions: first, that such procedures constitute the most valid forms of evaluation; second, that their arrival heralds the end of an earlier era of non-evaluation.

Throughout the discussion on this topic I have used the adjective 'formal' or 'formalised' in order to emphasise both the official and artificial character of such evaluation procedures, and to allow for a contrast with other sorts of evaluation which can reasonably be termed 'informal'. We can define evaluation in the curriculum theorist's terms as 'information for decision-makers' or as 'measurement of the extent to which objectives are achieved' (both of them problematic and prescriptive rather than neutral and descriptive); or we can seek a more open definition like 'making judgements of worth or effectiveness'. Note, as against this, how limited are the first two definitions in terms of our eight evaluation decisions listed above: one views evaluation mainly in terms of decisions 6 and 7 ('dissemination' and 'application') and the other in terms of decision 4 ('methods'). Both neglect the vital areas of values, criteria, control and accountability.

If we adopt the third definition, it allows for three extensions to our conceptual framework. One is to project to centre-stage the actual *judgemental process* at the heart of evaluation; the second is to free it from presuppositions about particular methodologies, contexts or uses; the third is to prompt a sense of evaluation as a continuum of many diverse types and modes of judgement, all of which can make a claim to be taken seriously, not because they are 'formal' rather than 'private' or 'informal' but because they happen, they occur in real life.

This judgemental continuum, in schools and classrooms, overwhelmingly comprises evaluations which are nearer its 'informal' than its 'formal' pole. Teachers' and heads' use of tests, checklists, profiles and so on constitutes a minute proportion of the evaluation on which their most important everyday decisions are made. The *focus* is children's personalities, their potential, their behaviour, their educational progress. The *aims* are diagnosis, making necessarily rapid decisions as a basis for further action. The *criteria* are personal, experiential, value-loaded, sometimes idiosyncratic, sometimes collectively evolved. The *methods* are watching, talking, listening, giving out and receiving non-verbal cues and signals, reflecting, hypothesising, discussing . . .

Evaluation in this sense is of fundamental importance in schools and classrooms because it is basic to human behaviour and interaction. It is a process of immense subtlety and, for the child or teacher being evaluated, of profound consequence. And it works no less effectively than tests and checklists in providing a reliable basis for diagnosis and action. Indeed, HMI argue in the 9–13 survey (DES 1983c, para.6.14) that such formal procedures tend to neglect this latter, diagnostic, dimension and concentrate overmuch on generalised and summative judgements of attainment.

Nor is it the case as we have seen that 'formal' procedures necessarily have a stronger claim to 'objectivity' than informal: formal procedures are more accessible to public scrutiny than informal and thus can more readily be checked for bias, but this does not of itself guarantee their objectivity.

The realistic approach in this matter would seem to be not to replace everyday informal evaluation but to refine it. It may or may not be always valid or reliable, but its ubiquity and dominance demand our attention.

School self-evaluation, then, would seem to require first that teachers and heads develop a proper self-consciousness about their everyday appraisals and judgements, then that they devise ways of refining them further, supplementing them where appropriate by more formalised procedures. The questions for schools are less 'How *shall* we evaluate?' than 'How *do* we evaluate?' and 'How valid and effective is our evaluation?'. The focus of such appraisal then becomes the school's central evaluations: the everyday, minute-to-minute ways in which teachers assess children's progress, define their needs, judge their potential, and decide what curriculum experiences to provide; the ways heads determine curriculum policies and priorities, and assess staff competence and progress. The dimensions of this appraisal can be those same decisions of which 'formal' evaluation is constituted — aims, focus, content, criteria, methods and so on.

The processes under scrutiny, in effect, are those we have examined in this book, though the word 'evaluation' was not necessarily used: the teacher's judgements about the nature and purposes of primary education (Chapter 1), about childhood and individual children (Chapters 2 and 4), about teaching strategies (Chapters 2 and 5), about appropriate curriculum experiences (Chapters 3 and 5); teachers' and heads' judgements about the whole curriculum (Chapters 3, 5 and 7), school staffs' individual or collective judgement about school policy and decision-making (Chapters 7 and 8). A large part of this book is essentially an examination of evaluations and evaluation capacities in primary education.

All this implies an important shift in consciousness. The evaluation movement has seemed to imply that hitherto teachers did not evaluate, or at least did so inadequately. The parallel with initial teacher education is not coincidental: there the assumption, we saw in Chapter 6, was that teachers operate without theory, without a valid view of children, curriculum teaching and learning. In teacher education a recipe theory has been imposed on students and teachers without regard to existing everyday theories and theorising processes. In evaluation a predetermined set of focuses, criteria and methods is imposed without regard for existing evaluative processes. Both tendencies are a consequence of factors we have touched on at various points in the book: the failure of the primary teaching profession to develop an adequately rational and generalisable language of discourse about its tasks and activities which could hold its own against that of academics, researchers and policy-makers; the acquiescence of the profession in the elevation of the one sort of language and the one sort of activity over their own; their acceptance of an over-simplified and scientistic view of knowledge which unduly favoured the claims to 'fact' and 'proof' of social scientists and evaluation technicists; the power differential in such matters between the class teacher on the one hand, and the academic researcher, LEA adviser or administrator on the other; the presumptuousness of some in the latter groups concerning the relative merits of their own and teachers' procedures; the exacerbation of these tendencies (a) by a dominant primary school culture which isolates and parochialises the class teacher and (b) by teachers' lack of influence, relative to other groups in the educational world, on the vehicles for generating and disseminating ideas — books, journals, conferences and professional networks.

The debate about school self-evaluation, like that about educational theory, has become skewed away from the teacher and from classroom actualities, not least because of teachers' failure to participate in it.

CONCLUSION: THE NEW MANAGERIALISM — A CAUTIONARY NOTE

There was a time when 'school management' referred exclusively to the peripheral activities of the group of people now termed 'governors', and 'administration' was something many heads resisted as a chore. This is not to say that primary schools were neither managed nor administered, but that 'running a school' tended to be conceived of without recourse to these words and the concepts they imply. Instead, the dominant elements were the head's charisma, his or her proven ability as a teacher, authority over teachers and pupils, and capacity to construct and enact a convincing 'philosophy'.

This chapter has been about change, and one of the many changes now confronting primary schools is the pressure to take internal management seriously, to redefine, explicitly and systematically, the tasks a school has to undertake and to devise ways of maximising the school's human and material resources in furtherance of those tasks. School management is now a growth industry — witness the current proliferation of books, journals, university, college, polytechnic, LEA and DES courses, training programmes for heads and deputies, management centres and headship centres. Other symptoms, closer perhaps to the class teacher, are the roles and technologies discussed in this chapter — reappraising the head's leadership role and redefining and enhancing posts of responsibility, systematising curriculum planning through schemes, guidelines and meetings, and developing evaluation and self-evaluation procedures both to meet accountability demands and to promote professional growth.

In many respects these developments are to be welcomed. In the first part of this chapter we considered the extent to which the established model of professional roles and relationships in the primary school can militate against the school's capacity to change or to respond to change, whether external or internal. We highlighted the deadening, parochialising effect of the traditional class teacher–head relationship, its tendency to de-skill and isolate one, over-inflate the other and protect both from proper and necessary appraisal. We examined the effectiveness and impact of different leadership styles and argued for those which combined positive initiative, guidance and support with a commitment to collegiality in decision-making and policy-formulation. We showed how class teacher initiative and a more productive (intellectual) autonomy can be fostered best in a climate of mutual accountability. We saw how the acknowledgement and development of the specialist strengths of individual teachers can have a powerful impact upon the culture and curriculum of the school as a whole. And, despite the criticism, we found the new emphasis on systematic curriculum planning and evaluation to be helpful, and a significant advance on the random, ad hoc arrangements such procedures seek to replace. These kinds of measures, therefore, seemed to have the potential at least to contribute to four much-needed changes: the enhancement of teachers' intellectual autonomy, the promotion of collective discourse about educational matters, the achievement in schools of a higher level of cultural and social awareness, and the generation of a coherent 'whole curriculum' as reality rather than mere rhetoric.

These are only *potential* consequences, however: change as fundamental as this requires more than procedural adjustment, and in any case we saw how some of the procedures appear to have limited chance of success even in their own terms. Specialist posts were little use without the necessary authority, time and resources. They necessitated considerable shifts in the attitudes of class teachers and heads. They needed to be evolved on the basis of comprehensive analysis of a school's educational and professional needs, and might require a concept of specialisation broader than the 'curriculum consultant' role advocated by HMI. Curriculum schemes and guidelines were worthless unless conceived as resources in a comprehensive strategy for curriculum development; in any event some were constructed on the basis of an alarming lack of self-consciousness of the models of human development and learning they exemplified. And similar reservations could be expressed about the dominant evaluation instrument, the checklist, with its spurious objectivity and its tendency to distort and over-simplify educational goals, learning processes and outcomes. We saw, too, how formalising evaluation in this way could militate against the more pressing need to analyse and refine those everyday informal judgemental processes on which class teachers' decisions about children more crucially depend.

Common to each of these strategies are three dangers. The first is *superficiality*. Documents and procedures do not of themselves produce curriculum change and evaluation. These are much deeper and more elusive processes depending on teachers' expanding knowledge of possibilities, their changing attitudes and their enhanced skills, on the professional culture of the school and on its capacity to promote such individual change. One can already detect an obvious cynicism in the primary sector in this regard: LEA curriculum policy documents produced to satisfy the requirements of DES Circular 6/81; school curriculum guidelines produced to keep the head and advisers quiet. Curriculum, as we have established and as the profession — as demonstrated by these responses — so clearly understands, is action and thought, not words on paper. Yet the production and discussion of documents and the completion of checklists, while they may help teachers penetrate to the deeper levels of educational discourse, can by virtue of the time and effort they consume counter-productively prevent that penetration.

The second danger is *mechanisation*: the reduction of pupils to objects with charac-teristics and functions which can be exhaustively listed in advance, of evaluation in the classroom to a merely technical matter of placing ticks or numbers in a box, of curriculum development to the 'implementation' of somebody's 'plan', of the teacher to an operative on the classroom production line. The emphasis in the mechanistic approach is on predictability and control: defining a precise path for the educational endeavour, anticipating all eventualities, specifying all outcomes, and ensuring that it is followed unswervingly.

There seems little doubt that checklists have become something of a management fad. Whitaker (1983) for example, in an otherwise useful discussion of primary headship, proposes checklists for virtually every aspect of management: curriculum planning, staff appointments, staff development, school self-evaluation, and pupil records. It has to be asked how far the checklist is appropriate to the particular conditions of educating children: education is value-laden, complex and debatable; children are only in certain respects predictable; teaching is idiosyncratic and uniquely compounded of the characteristics of teacher, taught and the situation within which they meet; some education outcomes are desired and worked towards but others are not known in advance not least because the educational claim to foster individuality and autonomy is in fact conditional upon allowing for and seeking the new and unpredictable response.

The third danger is *over-bureaucratisation*. Bureaucracy is, properly, a neutral word signifying a particular sort of institutional structure characterised by a clear demarca-tion of responsibilities, the obligation to abide by rules, the assumption that offices are filled by people having the most appropriate specialist or technical expertise, and the overriding assumption of consensus over institutional goals (Weber 1964). The last assumption has to be questioned in an educational institution, but otherwise the issue is not so much systematisation and specialisation as such, which we have seen is to some degree helpful in primary schools, but the undesirable consequences of these: a growing rigidity in the hierarchy of command, a concentration of power at the top, the fragmentation of the task (of educating) into segments which may lose their coher-ence, the formularising of discourse into 'procedures', whether documents or meet-ings, which eliminate tentativeness, the exposure of value-positions and indeed genu-ine dialogue. It might be argued that this is less of a danger for primary schools than for secondary schools and higher education institutions (where indeed these characteristics are increasingly dominant). Primary schools are small, their specialist functions are minimal, their traditional culture is informal and expressive. Nevertheless, some of the tendencies are already manifest.

Superficiality, mechanisation and bureaucratisation are dangers attendant upon a particular model of school management which is now strongly evident in the literature and the courses to which I referred earlier. It is, as Taylor (1977) points out, a 'mongrel' approach which combines ideas from a number of sources — classical management theory, systems analysis, industrial psychology and behavioural objectives-based curriculum planning, but nevertheless the dominant influence is industrial rather than educational in as far as 'management' as concept and practice originally evolved to meet the production requirements of industrial and commercial organisations and subsequent models have been developed from that base and translated into the educational context. In a fundamental sense, therefore, such a model is bound to be incongruent with the educational process. In Burns and Stalker's terms (1966) it is 'mechanistic' rather than 'organismic'. It is hierarchical, closed, consensus-oriented and premised on strict 'managerial' accountability as defined earlier. Information about performance is passed upwards, instructions and decisions are passed downwards. More critically still, it depends for success on stability, predictability and long-term planning. It is thus unsuited to the conditions, endemic to education, of change, unpredictability and the need constantly to adjust to new circumstances.

In contrast, 'organismic' management is adapted to unstable conditions; it demands role flexibility rather than excessive specialisation, shared rather than hierarchic control and decision-making; omni-directional rather than one-way communication; it necessitates each member having knowledge of the overall purpose and situation of the institution as a whole and of factors affecting its development; it emphasises loyalty to task rather than to superiors; and it is process rather than merely goal-oriented (Adelman and Alexander 1982).

It will be observed, therefore, to what extent a range of recent developments in primary education are consistent with, if not necessarily the product of, the mechanistic tradition: behaviourist views of children's development and learning with their distrust of introspection and neglect of mind as not being amenable to 'scientific' study and deduction; means-ends curriculum planning; the technology of guidelines and checklists; and the emergent process of management itself. In this respect the behaviourist emphasis of curriculum and evaluation and the new industrial management models are sides of the same coin.

Now it might be argued that these trends are so contrary to primary traditions that they will have little impact, or if so, will be assimilated and modified to re-emerge in a much diluted form. But this is to ignore the one factor which the new managerialism and the traditional approach to running primary schools have in common, namely the unquestioned power of the head. The established model, which we explored in detail in Chapter 7, is authoritarian and paternalist. The new models simply offer ways of maintaining the 'top-down' control more efficiently. Both models presume an 'employee' view of the class teacher. Non-specialisation in one is succeeded by heavily circumscribed and constrained specialisation in the other. The absence or arbitrariness of discussion in one is succeeded by tightly controlled and formulated debate in the other. The confrontation of value-issues is possible in neither.

If this seems a pessimistic characterisation, then we might reflect on the fact that such 'management' courses as are currently available are for heads (and occasionally deputy heads) only. Management then, is conceived of as something heads (or potential heads) do to other people. To manage a school is to define, determine and evaluate the lives of the children and teachers within it.

An alternative approach is possible. 'School management' is not a closed concept: it allows as strongly for the possibility that class teachers are also managers as that heads reserve this function to themselves. An 'organismic' concept of management would require a course in which all staff participated, for all would be seen as equally in need of developing managerial skills of some sort. Such a course might most appropriately be based on particular schools rather than in detached centres such as colleges, universities or management units. Instead of the head acquiring a generalised apparatus of management knowledge and skills which he takes back to the school and attempts to apply, strategies for management would be evolved to meet each schools' unique situation and needs. Instead of staff having to take at face value a set of assumptions about management, the exploration of which they were not party to, they would now participate in and have a chance to influence the conceptual framework for their subsequent practices. Instead of the concept of 'management' being treated as 'given', it would be treated as problematic and negotiable.

Emergent approaches to management training otherwise seem destined to emulate earlier traditions of initial and in-service training, of which, ironically, heads have often been the sternest critics: the reliance on all-purpose recipe knowledge, the physical separation of training from action, and the implied contempt for the everyday theorising of the class teacher.

However, this situational shift only partly meets the broader needs defined in these pages. Educational decisions, we have asserted, are ethical as much as technical, grounded in speculation as much as certainty, in values as much as facts, and depend on knowledge and qualities of judgement which few management courses can provide. It is perhaps the gravest weakness of the new managerialism that its instrumentality is so narrow: it concentrates on how schools can best be run but neglects the purposes they serve. It detaches the skill of managing from the act of educating. It emerges as hard to reconcile with the intellectual autonomy, individual theorising and collective deliberation which we saw as essential foundations for educational development. An educational manager, whether a head or class teacher, undoubtedly needs administrative skill; but he or she also needs these more fundamental attributes of intellect, imagination, understanding and judgement to provide the framework and justification. Without these, management in education is meaningless.

All these issues, and more besides, bear on what is likely to be a 1980s growth point in primary school management, the role of the curriculum consultant/postholder. It is clear from this book's analysis that the class teacher needs support in respect of curriculum and that the curriculum as a whole in many schools can benefit considerably from the application of specialist knowledge and enthusiasm. But it is also clear that the success of consultancy as an educational tool depends on how the role is conceived and implemented. The issue is not so much the practical and interpersonal difficulties highlighted in these last two chapters and in the Birmingham study — time, authority, credibility and so on (though clearly these need to be resolved) — but the ways of thinking about children, curriculum, teaching, planning, evaluation and management which underpin heads' and specialists' practices.

I see little sign as yet that consultancy/specialisation is predicated on assumptions other than those which I have criticised throughout this book, or indeed that there is much consciousness that such assumptions may be problematic. Thus, the DES has tended to offer a base-line of specialist curriculum knowledge as mainly mastery of subject matter. Many LEAs are busy promoting at an unseemly speed the conceptually dubious checklists, curriculum guidelines and management recipes we have discussed in this chapter. And the profession itself sometimes seems content to perpetuate an alliance of rigid developmentalism and narrowly pre-ordinate planning models which we have found to fall well short of the comprehensive concept of primary education which is needed. So, for example, 'Primary Practice', a widely circulated document with in some respects much to commend it, advocates yet again the tired and, I believe, discredited formula:

> a precise statement of aims and objectives, rooted firmly in what is known about children's growth and development. This must be our starting point.
>
> (Schools Council 1983, p.35)

Thus we have a network of assumptions about children and education, many of which are suspect, none of which, as we have seen in this book, has this sort of claim to be taken for granted, but which are nevertheless translated into professional dogma.

Specialisation, consultancy and the streamlining of headship may produce greater efficiency, but in respect of what? Ideas imposed more effectively on children and teachers than in the 1960s, but which remain, as ideas, as ill-conceived as ever?

Primary education certainly needs to review its professional procedures, but far more pressing is the need to review the ideas which such procedures seek to implement.

Postscript

The introduction invited those readers who wished to do so to treat each of the book's three parts as self-contained. But, even if read this way, and certainly if read, as intended, from cover to cover, it will have been evident that the book aimed not only to diagnose distinctive conditions in the worlds of classroom, school and training institution, but also to discover causal or contributory relationships between them.

Without offering a detailed resumé — which would be superfluous here since readers can refer to the summary with which each chapter ends — it is perhaps helpful to remind ourselves of the main features in terms of which the current character of primary education has been explored.

First, of course, there are the basic imperatives of 'whole child' and 'whole curriculum': a general education for children aged 5–11, representing the total spectrum of British multi-culture and almost the full range of abilities, attributes and potentialities; an education complete and comprehensible in its own terms, yet also a secure basis for subsequent educational experience.

Second, there is the class-teacher system which is used as the almost universal vehicle for this pattern of education.

Third, there are the professional knowledge and skills which, individually and collectively, primary class teachers need, possess or lack in relation to the considerable and comprehensive demands of their role.

Fourth, there are the confusions and contradictions in the rationale by which primary education is conducted; notably the persistence of the elementary tradition's values and practices and their juxtaposition with a child-centred doctrine by which they are supposedly repudiated.

Fifth, there is the accumulating evidence about the quality of primary practice: its strengths, anomalies and weaknesses; and its consistency or inconsistency with professional claims and rationale.

Sixth, there is the pervasiveness of an ideology which has to legitimise and sustain rationale and practice, notwithstanding their confusions and weaknesses, and indeed must offset the class teacher's consequent vulnerability to challenge on the grounds of expertise; as a result the expression of this ideology may be strident, crude and mindless.

Seventh, there is a system of teacher training which sometimes underestimates the demands of class teaching, fails to meet many of its most urgent needs, neglects the theorising capacities vital to educational development, and by so doing confirms and perpetuates the above tendencies.

Eighth, there is a culture and balance of power in the school which may tend to feed class-teacher insularity and cultural disengagement, discourage the growth of the professional towards intellectual autonomy, militate against an adequate response to change and generally provide little by way of individual or collective resources for breaking out of the established ways of thinking and acting.

Therefore, in as far as there are problems of primary practice, these require attention on not one front but many. Though teacher training, for example, seems to fail the class teacher in areas like curriculum, the reform of these aspects of training will not solve the problems. Nor, alone, will the introduction of curriculum consultancy, nor, alone, will any of the other strategies put forward in this book or implied by its analysis. But tackling initial training, *and* school organisation, *and* professional development will be productive.

This much is obvious, though the monocausal view is still widespread ('It's all the fault of teacher training/LEA advisers/the parents/society . . . '): that too is a consequence of class-teacher vulnerability. However, there is a much more general problem pertaining to all the contexts we have discussed: that of the language and conceptual frameworks available for evolving and communicating analysis and critique of current ideas and practices and for generating alternatives. Since language and conceptual framework are part symptom, part consequence and part cause of the conditions summarised above, they must be, as they stand, inadequate for the task which is indicated.

In Chapter 1 I suggested that the language of primary ideology, which frames or informs much of primary discourse generally, has become 'ritualised and sloganised beyond redemption'. Subsequently we considered the role of 'academic' and 'everyday' modes of analysis in initial training and I argued that there at least the former is pursued at the expense of the necessary development of the latter.

Hypothesised here, then, are three ways of externalising, exploring and communicating ideas about primary education: 'ideological', 'academic' and 'everyday'. The first two are less problematic than the third, since they are public and bound by discernible and consistent rules. Ideological language is a form of extreme conceptual restrictedness yet emotive power. Academic language has infinitely greater scope yet it too imposes restrictions deriving from the particular conceptual frameworks and methodological paradigms in which it is embedded. Everyday language, as the epithet indicates, is the basic means for ordinary human interaction. Since it is the raw material for philosophers, poets, novelists, linguisticians and others, it would be presumptuous in the present context to claim more than that it is ubiquitous, diverse and yet elusive.

My concern is not everyday language as such, but its use in the context of primary education. Both ideological and academic language provide forms of communication which can generate recognition and understanding across time and place. In contrast, everyday language, as used in primary education, is to a greater or lesser extent 'particularistic' (Bernstein 1971b): it evolves in and is therefore to some extent tied to unique school and classroom contexts. It is ideal for discussing what teachers call 'practicalities' — classroom events and circumstances, as and when they occur — about which, for as long as the exchanges are kept within the particular contexts which generate them, there is little ambiguity of meaning. Everyday language is as yet less adequate for two purposes which, as we have seen in these pages, are vitally needed for longer-term educational progress. One is ready communication across or apart from particular school contexts — a 'community of discourse' in which all concerned with primary education can participate. The other is the treatment of ideas at the level of abstraction and generality that freeing language from particular contexts requires, and especially those ideas concerning fundamental questions like what it means to be educated which introduce conceptual complexity and value-divergence. The deficiency in everyday language is not inherent. On the contrary, it is a tool of great subtlety both for the expression of ideas and the conduct of practice. The problem is that as yet it has been used mainly for the latter, with the consequence that there is a vacuum which is too frequently filled by the use of the most readily available alternative — ideological language — which is 'universalistic' in that as a form of communication it is not context-bound, but is in fact wholly incapable of handling the ideas and arguments which are needed before anything approaching universal principles can be hammered out.

This leaves academic language. It thrives on abstraction, on the generation and exploration of ideas which can exist independently of particular physical circumstances. Yet academic language is traditionally resisted in the profession.

Some of the causes of this resistance were discussed in Part 2, and undoubtedly it is the case that the way it is promoted can be highly alienating to students and teachers. Not only are its basic credentials regarded as suspect because it is used and advocated mainly by people who do not work in schools and do not have to cope with the everyday challenges of teaching children, but it has often been presented, in an arrogantly monopolistic manner, as the only valid or respectable means for talking and thinking about education: the rest, it is implied or even asserted, is mere intuition, reflex, or common sense, which neither wants nor is able to accommodate hard thinking, value complexity, ideas and generalities.

Unfortunately, the charge, if not the conclusion, is sometimes justified: where everyday language degenerates into personalised anecdote it is the antithesis of universalistic. But teacher educators may have made the mistake of characterising all everyday language as, *ipso facto*, anecdotal and all academic language as rational, qualified, subtle and sophisticated. Neither generalisation is sustainable.

More damning is the frequent hypocrisy of the academics' position. For in circumstances in higher education equivalent to those in which they argue that primary teachers should 'apply' academic perspectives and constructs — curriculum planning, the diagnosis of student needs, the evaluation of performance — language, thought and behaviour can be at least as irrational, emotive, stereotypical, ad hoc and above all atheoretical as those same academics disparagingly characterise it in schools. In these circumstances, teachers' rejection of both the language and concerns of academic inquiry as 'airy-fairy', 'irrelevant', 'mere theory' or whatever becomes understandable if not justifiable.

With everyday language restricted by the culture of primary education to the particular and concrete, academic language resisted or otherwise not incorporated, ideological language by its nature antithetical to considered analysis and discussion, the following scenario is all too familiar at professional gatherings, whether in school, at teachers' centres, on courses or elsewhere. All goes well for as long as discussion centres on tangible immediacies — resources, timetable arrangements, particular children and so on. But once it enters issues which necessitate some degree of abstraction and conceptual open-endedness (such as is the essence of any serious consideration of matters like aims for primary education, the nature of a whole curriculum, or principles for pedagogy or evaluation), language and ideas veer off sharply in one of a number of directions: into the cosy populist platitudes of ideology; into ever-ready personal anecdotes which all can savour; into argument-stopping appeals to 'authorities', whether bureaucratic/managerial ('the office'/'the adviser') or debased academic ('research has proved . . .', 'we must state our objectives first . . .', 'seven year olds aren't capable of that . . .'); into 'hard reality' ('the parents round here expect . . .', 'society demands . . .'); or into appeals to precedent and experience ('we've always done this and it's worked perfectly well so why should we change . . .', 'we've never done this before so it won't work and we won't change . . .'). Sometimes responses such as these may be not without validity, but assertion may be taken as proof, with no opportunity provided actually to test the assertion. Thus, whatever the potential strength of a response, each of these divergences is a U-turn back to where discussion started, or rather – since discussion can proceed in this way for a long time or on numerous consecutive occasions – a perpetual circumnavigation.

The point in a discussion where this happens, where the conceptual obstacle is encountered, briefly or barely surveyed, and smartly avoided, is palpable. In some it produces the illusion that progress has been made, in some an uneasy feeling that progress may have been more apparent than real, and in others having more perspicacity and commitment to intellectual effort a profound frustration.

It is stressed that the argument is not that everyday language is inherently inadequate for the task but that the history and circumstances of primary education have inhibited its development. It must also be noted that the argument that academic language can fill the vacuum is unproven for it too is restricted, by the conceptual syntax and history of the parent disciplines: that this is the case in the disciplines of educational studies, especially psychology, we saw in Chapters 2 and 4. Moreover, there must remain an uncertainty as to whether a language as formalised as this can ever truly convey the subtlety and nuance of behaviour, relationships, intentions and responses which contribute to life in primary schools: for it is a language which resists ambiguity and doubt, imposes order on what may well be unorderable, offers explanations for what may well be inexplicable, and despises or suspects, as threats to rationality, the affectivity and emotional engagement which are so powerful a part of the teaching and learning processes.

One of the consequences of this state of affairs — as this book has shown — is that ideas and practice, being trapped within inadequate linguistic and conceptual parameters, fail to progress. Another is that while the practice of individual teachers does progress the profession as a whole is unable to benefit because neither practice nor its underlying rationale can be adequately articulated. Hence that common but frustrating paradox of primary education, impressive classroom practice, demonstrating acute sensitivity to individual children's needs, explained in banal language which submerges this individuality under layers of ideologically loaded generalisations. For teachers of such talent and skill the words and structures whereby what is going on in their classrooms can be conveyed and explained seem not to be available, and in the discussion scenario above these teachers may be as frustrated in their own use of ideological language or anecdote as are the more articulate colleagues or observers who listen to it.

The unlocking of a language and conceptual framework is as important for the exploration of practice as ideas, for it is only through articulating *why* particular practice is good or bad that we can construct principles whereby practice generally can be improved.

It is in everybody's interests, therefore, jointly to seek to evolve a truly universalistic language for primary education. This must accommodate both abstraction and 'hard reality'. It must be able to be used in schools, training institutions and elsewhere. It must be capable of encompassing both particulars and universals. It must clarify obscurity and reduce ambiguity yet also tolerate the uncertainty and value-divergence which must always remain in educational discourse. It must achieve a greater degree of rationality but without the aridity, over-categorising and self-indulgent verbal acrobatics which sometimes characterises academic exchange. It must accept the power of affectivity in the teacher–pupil relationship.

Needless to say, I regard the systemic language of the new managerialism as no more adequate for these purposes than the atavism of ideological language: one imposes on human behaviour categories and structures of excessive and indefensible simplicity; the other is a hollow shell devoid of its vital core of argument and thought. There must be a middle ground, and it seems obvious that the growth point is not academic language (as teacher educators tend to assume) but everyday: for this is the language of that classroom thought which is so central a determinant of classroom action. But neither must academic language be rejected (as it so often is by teachers). What must be discarded is the language of ideology. Freed of this straitjacket but enriched by the critical sensitisation and access to the minds and actions of others which academic study at best provides, everyday language can provide the basis for both public and private theorising.

Reform of the language of primary education is inseparable from revision of its conceptual frameworks. Here again the ideological contamination is marked, as we saw in Part 1, and leads to the endemic mismatch between claims and practices. Thus: the 'whole child' but the horizontal and vertical fragmentation of the developmental matrix; the 'unified curriculum' but the schism of curriculum I and II; the rejection of subjects but the dominance of subject structures in the curriculum areas held to be most important, and the transparent re-labelling of subjects as 'areas of development'; the empiricist, 'discovery learning' claims, but the manifest *a priorism*; 'catering for each child's individual needs', but the reality of labelling, under-expectation and under-achievement. This means that revising the conceptual framework is only partly a matter of extending its focus into areas hitherto unexplored: equally important is the elimination of ideologically-governed censorship which prevents such areas from becoming legitimate objects of concern.

The main headings in a reasonably comprehensive framework or theory might be: (a) the child, (b) the curriculum, (c) the teacher and pedagogy, (d) the relationship between education, culture and social change, (e) the management and organisation of the school, (f) initial training and continuing professional development. Each of these headings subsumes diverse subsidiary themes which cannot be identified in detail here, but the principle of extending scope should apply within each heading as well as to the framework as a whole. Thus, curriculum discourse should include not merely content but the various dimensions discussed in Chapters 3 and 5 — values, epistemology, culture, psychology, pedagogy, planning and evaluation — and probably others. The child needs to be conceived of in terms more comprehensive than 'development'. Pedagogy is more than observable 'teaching method' or 'teaching style': the teacher's assumptions, expectations and intentions are equally significant. Evaluation is more relevantly about minute-to-minute classroom appraisals and the events and ideas which shape them than about tests and checklists. School management is about identifying and pursuing educational goals, maximising teacher motivation and expertise, as well as operational efficiency. And engaging with culture and social change involves societal analysis more comprehensive than either 'society expects . . .' or the purely ethnic preoccupations too often implied by 'multicultural', together with a fundamental commitment (which may prove difficult for some) to abandon the introverted, cocoon model of child-centredness for a stance which is more forward and outward looking but no less child-centred.

The goal is the liberation of primary discourse: from ideology and the sloganising of ideological language; from educational fashion; from both undue deference and unjustified cynicism towards educational research; from the head's keepership of those areas of values and policy which should concern all teachers; from the parochialising effect of working and thinking in terms of the immediate school context only; and from anti-intellectualism. The outcome, as we saw earlier, is an intellectual autonomy commensurate with the considerable executive freedom and responsibility of primary teachers.

The mechanism for achieving these goals is partly a matter of individual and collective will and effort, partly a matter of procedures. Initial training can make a major contribution by abandoning the narrower academic monopolies that we considered in Part 2 and encouraging analytical eclecticism, with students encouraged to draw on research, speculative theory and the ideas and practices of teachers and each other; they need to be engaged at first hand in argument and problem-solving rather than always handed ready-made conclusions and solutions. Schools can make comparable changes. Action research offers a potent methodology for both professional and curriculum development. The cosy, privatised equilibrium of 'my class' and 'my school' needs to be replaced by honest and perhaps uncomfortable collective analysis of shared issues and problems, by more delegation from the head and greater acceptance of school-wide responsibilities by individual teachers. None of the procedures available for encouraging change, as we saw in Part 3, is without its problems. But procedures have the virtue of being tangible while 'a climate of professional discourse', though we may recognise its presence or absence, is not; procedures can be tried, monitored, modified or abandoned. They are a sensible starting-point.

The transition in some schools and training institutions has begun. In others it will be less easy, and throughout there is the meta-problem that it is only by using *existing* language, constructs and human capacities that we can create the needed alternatives. Avoiding circularity, therefore, is not easy, and educational history is littered with 'innovations' which are nothing of the sort. But history suggests, equally, that abundant knowledge, a free-wheeling imagination, hard intellectual effort, moral commitment and a liberal dash of realism are the prerequisites for such progress as has been achieved. It is time these were more highly valued: without them, schools cannot hope to make a valid and constructive educational response to the perplexing, unjust and dangerous world in which our children are growing up.

References

Adelman, C. and Alexander, R.J. (1982) *The Self-Evaluating Institution*. London: Methuen.

Advisory Committee on the Supply and Education of Teachers (1983) *Criteria for the Approval of Initial Teacher Training Courses: Advice to the Secretaries of State*. London: DES.

Alexander, R.J. (1979) The problematic nature of professional studies. In Alexander, R.J. and Wormald, E. (ed.) *Professional Studies for Teaching*, pp. 2–14. Guildford: SRHE.

Alexander, R.J. (1980a) Towards a conceptual framework for school-focussed INSET, *British Journal of Inservice Education*, **6**, 3.

Alexander, R.J. (1980b) The evaluation of advanced inservice courses for teachers: the challenge to providers, *British Journal of Teacher Education*, **6**, 3.

Alexander, R.J. (1983) Training for primary class teaching: an agenda for progress, *Primary Education Review*, **16**.

Alexander, R.J. (1984) Innovation and continuity in the initial teacher education curriculum. In Alexander, R.J., Craft, M., and Lynch, J. (ed.) *Change in Teacher Education: Context and Provision Since Robbins*. pp. 103–160. Eastbourne: Holt, Rinehart and Winston.

Alexander, R.J., Craft, M., Lynch, J. (ed.) (1984) *Change in Teacher Education: Context and Provision Since Robbins*. Eastbourne: Holt, Rinehart and Winston.

Alexander, R.J. and Whittaker, J. (ed.) (1980) *Developments in PGCE Courses*. Guildford: SRHE.

Alexander, R.J. and Wormald, E. (ed.) (1979) *Professional Studies for Teaching*. Guildford: SRHE.

Ashton, P.M.E. (1981) Primary teachers' aims, 1969–77. In Simon, B. and Willcocks, J. (ed.) *Research and Practice in the Primary Classroom*. London: Routledge & Kegan Paul.

Ashton, P.M.E., Henderson, E.S., Merritt, J.E. and Mortimer, D.J. (1982) *Teacher Education in the Classroom: Initial and Inservice*. London: Croom Helm.

Ashton, P.M.E., Kneen, P. and Davies, F. (1975) *Aims into Practice in the Primary School*. London: University of London Press.

Ashton, P.M.E., Kneen, P., Davies, F. and Holley, B.J. (1975) *The Aims of Primary Education: A Study of Teachers' Opinions*. London: Macmillan.

Assessment of Performance Unit (1981) *Personal and Social Development*. London: DES.

Assessment of Performance Unit (1983) *Aesthetic Development*. London: DES.

Avon, County of, *Progress Record Card: Literacy*. County of Avon Education Department.

Bailey, C. (1980) The autonomous teacher. In Sockett, H. (ed.) *Accountability in the English Educational System*, pp. 98–111. London: Hodder and Stoughton.

Bailey, F.G. (1983) *The Tactical Uses of Passion: an Essay on Power, Reason and Reality*. Ithaca, NY: Cornell University Press.

Bantock, G.H. (1969) Conflicts of values in teacher education. In Taylor, W. (ed.) *Towards a Policy for the Education of Teachers*, pp. 122–134. London: Butterworth.

Barth, R.S. (1975) Open education: assumptions about children, learning and knowledge. In Golby, M., Greenwald, J. and West, R. (ed.) *Curriculum Design*, pp. 58–81. London: Croom Helm.

Bassey, M. (1978) *Nine Hundred Primary School Teachers*. Slough: NFER.

Becher, T., Eraut, M.R. and Knight, J. (1981) *Policies for Educational Accountability*. London: Heineman.

Bennett, N. (1976) *Teaching Styles and Pupil Progress*. London: Open Books.

Berlak, A.C., Berlak, H., Bagenstos, N.T. and Mikel, E.R. (1976) Teaching and learning in English primary schools. In Hammersley, M. and Woods, P. (ed.) *The Process of Schooling*, pp. 86–97. London: Routledge & Kegan Paul.

Bernbaum, G. (1977) The role of the head. In Peters, R.S. (ed.) *The Role of the Head*, pp. 9–36. London: Routledge & Kegan Paul.

Bernstein, B. (1971a) On the classification and framing of educational knowledge. In Young, M.F.D. (ed.) *Knowledge and Control*, pp. 47–69. West Drayton: Collier Macmillan.

Bernstein, B. (1971b) *Class, Codes and Control*. London: Routledge & Kegan Paul.

Blackie, J. (1967) *Inside the Primary School*. London: HMSO.

Blenkin, G.M. and Kelly, A.V. (1981) *The Primary Curriculum*. London: Harper and Row.

Blenkin, G.M. and Kelly, A.V. (ed.) (1983) *The Primary Curriculum in Action: a Process Approach to Educational Practice*. London: Harper and Row.

Blishen, E. (1969) *The School That I'd Like*. Harmondsworth: Penguin.

Blumer, H. (1969) *Symbolic Interactionism*. Hemel Hempstead: Prentice-Hall.

Blyth, J. (1979) Teaching young children about the past, *Education 3–13*, **5**, 1.

Blyth, W.A.L. (1965) *English Primary Education*. London: Routledge & Kegan Paul.

Blyth, W.A.L., Cooper, K.R., Derricott, R., Elliott, G., Sumner, H. and Waplington, A. (1976) *Place, Time and Society 8–13: Curriculum Planning in History, Geography and Social Science*. Glasgow and Bristol: Collins/ESL Bristol.

Board of Education (1931) *Report of the Consultative Committee on the Primary School* (Hadow Report). London: HMSO.

Board of Education (1944) *Teachers and Youth Leaders* (McNair Report). London: HMSO.

Boyson, R. (1982) Quoted in *Radio Times*, 21 September.

Brandis, W. and Bernstein, B. (1974) *Selection and Control: Teachers' Ratings of Children in the Infant School*. London: Routledge & Kegan Paul.

Bristol, University of (1983) *Guidelines for Review and Institutional Development in Schools (GRIDS): Handbook for Primary Schools* (Draft). School of Education, University of Bristol (mimeo).

Brown, G. and Desforges, C. (1979) *Piaget's Theory: a Psychological Critique*. London: Routledge & Kegan Paul.

Browne, J.D. (1971) The curriculum. In Hewitt, S. (ed.) *The Training of Teachers: a Factual Survey*, pp. 81–92. London: University of London Press.

Bruner, J.S. (1963) *The Process of Education*. New York: Random House.

Bruner, J.S. (1966) *Toward a Theory of Instruction*. Cambridge, Massachusetts: Harvard University Press.

Burns, T. and Stalker, G.M. (1966) *The Management of Innovation*. London: Tavistock.

Burstall, C. (1970) French in the primary school: some early findings, *Journal of Curriculum Studies*, **2**.

Central Advisory Council for Education (England) (1967) *Children and their Primary Schools* (Plowden Report), London: HMSO.

Chambers, P. (1971) The study of education in colleges: harking back. In Tibble, J.W. (ed.) *The Future of Teacher Education*, pp. 68–80. London: Routledge & Kegan Paul.

Chambers, P. (1979) The scope and direction of professional studies since James. In Alexander, R.J. and Wormwald E. (ed.) *Professional Studies for Teaching*, pp. 30–45. Guildford: SRHE.

Chambers, P. (ed.) (1982) *Making INSET Work: Myth or Reality?* Bradford: CUEDIN.

Child, D. (1981) *Psychology and the Teacher*. Eastbourne: Holt, Rinehart and Winston.

Child, D. (1983) *Psychology in the Service of Education: a Review*. Inaugural lecture, University of Leeds (mimeo).

Clift, P.S., Weiner, G.G. and Wilson. E.L. (1981) *Record-Keeping in Primary Schools*. London: Macmillan.

Coulson, A.A. (1977) The role of the primary head. In Peters, R.S. (ed.) *The Role of the Head*, pp. 92–108. London: Routledge & Kegan Paul.

Council for National Academic Awards (1982) *Content of Initial Training Courses for Teachers*. London: CNAA (mimeo).

Council for National Academic Awards (1983a) *Teaching in Schools: the Content of Initial Training. Council's Response to the HMI Discussion Paper*. London: CNAA (mimeo).

Council for National Academic Awards (1983b) *Initial BEd. Courses for the Early and Middle Years*: a Discussion Document. London: CNAA.

Cox, C.B. and Dyson, A.C. (ed.) (1971) *The Black Papers on Education*. London: Davis-Poynter.

Craft, M. (ed.) (1981) *Teaching in a Multi-Cultural Society: the Task for Teacher Education*. Brighton: Falmer Press.

Curriculum Development Centre (1980) *Core Curriculum for Australian Schools*. Canberra: CDC.

Dale, R., Esland, G. and MacDonald, M. (1976) *Schooling and Capitalism*. London: Routledge & Kegan Paul.

Dearden, R.F. (1968) *The Philosophy of Primary Education*. London: Routledge & Kegan Paul.

Dearden, R.F. (1976) *Problems in Primary Education*. London: Routledge & Kegan Paul.

Dearden, R.F., Hirst, P. and Peters, R.S. (ed.) (1972) *Education and the Development of Reason*. London: Routledge & Kegan Paul.

Delamont, S. (1976) *Interaction in the Classroom*. London: Methuen.

Department of Education and Science (1963) *Higher Education* (Robbins Report). London: HMSO.

Department of Education and Science (1972) *Teacher Education and Training* (James Report). London: HMSO.

Department of Education and Science (1975) *A Language for Life* (Bullock Report). London: HMSO.

Department of Education and Science (1977) *A New Partnership for our Schools* (Taylor Report). London: HMSO.

Department of Education and Science (1978a) *Primary Education in England: a Survey by HM Inspectors of Schools*. London: HMSO.

Department of Education and Science (1978b) *Statistics of Education, 4*. London: HMSO.

Department of Education and Science (1978c) Press notice, 26 September 1978. London: DES (mimeo).

Department of Education and Science (1979a) *Aspects of Secondary Education in England: a Survey by HM Inspectors of Schools*. London: HMSO.

Department of Education and Science (1979b) *Developments in the BEd. Degree Course: a Study Based on Fifteen Institutions*. London: HMSO.

Department of Education and Science (1980) *PGCE in the Public Sector: an HMI Discussion Paper*. London: HMSO.

Department of Education and Science (1981a) *The School Curriculum*. London: HMSO.

Department of Education and Science (1981b) *Teacher Training and the Secondary School: an HMI Discussion Paper*. London: HMSO.

Department of Education and Science

(1982a) *Education 5–9: an Illustrative Survey of 80 First Schools in England.* London: HMSO.

Department of Education and Science (1982b) *Mathematics Counts* (Cockcroft Report). London: HMSO.

Department of Education and Science (1982c) *The New Teacher in School: a Report by HM Inspectors.* London: HMSO.

Department of Education and Science (1982d) *Statistics of Education 1981.* London: HMSO.

Department of Education and Science (1983a) *Teaching in Schools: the Content of Initial Training.* London: HMSO.

Department of Education and Science (1983b) *Teaching Quality* (White Paper). London: HMSO.

Department of Education and Science (1983c) *9–13 Middle Schools: An Illustrative Survey.* London: HMSO.

Department of Education and Science (1983d) *Initial Teacher Training: Approval of Courses.* London DES (mimeo).

Desforges, C. and McNamara, D.R. (1979) Theory and practice: methodological procedures for the objectification of craft knowledge, *British Journal of Teacher Education*, **5**, 2.

Donaldson, M. (1978) *Children's Minds.* London: Fontana.

Dunlop, F. (1977) What sort of theory should we have?, *Journal of Further and Higher Education*, **1**, 1.

Eason, T.D. (1971) Main subject courses. In Tibble, J.W. (ed.) *The Future of Teacher Education*, pp. 81–93. London: Routledge & Kegan Paul.

East Sussex Accountability Project (1979) *Accountability in the Middle Years of Schooling: an Analysis of Policy Options.* Brighton: University of Sussex.

Eggleston, J.F. (1981) *The personal and professional education of primary school teachers*, CNAA conference paper. London: CNAA (mimeo).

Eggleston, S.J. (1977) *The Sociology of the School Curriculum.* London: Routledge & Kegan Paul.

Eisner, E.W. (1976) *The Arts, Human Development and Education.* Berkeley: McCutchan.

Eisner, E.W. and Vallance E. (ed.) (1974) *Competing Conceptions of the Curriculum.* Berkeley: McCutchan.

Elliott, G. (1980) *Self-Evaluation and the Teacher: an Annotated Bibliography and Report on Current Practice.* London: Schools Council.

Elliott, J. (1978) Classroom accountability and the self-monitoring teacher. In Harlen, W. (ed.) *Evaluation and the Teacher's Role*, pp. 47–90. London: Macmillan.

Elliott, J. (1980) Implications of classroom research for professional development. In Hoyle, E. and Megarry, J. (ed.) *Professional Development of Teachers: World Yearbook of Education*, pp. 308–324. London: Kogan Page.

Elliott, J. and Adelman, C. (1976) *Innovation at the Classroom Level Course E203, Unit 28.* Milton Keynes: Open University Press.

Ennever, L. and Harlen, W. (1975) *With Objectives in Mind* (Science 5–13 Teacher's Handbook). London: Macdonald.

Entwistle, H. (1970) *Child-Centred Education.* London: Methuen.

Etzioni, A. (1964) *Modern Organizations.* Hemel Hempstead: Prentice-Hall.

Fontana, D. (1977) Educational psychology: present and future, *Journal of Further and Higher Education*, **1**, 2.

Fontana, D. (1981) *Psychology for Teachers.* London: Macmillan.

Foss, K. (1975) *The Status of Professional Studies in Teacher Education.* Occasional Paper 4, Education Area. Brighton: University of Sussex.

Galton, M., Simon, B. (ed) (1980) *Progress and Performance in the Primary Classroom.* London: Routledge & Kegan Paul.

Galton, M., Simon, B. and Croll, P. (1980) *Inside the Primary Classroom.* London: Routledge & Kegan Paul.

Galton, M. and Willcocks, J. (ed.) (1983) *Moving from the Primary Classroom.* London: Routledge & Kegan Paul.

Glaser, B.G. and Strauss, A. (1967) *The Discovery of Grounded Theory.* London: Weidenfeld and Nicholson.

Goldman, R.J. (1965) *Readiness for Religion: a Basis for Developmental Religious Education.* London: Routledge & Kegan Paul.

Goodacre, E.J. (1968) *Teachers and their Pupils' Home Background.* Slough: NFER.

Goodson, I. (1982) *School Subjects and Curriculum Change*. London: Croom Helm.

Gray, J. and Satterly, D. (1981) Formal or informal? A reassessment of the British evidence, *British Journal of Educational Psychology*, **51**.

Griffiths, R. (1945) *Study of Imagination in Early Childhood*. London: Kegan Paul, Trench, Trubner.

Gulbenkian Foundation (1982) *The Arts in Schools: Principles, Practice and Provision*. London: Gulbenkian Foundation

Hamlyn, D.W. (1970) The logical and psychological aspects of learning. In Peters, R.S. (ed.) *The Concept of Education*, pp.24–43. London: Routledge & Kegan Paul.

Hargreaves, D.H. (1967) *Social Relations in a Secondary School*. London: Routledge & Kegan Paul.

Hargreaves, D.H. (1972) *Interpersonal Relations and Education*. London: Routledge & Kegan Paul.

Harlen, W., Darwin, A. and Murphy, M. (1977) *Match and Mismatch: Raising Questions*. Edinburgh: Oliver and Boyd.

Harris, M. (1972) *Environmental Studies: a Teacher's Guide*. London: Hart-Davis.

Hebb, D.O. (1977) What psychology is about. In Child, D. (ed.) *Readings in Psychology for the Teacher*, pp.30–36. Eastbourne: Holt, Rinehart and Winston.

Hirst, P.H. (1965) Liberal education and the nature of knowledge. In Archambault, R.D. (ed.) *Philosophical Analysis and Education*, pp. 113–138. London: Routledge & Kegan Paul.

Hirst, P.H. (1974) *Knowledge and the Curriculum*. London: Routledge & Kegan Paul.

Hirst, P.H. (1979) Professional studies in initial teacher education: some conceptual issues. In Alexander, R.J. and Wormald, E. (ed.) *Professional Studies for Teaching*, pp. 15–29. Guildford: SRHE.

Hirst, P.H. and Peters, R.S. (1970) *The Logic of Education*. London: Routledge & Kegan Paul.

Hoyle, E. (1975) The creativity of the school in Britain. In Harris, A., Lawn, M. and Prescott, W. (ed.) *Curriculum Innovation*, pp. 329–346. London: Croom Helm.

Inner London Education Authority (1977) *Keeping the School under Review*. London: ILEA.

Inner London Education Authority (1979) *Primary Yearly Record Summary, Age 6–11*. London: ILEA.

Jackson, P.W. (1968) *Life in Classrooms*. New York: Holt, Rinehart and Winston.

Jonathan, R. (1981) Empirical research and educational theory. In Simon B. and Willcocks, J. (ed.) *Research and Practice in the Primary Classroom*, pp. 161–175. London: Routledge & Kegan Paul.

Jones, R. (1980) *Primary School Management*. Newton Abbott: David and Charles.

Joyce, B. and Weil, M. (1980) *Models of Teaching*. Hemel Hempstead: Prentice-Hall.

Keddie, N. (1971) Classroom knowledge. In Young, M.F.D. (ed.) *Knowledge and Control*, pp. 133–160. West Drayton: Collier Macmillan.

Keiner, J. (1981) *Cross-curricular concerns for primary BEd. degrees: beyond the 'bolt-on' approach*. CNAA conference paper. London: CNAA (mimeo).

Kellmer-Pringle, M. (1980) *The Needs of Children*. London: Hutchinson.

Kellogg, R. (1969) *Analysing Children's Art*. Palo Alto, California: National Press Books.

Kerr, J.F. (ed.) (1968) *Changing the Curriculum*. London: University of London Press.

King, R. (1978) *All Things Bright and Beautiful? A Sociological Study of Infants' Classrooms*. Chichester: Wiley.

Kirby, N. (1981) *Personal Values in Education*. London: Harper and Row.

Lawton, D. (1983) *Curriculum Studies and Educational Planning*. London: Hodder & Stoughton.

Lortie, D.C. (1969) The balance of control and autonomy in elementary school teaching. In Etzioni, A. (ed.) *The Semi-Professions and their Organization*. New York: Free Press.

Lortie, D.C. (1975) *School Teacher: a Sociological Study*. Chicago: University of Chicago Press.

Lowenfeld, V. and Brittain, W.I. (1982) *Creative and Mental Growth*. New York: Macmillan.

Lynch, J. (ed.) (1981) *Teaching in the Multicultural School*. London: Ward Lock.

McCulloch, M. (1979) *School Experience in Initial BEd./BEd. Honours Degrees*

Validated by the Council for National Academic Awards. London: CNAA.

McDowell, D. (1971) The values of teacher education. In Burgess, T. (ed.) *Dear Lord James: a Critique of Teacher Education*, pp. 61–77. Harmondsworth: Penguin.

McIntyre, D. (1980) The contribution of research to quality in teacher education. In Hoyle, E. and Megarry, J. (ed.) *Professional Development of Teachers: World Yearbook of Education*, pp. 293–307. London: Kogan Page.

McNamara, D.R. (1976) On returning to the chalk-face, *British Journal of Teacher Education*, **2**, 2.

McNamara, D.R. and Desforges, C. (1978) The social sciences, teacher education and the objectification of craft knowledge, *British Journal of Teacher Education*, **4**, 1.

McNamara, D.R. and Ross, A.M. (1982) *The BEd. Degree and its Future*. Lancaster: University of Lancaster.

Marsh, L.G. (1973) *Being a Teacher*. London: A. & C. Black.

Marshall, S. (1963) *An Experiment in Education*. Cambridge: Cambridge University Press.

Marshall, S. (1978) Language — Arts?, *Education 3–13*, **4**, 1.

Ministry of Education (1959) *Primary Education: Suggestions for the Consideration of Teachers and Others Concerned with the Work of Primary Schools*. London: HMSO.

Modgil, S. and Modgil, C. (1982) *Jean Piaget: Consensus and Controversy*. Eastbourne: Holt, Rinehart and Winston.

Morrison, A. and McIntyre, D. (1973) *Teachers and Teaching*. Harmondsworth: Penguin.

Musgrove, F. (1971) *Patterns of Power and Authority in English Education*. London: Methuen.

Naish, M. and Hartnett, A. (1975) What theory cannot do for teachers, *Education for Teaching*. **96**.

Nash, R. (1973) *Classrooms Observed*. London: Routledge & Kegan Paul.

Nash, R. (1976) *Teacher Expectations and Pupil Learning*. London: Routledge & Kegan Paul.

National Union of Teachers (1979) *Primary Questions: the NUT Response to the Primary Survey*. London: NUT.

Nias, J. (1980) Leadership styles and job-satisfaction in primary schools. In Bush, T, Glatter, R., Goodey, J. and Riches C. (ed.) *Approaches to School Management*, pp. 255–273. London: Harper and Row.

Nisbet, R.A. (1967) *The Sociological Tradition*. London: Heinemann.

Nixon, J. (ed.) (1981) *A Teacher's Guide to Action Research*. London: Grant McIntyre.

Nuffield Mathematics Project (1975) *I Do and I Understand*. Edinburgh: Chambers.

Ogilvie, E. (1973) *Gifted Children in Primary Schools*. London: Macmillan.

Oliver, D. (1975) Skill-centred teaching: an alternative to integration, *Education 3–13*, **3**, 1.

Open University/Schools Council (1980) *Curriculum in Action: an Approach to Evaluation*. Milton Keynes: Open University Press.

Paisey, A. (1981) *Organization and Management in Schools*. Harlow: Longman.

Parlett, M. and Hamilton, D. (1976) Evaluation as illumination. In Tawney, D. (ed.) *Curriculum Evaluation Today: Trends and Implications*, pp. 84–101. London: Macmillan.

Patrick, H., Bernbaum, G. and Reid, K. (1981) *The way we were: the staff of university departments of education*, UCET conference paper. London: UCET (mimeo).

Peatling, J.H. (1982) On beyond Goldman: religious thinking and the 1970s. In Hull, J. (ed.) *New Directions in Religious Education*, pp. 5–22. Brighton: Falmer Press.

Pluckrose, H. (1975) *Open School, Open Society*. London: Evans.

Pluckrose, H. (1979) *Children in their Primary Schools*. Harmondsworth: Penguin.

Primary Schools Research and Development Group (1983) *Curriculum Responsibility and the Use of Teacher Expertise in the Primary School*. Birmingham: University of Birmingham School of Education.

Pring, R.A. (1976) *Knowledge and Schooling*. London: Open Books.

Reid, K., Bernbaum, G. and Patrick, H. (1981) *On course: students and the PGCE*, UCET conference paper. London: UCET (mimeo).

Reid, W.A. (1978) *Thinking about the Curriculum: the Nature and Treatment of*

Curriculum Problems. London: Routledge & Kegan Paul.

Renshaw, P. (1971) The objectives and structure of the college curriculum. In Tibble, J.W. (ed.) *The Future of Teacher Education*, pp. 53–67. London: Routledge & Kegan Paul.

Renshaw, P. (1974) Education and the primary school: a contradiction?, *Education for Teaching*, **93**.

Richards, C. (1982) Curriculum consistency. In Richards, C. (ed.) *New Directions in Primary Education*, pp. 47–62. Brighton: Falmer Press.

Rochdale, Metropolitan Borough of (1978) *Record-Keeping in Primary Schools*. Rochdale Borough Education Department.

Ross, A.M. (1973) The development of teacher education in colleges of education. In Lomax, D. (ed.) *The Education of Teachers in Britain*, pp. 135–147. Chichester: Wiley.

Rousseau, J.-J. (1911) *Émile*. London: Dent.

Ruddock, J. (1976) *Dissemination of Innovation: the Humanities Curriculum Project*. London: Evans/Methuen.

Salford, City of (1977) *The Primary School Profile*. Salford City Education Department.

Salford, City of (1982) *Profile 82*. Salford City Education Department.

Scheffler, I. (1971) *The Language of Education*. Springfield, Illinois: Thomas.

Schools Council (1983) *Primary Practice*. London: Methuen.

Selleck, R.J.W. (1972) *English Primary Education and the Progressives, 1914–1939*. London: Routledge & Kegan Paul.

Sharp, R. and Green, A. (1975) *Education and Social Control: a Study in Progressive Primary Education*. London: Routledge & Kegan Paul.

Shayer, M. (1979) Has Piaget's construct of formal operational thinking any utility? *British Journal of Educational Psychology*, **49**, 3.

Silver, P. and Silver, H. (1974) *The Education of the Poor: the History of a National School 1824–1974*. London: Routledge & Kegan Paul.

Simon, B. (1981) The primary school revolution: myth or reality? In Simon, B. and Willcocks, J. (ed.) *Research and Practice in the Primary Classroom*, pp. 7–25. London: Routledge & Kegan Paul.

Simon, B. (1983) The study of education as a university subject in Britain, *Studies in Higher Education*, **8**, 1.

Simon, B. and Willcocks, J. (ed.) (1981) *Research and Practice in the Primary Classroom*. London: Routledge & Kegan Paul.

Skilbeck, M. (1969) The balance of studies in colleges of education: commentary. In Taylor, W. (ed.) *Towards a Policy for the Education of Teachers*, pp. 110–17. London: Butterworth.

Skilbeck, M. (1970) Graduate training and curriculum development, *Education for Teaching*, **82**.

Southgate, V., Arnold, H. and Johnson, S. (1981) *Extending Beginning Reading*. London: Heinemann.

Stake, R.E. (1975) *Evaluating the Arts in Education: a Responsive Approach*. Columbus, Ohio: Merrill.

Stenhouse, L. (1975) *An Introduction to Curriculum Research and Development*. London: Heinemann.

Stonier, T. (1982) Changes in western society: educational implications. In Richards, C. (ed.) *New Directions in Primary Education*, pp. 287–300. Brighton: Falmer Press.

Storr, A. (1960) *The Integrity of the Personality*. Harmondsworth: Penguin.

Taylor, P.H. (1970) *How Teachers Plan their Courses*. Slough: NFER.

Taylor, P.H., Reid, W.A., Holley, B.J. and Exon, G. (1974) *Purpose, Power and Constraint in the Primary School Curriculum*. London: Macmillan.

Taylor, W. (1969) *Society and the Education of Teachers*. London: Faber.

Taylor, W. (1977) The head as manager: some criticisms. In Peters, R.S. (ed.) *The Role of the Head*, pp. 37–49. London: Routledge & Kegan Paul.

Tempest, N.R. (1974) *Teaching Clever Children 7—11*. London: Routledge & Kegan Paul.

Tibble, J.W. (1966) Some applications. In Tibble, J.W. (ed.) *The Study of Education*, pp.216–233. London: Routledge & Kegan Paul.

Tibble, J.W. (ed.) (1971) *The Future of Teacher Education*. London: Routledge & Kegan Paul.

Times Educational Supplement (1982) HMI teacher training document alarms primary specialists, *Times Educational Supplement*, 8 October.

Tough, J. (1976) *Listening to Children Talking*. London: Ward Lock Educational.

Tough, J. (1977) *The Development of Meaning*. London: George Allen & Unwin.

Tough, J. (1979) *Talk for Teaching and Learning*. London: Ward Lock Educational.

Universities Council for the Education of Teachers (1979) *The PGCE Course and the Training of Specialist Teachers for Secondary Schools: a Consultative Report*. London: UCET.

Universities Council for the Education of Teachers (1982) *Postgraduate Certificate in Education Courses for Teachers in Primary and Middle Schools: a Further Consultative Report*. London: UCET.

Walberg, H.J. and Thomas, S.C. (1971) *Characteristics of Open Education: Towards an Operational Definition*. Newton, Massachusetts: Education Development Center.

Weber, M. (1964) *The Theory of Social and Economic Organizations*. West Drayton: Collier Macmillan.

Whitaker, P. (1983) *The Primary Head*. London: Heinemann.

White, J. (1982) The primary teacher as servant of the state. In Richards, C. (ed.) *New Directions in Primary Education*, pp. 199–208. Brighton: Falmer Press.

Whitfield, R.C. (1970) A study of education for teachers. *Education for Teaching*, **82**.

Whitty, G. (1981) Curriculum studies: a critique of some recent British orthodoxies. In Lawn, M. and Barton, L. (ed.) *Rethinking Curriculum Studies*, pp.48–70. London: Croom Helm.

Wicksteed, D. (1982) *Surviving, relating and celebrating: towards a new definition of the basics*. Unpublished mimeo.

Wilcox, B. and Eustace, P.J. (1981) *Tooling Up for Curriculum Review*. Slough: NFER.

Williams, R. (1976) *Keywords: a Vocabulary of Culture and Society*. London: Fontana.

Wilson, J.B. (1975) *Education Theory and the Preparation of Teachers*. Slough: NFER.

Wilson, J.B. (1977) *Philosophy and Practical Education*. London: Routledge & Kegan Paul.

Young, M.F.D. (1971) *Knowledge and Control*. West Drayton: Collier Macmillan.

Name Index

Subject Index